SportsWars

SportsWars

Athletes in the Age of Aquarius

David W. Zang

The University of Arkansas Press
Fayetteville
2001

08 07 06 05 04   5 4 3 2 1

Designer: John Coghlan

⊚ The paper used in this publication meets the minimum requirements
of the American National Standard for Permanence of Paper for Printed
Library Materials Z39.48-1984.

The Library of Congress has cataloged the hardcover edition as follows:

Zang, David.
  SportsWars : athletes in the age of Aquarius / David W.
      p. cm.
Includes bibliographical references (p.   ) and index.
  ISBN 1-55728-713-9 (cloth : alk. paper)
  1. Sports—Social aspects—United States—History. 2.
Counterculture—United States—History—20th century. I. Title: Sports
wars. II. Title.
  GV706.5 .Z35 2001
  303.4'83'0973—dc21

                                                                    2001003221

To Bob Osterhoudt and Don Steel: mentors, colleagues, and friends whose good works and generosity are exceeded only by their humility

Acknowledgments

Many people supported the writing of this book. I thank Larry Malley, director and editor of the University of Arkansas Press, who expressed interest in the idea many years ago and sustained it until I brought it to publication. Professors Larry Gerlach, of the University of Utah, and Dick Crepeau, of the University of Central Florida, waded through full drafts and steered me toward better results. Professors Elliott Gorn and Randy Roberts of Purdue University also offered many constructive suggestions that shaped the final text. Dave Wiggins of George Mason University, Dan Nathan of Miami (Ohio) University, Debbie Shaller of Towson University, and Steve Gietschier of *The Sporting News* contributed their expertise and assistance with one or more portions. Thanks to John Irving for his suggestions regarding the Rick Sanders story.

I am grateful to many interviewees for the remembrances entrusted to me. In particular, Jose Feliciano, Dan Gable, Fred Shabel, and Bob Ward, all of whom are central figures in chapters, were generous and candid in speaking with me at length. I also appreciate the interviews of the coaches and athletes of the 1972 U.S. Olympic wrestling team, and the above-and-beyond contributions of Susan Feliciano, Ernie Harwell, John Hoke, Mike Gerald, and Ron Good of *Amateur Wrestling News,* David Stockner (stepbrother of Rick Sanders), Ernie Torain, and John Wooden.

Many librarians and archivists enriched my research experience. Thanks to those at the University of Pennsylvania; Towson University; the Wrestling Hall of Fame in Stillwater, Oklahoma; the Philadelphia Public Library; the Library of Congress; and the University of Maryland. Particular thanks go to Sarah Sherman at the Urban Archives at Temple University, Kristine Krueger at the National Film Information Service of the Center for Motion Picture Study, Cynthia Gabel of the NCAA, Roland Baumann of Oberlin College, and David Azzolina of Penn's Van Pelt Library. Thanks also to the Sports Information Offices at the Universities of Maryland and Pennsylvania.

Finally, thanks to my wife, Joanie, and family and friends, who have supported my work in countless ways.

Contents

I believe that sports—all sports—is one of the few bits of glue that holds society together, one of the few activities in which young people can proceed along avenues where objectives are clear and the desire to win is not only permissible but encouraged.
  —Vice President Spiro T. Agnew, Address to Touchdown Club of Birmingham, Alabama, January 18, 1972

Football is the strongest remaining unquestioned remnant of an old culture, and the struggle to change its current form is no less than the conflict between an old culture and a new culture.
  —Gary Shaw, University of Texas football, 1972

Introduction

If the '60s were any kind of revolution, were they a break from the past or from the future, an inauguration or a culmination? Do those times fail to measure up to narrative, or do the narratives we have fail to take the measure of those times?
—*Nick Bromell,* Tomorrow Never Knows, 2000

In the fall of 1970 I journeyed to Ohio State from nearby Wittenberg University and surrendered to the times. Joining a mob of tens of thousands, I marched for hours up and down Columbus's High Street, a one-mile strip of shops, bars, and fast-food joints that adjoins the Ohio State campus. Solitary police cars sat at each end of the street while in between them a demonstration of unfathomable intensity played itself out. Industrial trash dumpsters rolled through the street ablaze and pilotless. In front of bars drunken males fought with inept violence. Clouds of marijuana smoke floated above small gatherings of newly formed acquaintances. Longhaired youths threw rocks through the lit sign of a hamburger stand while patrons queued inside for food.

What was this? Was I in the midst of revolution? Not by conventional standards, surely. I was part of a demonstration in support of Ohio State's football victory over rival Michigan. The Buckeyes's legendary and reactionary coach, Woody Hayes, had put in an early appearance, proclaiming this to be "the biggest party we've ever had."[1] Later, a riot-equipped police force, some with bayonets mounted, moved down the street and met with a hailstorm of rocks and bottles. The police responded first with tear gas and then with fire hoses and wooden pellets fired into the crowd.

The moment's meaning was crystalline: sports had not escaped the firestorm of the Vietnam era. Whether you call the times the sixties, allowing the aura of upheaval to stand for the entire decade, or extend them until the United States pulled its troops from Saigon in 1975, that is what I was most surely in the midst of—a stretch of ten or fifteen years when sparks of change sometimes threatened to burst into flames of social and cultural revolution.*

Within organized sport, the era's push and pull—between change and resistance, black and white, young and old, male and female, hawk and dove, jock and puke—ended nearly a century of consensus. At stake was a sports ideology that began in the late nineteenth century as a general agreement on the desirability of athletic participation and that grew into a widespread and unshakable conviction in sports' ability to build character. The belief invited sports-loving Americans into a refuge that *New York Times* writer Robert Lipsyte termed "SportsWorld," a place he described in 1975 as "a sweaty Oz you'll never find in a geography book, . . . an ultimate sanctuary, a university for the body, a community for the spirit, a place to hide that glows with that time of innocence when we believed that rules and boundaries were honored, that good triumphed over evil."[2]

The arrival of riot police and tear gas in the sanctuary was evidence that the mythic qualities of SportsWorld would not survive the '60s as the framework for public perceptions of sports. Many factors impinged on the old sports ideology—the quest for profits, television ratings points, and advertising dollars. Certainly, beginning in the 1950s, big money, television, and critical media helped to create a climate of inescapable scrutiny and overexposure that was inhospitable to myth-making. But these things, along with a large influx of black athletes and the beginnings of female insistence on sharing the playing fields, were only parts of a fuller explanation.

Money and celebrity were always a part of our sports, but what you cannot trace back beyond the Vietnam era is the cultural tension that undermined SportsWorld's claims to character-building and the tenets by which organized sports were conducted: sacrificial effort, submission to authority, controlled physical dominance, victory with honor, and manliness (for, above all, organized sports were self-consciously male before this time). This book is about that tension and the issues that arose around those tenets.

---

*Herein, where observations are not tied to a specific date, the terms *Vietnam era, sixties,* and *'60s* are used interchangeably for stylistic reasons.

Many conditions of Vietnam-era life contributed to the tension. Primary in raising questions about the direction of American sport were the influence of youth culture, the subsequent ascendancy of the counterculture, and the United States' involvement in the Vietnam War.

The gap between old traditions and new possibilities was widest among children of the baby boom, a period that ran from 1946 to 1964 and peaked in 1957. The boom created a huge mass of youth moving through time and society like a pig in a python.[3] Between 1964 and 1970 the first baby boomers hit the ages of eighteen to twenty-four, what psychologists like Yale's Kenneth Keniston called the "dangerous years."[4] In conjunction with unparalleled prosperity, the result was an army of young people with the awareness, leisure time, and psychological predisposition to act. They were a cohort so invested in the possibilities for change that many entered adolescence with the folksy Kingston Trio and left it under the thrall of the psychedelicized Jimi Hendrix. What they thought about sport, an institution that had long obsessed youth, mattered.

Much of the assault on old ways, including old ways of conducting sport, came from the counterculture—an amorphous segment of the boomers identified often after the mid-'60s as simply "hippies." They were, in many concrete practices, distinct from those of the "New Left," the political brotherhood that stressed discipline and organization in its opposition to the establishment. However, as Todd Gitlin, a former leader of the radical Students for a Democratic Society (SDS), has acknowledged, around 1967—the "Summer of Love"—"many were the radicals and cultural revolutionaries in search of convergence, trying to nudge the New Left and the counterculture together, trying to imagine them as yin and yang of the same epochal transformation." In a succinct summation of how many perceived the younger generation, Gitlin wrote: "Thanks to the sheer numbers and concentration of youth, the torrent of drugs, the sexual revolution, the traumatic war, the general stampede away from authority, and the trend-spotting media, it was easy to assume that all the styles of revolt and disaffection were spilling together, tributaries into a common torrent of youth and euphoria, life against death, joy over sacrifice, now over later, remaking the whole bleeding world."[5]

The counterculture, in its often playful but deadly serious subversions of everything mainstream, demanded response and made conflict inevitable.

Simultaneously, the Vietnam War became for many Americans, and for most young adults, the central event in their lives. As television journalist Bryant Gumbel recalled years later: "it's hard to explain to people today how dominant Vietnam was in a young guy's life then. It tailored everything from the girl you went out with who you might not see again to your grades in school."[6] If war and victory had served in the past as regenerative experiences for America, the Vietnam War was a jolting affront to tradition. In 1988, speaking of Vietnam at a Veterans Day ceremony, President Ronald Reagan drew the day's loudest applause for this remark: "At this late date we can all agree that we've learned one lesson—that young Americans must never again be sent to fight and die unless we are prepared to let them win."[7] In 1991 President George Bush openly asserted that the success of Operation Desert Storm had healed the wound of Vietnam. For many reasons—its perceived injustice, its break with American winning tradition, its overtones of racism and genocide, its charges of corruption, bullying, and impotence—the war in Vietnam held loaded meanings for all American institutions.

It is dangerous to claim disjuncture as the distinguishing mark of a decade. Nonetheless, a glance at the titles of histories written closer to the time reaffirm the era's apocalyptic aura: *Coming Apart; A Troubled Feast; Decade of Disillusionment; The Unraveling of America.* The sense of division grew, like other trends of the Vietnam era, from inflated perceptions that eventually outstripped numbers to become conscious reality. If every teenaged male did not have long hair, if free sex was not being flaunted on all four corners of San Francisco's Haight-Ashbury intersection, and if marijuana was not the drug of choice on college campuses, it sure *felt* that way.

It is not my contention that the '60s produced all of the ideas and behaviors that strained American culture. In fact, it is possible to see many of them emerging in the 1940s and 1950s. But it was the blend of Vietnam era conditions that led to the heightened awareness, expression, and judgments that fostered a sense of change.

Though the Vietnam era has elicited books on its war, its political movements, and the media, and books on many facets of its popular culture, there have been no books about sport other than those that appeared during the era. This despite the fact that sport presented a visible battleground for most of the issues confronting the broader culture. Indeed, it is strange that studies of the period dwell on John F. Kennedy and Richard M. Nixon but take little account of the former's belief in sports as tests of individual and collective vigor or the latter's reliance on sports metaphors to explain his policies. It is an incomplete reckoning that causes Muhammad Ali, arguably the most recognized and photographed figure in American history, to have his place in conventional texts marked by mention of his political dissent yet also by a disregard for his meaning as an athlete.

The sixties were unique in three ways for sport: first, the critiques of SportsWorld challenged not just abuses therein, not just the proposition that athletic participation builds character even, but the very nature of that character and the methods used to build it. Second, for the first time in history the critics included a substantial number of athletes—some highly visible and influential, like Ali and Bill Walton—and others once encamped within the community of athletics, such as sportswriters like Lipsyte. Finally, sport's entrenched position as standard-bearer for American values—as the glue that was holding the country together—made it an appealing target in a time of general disenchantment.

Like many of the other dissenting groups in America, those disillusioned with sports were a loosely confederated faction. With the 1971 publication of *The Athletic Revolution,* a call for greater athlete autonomy, Jack Scott, a sociology professor, coined the term that covered the efforts of many to close the gap between sport's ideals and its realities. Scott himself got the chance to put his preachings into practice as the athletic director at Oberlin College in Ohio from 1972 to 1974. He hired "liberated" coaches and did his best to give athletes a greater voice in athletic program decisions.

Before Scott, others had initiated their own brands of revolt. National Basketball Association (NBA) star Bill Russell's autobiography, *Go Up for Glory* (1966), expressed race-related reservations about professional basketball. Dave Meggyesey, an All-Pro lineman with the St. Louis Cardinals, denounced football as a brutal, militaristic game run by dehumanizing administrators and coaches in *Out of Their League* (1970). Gary Shaw took the same view of college football in 1972's *Meat on the Hoof,* an exposé of demeaning practices at the University of Texas. Jim Bouton exposed some of his ex–New York Yankee teammates as less-than-heroic characters in his popular *Ball Four* (1970). The baseball establishment

Former all-pro lineman Dave Meggyesy's *Out of Their League* attacked football's "dehumanizing" practices. *(Micki Scott)*

was outraged at Bouton's revelation of locker-room hijinks and after-hours escapades.

There were, as well, a number of "radical jocks" at American colleges

Jack Scott, who coined the term "Athletic Revolution."

and universities. These were athletes who may not have openly proclaimed revolution, but nonetheless rejected some of the restraints imposed by the standards of character-building. Often, these athletes participated in the so-called minor sports, like rowing, fencing, or swimming. Some, such as the Harvard crew, were highly successful in competition while maintaining a political awareness encouraged by their coach, Harry Parker. But in many cases it was difficult to reconcile a way of life endorsed by the counterculture with that demanded by a coach. As writer James Simon Kunen noted of his rowing experience at Columbia: "When the men of

Columbia row past the Consolidated Edison power plant on the river, they know that the same men run their school who run Con Ed and they see the air being polluted . . . and they know *that* is not a game . . . It begins to seem that crew may be a waste of time."[8]

A media increasingly curious about sport's ties to the larger world turned a bright light on the association of athletics and values. Lipsyte's *SportsWorld* was one of several books by journalists that abandoned the adulatory tone that had characterized the sportswriting of earlier times. Jerry Izenberg's *How Many Miles to Camelot?* (1972) and Leonard Shecter's *The Jocks* (1970) were others. Paul Hoch, in *Rip Off the Big Game* (1972), offered a neo-Marxist perspective of sport. Finally, the famed James Michener's lengthy and moderately critical *Sports in America* (1976) certified that the state of American sports was worthy of close examination.

Some, such as Harry Edwards and Curt Flood, joined Ali in active revolt. Edwards, then a sociology professor at San Jose State and a former track and field athlete, organized a black athletes' boycott of the 1968 Olympic Games at Mexico City. Though few athletes actually stayed away from the Games, Edwards called attention to the plight of blacks in sports and the general powerlessness of all athletes. The black power salute by John Carlos and Tommie Smith on the victory podium grew out of the ferment Edwards recapped in his 1969 book, *The Revolt of the Black Athlete.* Curt Flood, an All-Star outfielder with the St. Louis Cardinals, walked away from baseball that same year when the Cards tried to trade him to the Phillies. His suit asking for control over his own career helped a few years later to topple baseball's reserve clause, which had bound players to a team for life. The resulting free agency made all professional athletes freer and richer.

Though the "athletic revolution" prodded the consciousness of many, resistance to it lent the era as much significance. When Vice President Spiro Agnew addressed the First Annual Vince Lombardi Award Dinner in 1971 he referred to discipline, ethics, "manhood," and a "desire to prevail" as abiding values that had molded American society. While they were still practiced and taught by men such as Lombardi, Agnew said, there was a faction of countrymen who found them "inapplicable to modern life." Though he feared the stridency of these critics, he also characterized them as a minority, as "the Americans out of touch with what's going in our country today."[9] A large percentage of America's youth agreed with

Vice President Spiro Agnew, staunch defender of sport's claims to character-building.

Agnew. In harkening back to older times, older ideals, and the idea of an undivided America sustained by the kind of character associated with its playing fields, they contributed just as surely as the "revolutionaries" to the debate over the conduct of sport.

Harry Edwards, who proposed a boycott of the 1968 Olympics by black athletes.

The following chapters represent a selective approach. The stories I tell here address sports such as boxing, wrestling, and football; look at Olympic, collegiate, and professional athletics; and examine white and black, as well as counterculture and establishment. Still, there are biases. The material is more middle class than not, more attuned to the sites at which character-building was acclaimed and understood (there is, for example, nothing here related to auto racing, bowling, or skiing). Often that turned out to mean something related to the college experience. Colleges were, in the words of one historian, the "flash-point" of America's "canker of rage and frustration."[10] They had also long been sites of the "athletics build character" ethic; as such, they now became battlegrounds for the soul of sports.

The stories, while representative, are not always about the most famous or incendiary events. Instead, they are meant to show how deep and wide the sensibility of the '60s ran through not just boycotts, Olympic black power salutes, and stripped titles, but through the everyday routines and issues that absorbed most Americans.

Though a great deal of the book explores gender, the lack of a chapter devoted to women in sport may seem negligent. After all, Billie Jean King's defeat of Bobby Riggs in 1973 was one of the era's most memorable national television events, and the passage of Title IX of the 1972 Educational Amendments Act made possible expanded opportunities in sport for girls and women. Nonetheless, the explosion of women's sports awaited the critiques of the character-building ideology: a belief system that had theretofore dismissed women at play. Not until the beliefs were shaken did women make strides toward equity, that is, not until after the Vietnam era.

Perhaps the notion of character defined by Victorian sensibilities—and enshrined in sporting ideology—was destined to be archaic in the twentieth century, a time when the idea that one *becomes* surrendered constantly to the idea that one *is*. The emergence of Freud left us reeling under the sway of something as powerful as social ideologies: our own unknowable egos. As Jacques Barzun pointed out in 1974, compound words beginning in *psycho-* had doubled to 140 in the preceding thirty-five years.[11] A society overrun by personality and steeped in neuroses is not one conducive to consensus about what character is and who has it. In the flux of the Vietnam era it was easy to get mixed up. Indeed, the infamous Nixon White House tapes find the president, after a sixteen-second gap, blending the old—character—with the new—personality—in a 1971 appraisal of Baltimore quarterback Johnny Unitas: "He's a leader of men, no question about it, a leader of men. Strong. Intelligent. A fine personality, a fine character." [12]

Still, as obsolete as the old sporting ideals sometimes appear, they did not die with the '60s. The virtues associated with sports character still represent what many Americans *wish* to see when they look at the team portrait. Much of the lamentation over the perceived loss of heroes ("Where have you gone, Joe DiMaggio?") stems from the fact that, though the Vietnam era pushed the nation's reality a few degrees in a new direction, it did not unseat the feeling about what sports ought to provide. Lipsyte wrote in 2000 that lawyers and agents have made the "performer who can deliver the audience more important than any designated moral authority."[13] True. No one at the turn of the century is calling sports "the glue holding the nation together." But we still look to sports to be morality plays staged by heroes, villains, and fools. We still seek parables and lessons that give our games a meaning that can't be explained by a vault full of money, multiple camera angles, or press conferences. The Vietnam era made the search harder.

SportsWars

CHAPTER ONE

A Star-Spangled Collision: Sports and Rock 'n' Roll in the '60s

*Therefore the music of a well-ordered age is calm and cheerful,
and so is its government. The music of a restive age is excited and
fierce, and its government is perverted . . .*
　　　　　　　—Herman Hesse, citing an ancient Chinese source in
　　　　　　　The Glass Bead Game, *1969*

On Monday, October 7, 1968, moments before Game Five of the World Series between Detroit and St. Louis, twenty-three-year-old Jose Feliciano, accompanied by his guide dog, Trudy, took up a spot in the vast emerald of Tiger Stadium's centerfield. His long dark hair and dark glasses hinted at sinister possibilities. A small mike for NBC's audio feed was taped to the stadium's microphone stand to preserve the moment ahead. "I had about ten seconds of should I or shouldn't I," the singer recalled later.[1] Then, backed only by his guitar, before a sold-out crowd and a live television audience estimated at 55 million, Feliciano decided he should.

His national anthem was one for the ages. Each note of the performance—hauntingly gentle and beautiful in retrospect[2]—seemed wildly unorthodox at the time. It was nuanced in a way that the prideful, bombastic versions of singers like Broadway's Robert Merrill were not. It seemed to some bluesy and "languid." Feliciano changed single sounds into multiples; his voice played with the melody, keening one moment, dropping to near-whisper the next. As he finished, tagging a protracted and flowery "yeahhh, yeaahhhhhhhhhh" onto "the home of the brave," the Tiger Stadium crowd's stunned murmuring blended with cascading boos and puzzled applause to produce a sound like distant, rumbling thunder.

Jose Feliciano sings the national anthem before game five at Detroit's Tiger Stadium. (Detroit Free Press)

Feliciano had created a volatile mix, as response made immediately clear. Military veterans in a Phoenix hospital threw their shoes at the television set. Switchboards lit up in explosive protest. KSD-TV in St. Louis received 200 calls in five minutes. Tiger Stadium fielded 2,000 complaints in the first hour. The Tigers claimed the ratio of negative to positive responses was 100 to 1. The story was front-page news not only in Detroit and St. Louis but also in New York and Los Angeles. Sportswriters characterized the performance as "bizarre," as a "star-spangled goof," and as having all the musical appeal of a "tiger tootling on a tin can." One press box resident thought Feliciano "forgot the tune," and another cracked, "I thought the dog was singing instead of the guy." Though the Tigers won, winning pitcher Mickey Lolich tossed gas on the fire, claiming that the length of Feliciano's rendition had him "so upset that I couldn't straighten myself out in the first inning."[3]

Many thought the version smacked of rock 'n' roll, and in 1968, a year when it seemed the whole world might turn upside down, sports and rock 'n' roll sat on opposite shores of a divided culture. As political assassinations and war-related abominations seemed to ring the death knell that year for national togetherness, the older generations blamed the young for all American losses: for the pathetic inability to bomb tiny North Vietnam into submission; for the disappearance of a work ethic; for the discarding of romance's courtship phase; for the mockery of manly appearance; and for the corruption of melody. The last of these, embodied in the rhythm that drove rock 'n' roll, ignited hysteria in its detractors. A national leader of the Christian Crusade was convinced that rock 'n' roll was a Communist plot to render American youth useless through "nerve-jarring mental deterioration and retardation."[4]

By October of 1968, a month before the most divisive election in the most divisive year of the Vietnam War, the youth counterculture had rolled Elvis Presley's sneer, the long hair of the Beatles, the fantasia of hallucinatory drugs, and the biting political lyrics of folk singers into one long, loud soundtrack to accompany its ridicule and rejection of old ways.

Cloaked in the mythic mantle of character-building, sport was rock music's perceptual opposite, an institution bound tightly to tradition and the habit of acceptance. To some, then, Feliciano's decision to bring the two together at the high mass of American sports rituals was akin to appointing Yippie leader Jerry Rubin as commissioner of baseball. Few observant Americans were unaware of the place of athletics in withstanding the countercultural attack that pop music seemed to amplify. Already in 1968 college football players had been called upon to break up campus protest rallies, going so far in April as to surround student-occupied buildings at Columbia University to keep food from reaching the long-haired squatters inside. Ted Gold, a member of the radical political faction, the Weathermen, acknowledged the rift between sport and counterculture. Before dying in a self-rigged terrorist bombing, he admitted that he could never become a full-fledged revolutionary until he had shed his affection for Giants' center fielder Willie Mays.[5]

Tiger announcer Ernie Harwell, who invited Feliciano to sing and then suffered the wrath of angry fans. *(Photo courtesy of Ernie Harwell)*

Feliciano was less fearful of crossing boundaries (Jimi Hendrix had experienced the same edginess as Feliciano a year earlier at the Monterey Pop Festival. He decided against an electrified "Star Spangled Banner," postponing it until 1969's Woodstock Festival). Born blind in Puerto Rico and raised in the Bronx, Feliciano was self-taught, and his virtuoso guitar work shared space with a voice and arrangements that were unique and visionary. In his folk days he had shared a Greenwich Village stage with Bob Dylan. He had come to national prominence a few months before the World Series when he dared to record a cover of the Doors' "Light My Fire" that hit the top of the *Billboard* charts. His initial album brought him two Grammys (and six nominations), one for best vocal performance. He was also a New York Yankees fan, and before the game he had bantered playfully with the Tigers in their clubhouse.

Those who disliked his anthem cared little for his love of baseball, hearing only the sounds of a patriotic ritual bent to the breaking point. As expected in a time when divisiveness fueled media reporting, the man-on-the-street commentary that found its way into print ran toward the inflammatory. Ernie Harwell, the Tiger announcer responsible for inviting Feliciano to perform, would later say that his mail was divided down the middle, but, he agreed, most "editorials lambasted it, [and] civic groups passed angry resolutions." One caller railed at the announcer: "Anybody who'd let that long-hair hippie ruin our 'Star-Spangled Banner' has got to be a Communist."[6]

The Detroit *Free Press* published a litany of howls:

"[It was] . . . just a desecration to hear it sung that way."

"Are there no groups about who are prepared and willing to sing this difficult song the way it is meant to be sung?"

"I got sick. No wonder our country is losing its dignity."

"I must be old by today's standards, 26, because I didn't appreciate the way Jose Feliciano interpreted our national anthem."

"No matter how wrong our country might seem to some people, it did not deserve the horrible rock-and-roll rendition given the anthem . . . it makes one ashamed . . . Our only hope is that no other country is receiving the games."[7]

Over the years many people have complimented Feliciano on his version, but those who loved it were, in 1968, less vocal than its opponents. The press cited only a few of the people who saw its departure from tradition as positive: "his clear emotion-packed voice gave a truly contemporary flair to a song old yet relevant," wrote one. "If we aren't willing to accept a different rendition occasionally, with common sense and tolerance . . . we are not fostering goodwill," added another. Harwell, ever decent and honorable, also came to the young singer's defense. "I feel a fellow has a right to sing any way he can sing it."[8] It is a stance he maintains to this day. That a large number of people enjoyed the performance was undeniable, evidenced by RCA's decision to release the stadium recording as a 45 rpm single.

Without doubt, age was a factor in one's response. Beatle George Harrison had opined in 1968 that: "music is the main interest of the younger people. It doesn't really matter about the older people now because they're finished anyway." NBC's color analyst, Tony Kubek, offered partial agreement. "I think he [Feliciano] did one heckuva job," he said. "I feel the youth of America has to be served and this is the type of music they want." But age was not all. Joe Oyler (whose brother, Ray, played for the Tigers) responded: "I'm young enough to understand it, but I think it stunk."[9]

Two days after the performance an editorial writer noted that Feliciano "gave expression to the feelings of another America too rarely felt in our national and patriotic institutions. Feliciano was saying that nothing is static, that nothing lies beyond examination or change, that this too is America."[10] What Feliciano said literally was, "I sang it that way to express my love for my country. I am very happy that I did it that way. It's the way I feel." He also told the Associated Press that although his stadium performance was his first in public, "I had worked on the arrangement for sometime by myself awaiting the opportunity."[11]

Feliciano left Tiger Stadium after a few innings, bound for another engagement, but the controversy followed him. Shortly thereafter his career lay in shambles, many radio stations refusing to play his records.[12] During guest spots on late-night television shows, he was unable to appease the fury of America's older generations, who did not see the irony in the singer's claim that, "I owe everything to this country. I wanted to contribute something to express my gratitude for what it has done for me . . . I'm for everything it stands for."[13]

In 1968 it was hard, however, to find consensus about what the country stood for. Sports and rock music, in particular, were nations unto themselves, with different constitutions, dress codes, and values. And though many young people had begun engaging in cultural play, darting back and forth between them, the ideals of sports and rock music were oil and water; in the antipathy between them one could feel the tensions running through American society.

Feliciano's blindness had closed the door to sports but opened another just as alluring. Of all the career paths open to young males in the latter half of the twentieth century, only those of rock star and professional athlete seemed so desirable yet remote that their attainment required the intervention of gods. Prior to Elvis this parity had not been the case. Rocket scientist Homer Hickam neatly summed the low accord musicians had relative to athletes before the arrival of rock 'n' roll: "When I went to Big Creek, Coach Merrill Gaines, the winningest coach in southern West Virginia history, took one look at me lost inside the practice gear and ordered me off his football field. I joined Big Creek's marching band . . . Dad had no comment . . . but I noticed he and [brother] Jim exchanged a look of what I took to be agreement about the shame of me being in the band."[14] The rise of rock 'n' roll changed that, adding a glamorous rival to the role of sports star, both being pathways to what seemed a life of ceaseless pleasure, adulation, and satisfaction. In the '60s dreaming of one meant forgetting the other.

Those like Ted Gold, who thought of revolution, of betraying the nation's established institutions, would by necessity have to break with organized sport. It had, in the years following World War II, become the institution standing most clearly for the idea of an American One Way, a reductive construct that honored democracy, suburbia, whiteness, middle classness, Christianity, and consumerism. The One Way promoted the illusion of an America singularly disposed toward all things social, cultural, intellectual, and moral. The idea could be stretched too far, as Sen. Joe McCarthy had demonstrated, but it also found persuasive ways to present itself, as in 1959's famous "kitchen debate." At a Moscow trade show that featured a mock American kitchen as an exhibit, Vice President Richard Nixon countered Soviet Premier Nikita Krushchev's claims of national superiority not with a show of military technology, but rather with a prideful demonstration of America's latest time-saving appliances. Explicit in the demonstration was an absolute conviction that the appliances were de facto evidence of an irresistible and surpassing lifestyle, a notion seemingly borne out when Krushchev later had some of the appliances quietly shipped to the Soviet Union for his own use. Implicit in such certitude was an intolerance for diversity. The One Way was single-minded enough, in fact, to spawn, during the upheaval of the '60s, the slogan "Love It or Leave It."

The February 1964 landing of the Beatles in the United States revealed that the first step in leaving it might be accepting the possibility of

Somewhere Else. As Beatle publicist Derek Taylor later wrote, "there must in 1964 have been a basic longing to find something outside themselves and their experience, or Americans could never have taken to the Beatles in the way they did."[15] Until then even disaffected and alternative experiences like those of Jack Kerouac's *On the Road* (1955) had been "our" experiences. Actually, in retrospect, it isn't hard to see that the mythical California surf culture that the Beach Boys had created just prior to the British invasion of rock bands aimed at the same thing—a utopian "somewhere else" that invited youth to step across the borders of the One Way.

But the media depiction of the Beatles as invaders helped make their singing, rollicking mockery of the One Way apparent. Drug guru Timothy Leary claimed that the Beatles had been sent to create a young race of laughing freemen, a stance that—at least in Leary's estimation—made them "the wisest, holiest, most effective avatars the human race has ever produced."[16] A 1979 survey of members of the "Woodstock generation" confirmed their effect, identifying the Beatles as the most influential and admired of all 1960s newsmakers. The survey had an admitted self-selected bias among those polled, but the Beatles enjoyed such an advantage over even the closest of other figures that their influence cannot be doubted.[17]

There were other signs that the influence was not limited to those who later identified with the counterculture. Beatle biographer Philip Norman reported that on the first Sunday night appearance of the Beatles on the *Ed Sullivan Show,* a single riveting moment for American culture, the country's crime rate was lower than at any time during the previous half century. There was a dramatic drop in New York City of juvenile offenses. "In all the five boroughs, not one single car hubcap was reported stolen."[18] And in 1964, with the issuance of Beatles trading cards, the singers moved formally from ephemera to artifact, their significance certified by sharing space on collectible cardboard with the likes of Mickey Mantle.

Of course, rock 'n' roll was by its very nature about an alternative. Rock journalist Greil Marcus wrote that Elvis's manager, Sam Phillips, found Presley by looking for "music that didn't fit, didn't make sense out of or reflect American life," but in fact "made it beside the point."[19] This alternative encapsulated Top 40 radio, where, according to one writer, "cliches and junkiness and triviality take on the epic sweep of a myth and the depth of a common unconscious."[20] Similarly, as Marcus later ventured, "rock 'n' roll is a combination of good ideas dried up by fads, terrible junk, hideous failings in taste and judgment, gullibility and manipulation," but it also has "moments of unbelievable clarity and invention, pleasure, fun, vulgarity, excess, novelty, and utter enervation."[21] All of those things lived on the fringes of respectability in America.

Sport was closer to the heartland and thus closer to country music in its "no surprises" approach. It is no coincidence, then, that "Love It or Leave It" had produced a parallel among coaches: "My Way or the Highway." As youth culture generally yearned for somewhere else, sport seemed to go out of its way to become more insular, more entrenched in the "here," more paranoid about what was out "there." Two incidents illustrate. In 1971 the Howard University soccer team won the NCAA national championship. It was the first collegiate championship in any sport ever won by a predominantly black school. More important, the starting eleven all came from the Caribbean or Africa. The NCAA stripped Howard, which had beaten a team of homegrown Americans from St. Louis University, of the title, claiming that some of the players had not met NCAA entrance requirements. Eventually, Howard sued. The court ruled that an NCAA regulation concerning foreign eligibility was illegal, but the championship remained lost, and the record books still list the title as "vacated."[22]

Perhaps more notable was the case of Little League baseball. Born in the aftermath of the Great Depression, Little League had spread the gospel of American baseball and sportsmanship for decades. With the exception of two victorious teams from Monterrey, Mexico, its World Series had been a showcase for American victory until late in the '60s. In both '67 and '68, however, Japanese teams beat the American champions in the final game. In five of the next six years—through 1974—teams from Taiwan extended the Asian domination over the United States. Little League responded in 1975, the year the American military left Vietnam in ignominy, by simply banning all foreign competition. This solution proved too blatant, and the ensuing uproar forced the lifting of the ban: various teams from the Far East carried the championship trophy back to Asia for the next six years, a particularly galling occurrence to Americans already undone by the U.S. military's inability to defeat the North Vietnamese.[23]

Though *ABC's Wide World of Sports* gave a hint of Somewhere Else with a mix begun in the early '60s of such exotica as barrel jumping, hurling, and demolition derbies, Americans continued to reserve their greatest interest for activities that they regarded as peculiarly theirs. Baseball, basketball, and football were sports that a century's worth of parents, politicians, educators, businessmen, coaches, and playground leaders had promoted as crucibles for American values.

During the Vietnam era, sport and rock 'n' roll diverged noticeably on questions about those values: the nature and worth of manliness, physical prowess and competition, hard work, and authority. At nearly every turn, it seemed, rock music issued a challenge that undermined the belief system of organized sport and tugged American youth a few degrees in a new direction.

In the case of manliness, the challenge arrived with the Beatles. Wearing "pudding basin" haircuts that concealed the top half inch of their ears, the English rock musicians ensured that at the very least the cosmetics of manliness would change. In a 1971 interview John Lennon claimed, "When we got here you were all walkin' around in Bermuda shorts with Boston crewcuts and stuff on your teeth . . . The chicks looked like 1940's horses. There was no conception of dress or any of that jazz."[24]

Adult Americans showered the longhaired quartet with hostility during their first tour of the United States. A sampling from Philadelphia: "homosexual retards"; "uncivilized"; "filthy"; "the truly nonsensical work of fanatical screwballs."[25] Teenaged American girls felt differently; when they fainted in adulation, it was evident that it would be just a matter of time before teenaged American boys let their own hair grow, a fashion choice of portentous meaning.

At the turn of the century, when anthropology was absorbed in the study of "primitive" cultures, learned observers noted that savage men allowed their dress to become womanly, sometimes even wearing skirts and jewelry.[26] From the Victorian age into the 1960s, distinctive gender appearance coincided with popular belief in America as an advanced form of civilization. So it was that acceptance of the Beatles' "girlish" looks came as a threat, particularly to those in the sports world. There, proper masculine appearance in post–World War II years meant short hair stood on end by a barber and kept there through the miracle of Butch Wax, or moderate length hair parted and held neat and steady by a little dab of Brylcreem or a palmful of Vitalis.

Beginning in the mid-'60s, as flamboyant fashions and colors from London's Carnaby Street began to find favor with the youth counterculture, and as the mainstream co-opted counterculture fashion, associations of gender and dress became more fluid and nonrestrictive, and appearance became an exaggerated source of identity. Indeed, a London hipster who had helped create the Carnaby Street fashions saw in the end of the '60s "the idea of multiple identity in fashion—of clothes worn not in a uniformity of caste or taste, but in a riotous confusion of colours, eras and nationalities."[27] As athletes began to meld dangerously with the masses, organized sports fought a losing battle against stylistic syncretism. As early as 1966 the American Football League (AFL) had outlawed facial hair other than mustaches,[28] but by 1969, the year when the title song of the popular Broadway rock musical *Hair* celebrated the wonders that awaited men who let their hair fall "shoulder length or longer," high school and college yearbooks—and college and pro press guides—reflected a marked increase in longer, more unkempt hair, as well as mustaches, beards, and flaring sideburns.

The new look was especially offensive to many coaches. As a father figure writ large, the modern-day coach had responsibility under the character-building ideology to transform boys into men. Coaches paid great attention to appearance in the late '60s, deeming it an important element in the assessment of manly traits. Paul Dietzel, the outspoken football coach at the University of South Carolina, made hair length a condition of scholarship, telling his players in no uncertain terms "that you cannot wear these girl haircuts, because I like to make sure we are coaching boys."[29] Penn's football coach Bob Odell, recalling years later a hassle with a player over appearance, tried to explain his dislike of long hair. In a painfully drawn-out effort, he admitted, "I would say that I-I-I just didn't like it and I can't—just because—it looked like a girl."[30]

For wrestling coaches, a particularly conservative lot, the hair issue was so controversial that the NCAA Wrestling Rules Committee felt compelled to police it. Beginning with the 1968–69 season, wrestlers were required to be clean shaven and well groomed. Long hair was officially discouraged. The following season the rules limited sideburn growth, and

Fans stood outside football stadiums just to look at Joe Namath. *(Photo courtesy of New York Jets)*

the previous year's standards were reemphasized "in the interest of good health habits." Nonetheless, wrestlers resisted these hygienic appeals to good sense. Thus, for the 1971–72 season, the rules specified that "because of the body contact involved, . . . the hair in the back shall not extend below the top of an ordinary shirt collar and on the sides the hair shall not extend over the ears." Referees had the mandate to measure and clip hair before matches.[31]

Coaches continued into the early '70s to demand short hair, neatness, and conformity in dress. It was an increasingly futile stance. Many of America's best athletes had decided to opt for the new look, and their celebrity opened the doors for the others. Standout black basketball players like Walt "Clyde" Frazier of the New York Knicks adopted an extravagant style labeled as "Superfly," after the 1972 movie of the same name: tailored suits, full-length overcoats, wide-brimmed hats, and plenty of jewelry. New York Jets quarterback Joe Namath put on a pair of Beautymist pantyhose for a television ad and wore long fur coats and a Fu Manchu mustache. Pro footballer Peter Gent later recalled that people began to show up outside stadiums "just to look at him."[32] When his hair started to curl out the back of his helmet in the late '60s, Namath told critics, "I wear my hair the way I like to wear my hair. What does that possibly have to do with how well I throw a football?" Nothing, he thought, but as Jack Concannon of the Chicago Bears shrewdly observed in 1971, "They want us to play like Joe Namath but we can't look like him."[33]

Some coaches made no concessions to stars or playing ability. When UCLA's Bill Walton, the nation's outstanding college basketball center of the early '70s, walked into John Wooden's office one Monday wearing a weekend's growth of beard and mustache, he pleaded his case. The new look supported, he said, his political convictions. In a story oft told by both men, Wooden told Walton that he admired conviction in a man, before adding, "We're sure going to miss you around here, Bill." Walton shaved before practice. Asked to explain his policy on hair many years later, Wooden expressed genuine concern for the efficiency and welfare of his players. The hair could foster colds and flu if gotten wet and worn in the cold; it could make players perspire more and thus hamper ball handling. Mostly, though, it could contribute to a lessening of discipline and team unity.[34]

Some of the anxiety that changing appearances created was tied to deeper philosophic issues. Adults had shuddered involuntarily at first sight of the Beatles because they feared that once the hair came down, boys would be just a leap of the imagination from acting like girls, and, Lord forbid, feeling like girls. Sure enough, it came to pass. Critics who accused the Beatles of turning "men into morons and girls into swooning ninnies" fought a hopeless cause.[35] By decade's end the Beatles were indisputable agents of cultural change. Beatle John Lennon later recalled that they were "flags on the top of the ship," but, he pointed out, "the whole boat was moving."[36] Lennon was being too modest. As beat poet Allen Ginsberg later recalled, "I heard that high, yodeling alto sound of the OOOH that went right through my skull, and I realized it was going to go through the skull of Western civilization . . . The Beatles changed American consciousness—introduced a new note of complete masculinity allied with complete tenderness and vulnerability."[37]

It was no coincidence, then, that things like long hair, flowered shirts, and love beads—fashion championed by pop music lyrics and by pop musicians' dress—became powerful symbols for attitudes that would eventually encompass political radicalism, emotional sensitivity, and compassion—the last two regarded theretofore as feminine traits. As the youth population billowed and politics turned divisive, appearance was more than a look, it was one's essence. Eventually things like hair length came to serve as a man's identity badge—a key to his political, social, and emotional convictions.

James Kunen, student activist and author of a manifesto of counter-cultural thought, *The Strawberry Statement,* understood this well. Kunen recalled that his long hair had turned a day at Boston's Fenway Park in 1968 into an afternoon of paranoia. "There were 35,000 people, a great many of them staring at me," he wrote. "It seemed that they were saying, 'Get out. This is our place.'" He got off easy. In 1971 the lead singer of the rock group Chicago was beaten at a ballgame by four fans who objected to his hair length.[38]

To many, wearing long hair—flying the "freak flag"—implied a rejection of traditional masculine virtues, notably competition, aggression, and violence legitimized, measured, and rewarded by military and athletic valor. And, in the eyes of many coaches, an athlete could not carry out manly behavior if he looked like a girl. In 1969 Tommy Prothro, UCLA's football coach, estimated that about half of athletes had tried pot. "The boys who are giving in," he said, "you can spot. The long hair, not bathing, not caring."[39]

In the very same month that the Beatles first came to America, a college newspaper sports editor complained that the Army and Marines no longer presented manly challenges, and that moves to prohibit boxing and high school football programs were sissy ideas. America was, he claimed, drifting toward an asexual makeup "in which one sex cannot do anything the other cannot do." He urged that Americans confront "the understanding that, for the male, physical integrity is the key to mental integrity."[40]

Physical integrity meant different things in the ideologies of sport and rock 'n' roll. Sports, along with the military, were male-only places, a visible vanguard of patriarchy. Before the Vietnam era they were connected in their presentation of physical prowess as an eternal yardstick for measuring real power.

The attachment of sports to manliness is backed in Western culture by a long history of speculative wisdom, one begun with an idea of ancient imbalance between two distinct strains of male roles required by hunting and agricultural communities. Judeo-Christian doctrine updated this dichotomy to make the conflicting roles of the warrior and the priest the two most powerful symbols of masculine authority.

By the late nineteenth century many men believed that the restrained nature of Victorian culture and the shift from labor of the body to labor of the mind had wrought an unhealthy imbalance. Thereafter, for reasons both social and economic, a conception of physical integrity prevailed in which the natural warrior urges for dominance and aggression were deemed to be superior and more natural than the asexual and passive behavior of the priest.[41]

Through the Korean War years, the tradition of masculine heroism required combat service in the name of democracy. The United States was involved in twenty-seven separate military actions between 1900 and 1971, one every 2.6 years.[42] American popular culture reflected this bellicosity. For example, an adversarial view of the world characterized Hollywood films, which presented an us-versus-them mentality in the twentieth century.[43] The American people came to expect confrontation, and the heroic tradition, combined with the post–World War II fear of communism, exerted pressure on American males to fight.

When this warrior behavior met the '60s, however, it foundered. The Vietnam War imposed heavy strains on males who believed that physical prowess and integrity were inseparable. During that conflict, undefined ramifications of the nuclear bomb, the nontraditional guerilla fighting tactics of the Vietcong, the inability to win the war, and the cultural stress on violence and aggression as inappropriate modern behaviors exerted pressures on males not to fight. The result was that, unlike in past wars, men did not rush to combat.

The situation left little room for good feeling. Males either went to Vietnam and fought or they stayed behind with the knowledge that others less fortunate were fighting. Dr. Seymour L. Halleck, a psychology professor at the University of Wisconsin, had claimed before President Nixon's 1969 institution of a draft lottery that students with deferments were "plagued with guilt, an unremitting quiet which dominates every aspect of their existence."[44]

While the lottery relieved some of the guilt that accompanied deliberate draft evasion, it highlighted a new problem—that others less lucky were still being drafted and killed, but they were also being abandoned by former sympathizers whose luck in the lottery now let them off the hook. The ebbing of antidraft sentiment after the lottery showed to at least one college student the clarity of the antiwar movement's "impotence." He had been part of a crowd of 300 who had stood outside a draft induction center in 1970 "and watched and felt as our manhood and dignity slowly seeped out of our war-riddled selves."[45]

The reference of a noncombatant to himself as "war-riddled" was a reflection of a peculiar reversal in public perceptions. As the war stretched on, growing increasingly unpopular with the public, American soldiers were increasingly demonized while those who resisted the service gained sympathy. The difficulty of reconciling this new vantage with the traditional heroism of American military enterprise was obvious.

Rock 'n' roll didn't even try to reconcile. Like Jose Feliciano, Bob Dylan, and the Beatles, many pop musicians opposed war generally and the Vietnam War specifically. Credence Clearwater Revival's "Who'll Stop the Rain," Tommy James and the Shondells' "Sweet Cherry Wine," and Marvin Gaye's "What's Going On" decried war in their lyrics. Edwin Starr's 1970 hit, "War," took dead aim at the absurdity of fighting, its chorus repeatedly asking, "What is it good for?" before answering, "Absolutely nothing." At the 1969 Woodstock music festival, Country Joe and the Fish indicted America's intervention in Vietnam with their notorious "Feel-Like-I'm-Fixin'-to-Die Rag." Combined with their unabashed adoption of formerly feminine dress and hair styles, the opposition of rock stars to physical aggression was in step with what a writer later described as a feeling that "femininity was the garden of life, masculinity the landscape of death."[46]

Sports tried to connect to the virtues of military heroism despite a decidedly awkward gap between rhetoric and deeds. Military planes flew overhead at sporting events, athletes like Namath went to Vietnam to visit the troops, and coaches like Woody Hayes often drew positive parallels between sport and war. Some athletes likened their contests to symbolic battlefields. Olympic wrestler Gene Davis described the team mood just before the '72 Games in Munich by noting that, "We'd been doing combat for a month or two and we knew we had combat to do ahead of us." The Soviet-American matchups, his teammates agreed, brought a great deal of pressure and tension. Wayne Wells, the captain, said, "Just right below the surface was this political confrontation, and it was a significant deal in a sport like wrestling where the Russians were almost totally dominant." Ben Peterson, who won gold in '72, as Wells did, said that he and brother John "talked all the time that we had to beat the 'Dirty Borises.'"[47]

Nonetheless, unlike World War II and the Korean War, during which many athletes had served active duty, the Vietnam War elicited little more than occasional patriotic talk from athletes, and it became obvious to many that the one thing sport was not contributing to war was warriors. "The Vietnam War," sportswriter Frank Deford told a documentary filmmaker, "was fought by poor people. And the rich people included the athletes—and they simply were not called."[48] Economics and politics were at work, though probably the interests of professional teams ran ahead of those of individual players. According to one published report in 1966, only 2 of 960 professional athletes were serving in the military.[49] That year, M. Sgt. Hurst Loudenslager of the Maryland National Guard appeared in a *Life* magazine photo toting a football while wearing a Baltimore Colts uniform. "We have an arrangement with the Colts," his superior, George Gelson Jr., told the magazine. "When they have a player with a military problem, they send him to us." Many athletes received National Guard duty in exchange for team tickets and other favors. The Dallas Cowboys at one time had ten players assigned to the same division.[50] At least one college football player, drafted by both the Detroit Lions and a team from the lesser regarded Canadian Football League, chose the latter so that he would not have to return to the States if Uncle Sam beckoned.[51] By 1971 the government had 209,517 cases of accused draft offenders, but only one in eight of them were being indicted,[52] so he was hardly more privileged in his position than most who were fleeing the draft. Still, the indifferent stance of elite and professional athletes toward military service was unique and noticeable in the apparent contradiction it offered to sport's claim that it produced leaders.

Aside from the hypocrisy of athletes sitting out the war, a social atmosphere tilting toward pacifism and away from aggression exposed other areas in which sport seemed to be out of step with youth culture in ways that rock music was not.

Pacifism was connected to passivity. Sport, by its nature, has little room for either. But rock 'n' roll was able to successfully disconnect the two, thereby tapping into the anticompetitive rhetoric of youth rebellion (pacifism) while furthering the quest for active experiences (the antiwar movement was hardly pacifist, leaning upon physical confrontation and intimidation as much as passive protest) that energized the generation. Rock offered the contradictory images of tough guys like the Rolling Stones (described by one journalist as "five unfolding switch blades," whose speech and songs were "part of some long, mean reach for the jugular")[53] and the Beatles, who sincerely sang that "All You Need Is Love."

Lyrically, rock offered a new diversity of themes able to accommodate unresolved or unexplored gaps in youth sensibility. Despite its odes to teen independence, rock had first seduced the young in the '50s with songs of June and the moon, following an accepted and safe pattern of popular lyric themes of romance and teen love. When lyrics turned more complex after the mid-'60s, however, they revealed two sides—both a utopian idealism that emphasized nurturance, universal love, and sensory gratification,[54] but also nearly as much "dread and foreboding as flowerpower goofiness," as a recent Janis Joplin biographer noted. "For every 'Get Together' or 'Wooden Ships' there's a song like the Buffalo Springfield's 'For What It's Worth,'" calling attention to the paranoia striking deep in America's heart.[55]

With the 1967 release of "Sergeant Pepper's Lonely Hearts Club Band," with its lyrics printed on the back cover, the Beatles also introduced a new twist to the rock music experience. Until then, the energy of the rhythm had demanded a physical response—it was music that compelled dance. Now the lyrics themselves became self-consciously crucial—cultural signposts, ads, and dicta that required careful listening. Ironically, despite the era's civil rights movement, Motown's cadre of black singers and songwriters continued to supply both dance music and romantic ballads, not joining the musical critique of society in a substantial way until the release of Marvin Gaye's "What's Going On" in 1971.

Though music of lyrical complexity could promote a passive cerebral experience, when complemented by psychedelic drugs it also offered a kinesthetic adventure. Sports, entering an era of pharmaceutically enhanced performance, dealt uncomfortably with drugs. Many athletes drew a moral distinction, seeing therapeutic benefit in performance-related drugs but sneering at the recreational use of marijuana or LSD. The Dallas Cowboys' Peter Gent later laughingly recalled that athletes on uppers and downers dismissed pot as a "hippie drug."[56]

Rock music embraced drug imagery in its psychedelic riffs and paeans like "Lucy in the Sky with Diamonds." It was another way in which the music invited the young to leave a reality that seemed unexplainably oppressive while connecting them to a more intensely experienced sense of the world.[57] This could again support dichotomous aims: both fulfilling a need for physical expression that some writers of the era said was required to counter the deadening effects of advanced culture,[58] and passivity.

Few athletes admitted to an exploration of that kind of sensation. It is possible that sports, in its suspension of real time and real space, already provided the transgressive experience that many in the counterculture found for the first time in music and psychedelic drugs. The most notable athlete to admit to experimentation may have been Pittsburgh's Dock Ellis, who claimed to have pitched a no-hitter in 1970 while under the influence of LSD.

If, as Rutgers professor Leslie Fiedler stated, the cult of drugs was a "revolt against masculinity," nothing being more womanly "than permitting the penetration of the body by a foreign object,"[59] then drug use revealed something about sexuality as well. It was another area where the tenets of sport and rock 'n' roll diverged.

Rock 'n' roll was, from its inception, sexually charged. The first serious attempts at rock music censorship had come when rhythm and blues, the code name for black music, began to cross over into the white marketplace. In 1954 the host of television's "Juke Box Jury" moralized: "All rhythm and blues records, obscene and of lewd intonation, are dirty and as bad for kids as dope."[60] Indeed, both "jazz" and "rock and roll" were early black euphemisms for sexual intercourse. Rock musicians in the '60s, even as they invested their songs with social and political weight, never abandoned suggestibility. Thus, in an era when some people thought the young regarded the right to "sexual intercourse as an unalienable right like free speech and as a medical necessity, like breathing,"[61] rock music remained in tune.

As the '60s began, the sexual aspects of athletics tread a fine line between suppression and exhibition that had been drawn for a century. On the one hand, sport was one of the few permissible outlets for public display and praise of the body. On the other, it promoted a manliness publicly devoid of sexuality—in fact, opposed to its expression. The Victorian idea of the libidinous male wishing to ravish the demure female but able to resist doing so rested on the idea of very distinctive physiologies, sensibilities, ambitions, and desires of men and women, and in the belief that certain involvements—sport, fraternity life, the military—could help diminish the danger.

The official party line among coaches was that manly prowess sought inevitable release and that athletic participation was a socially beneficial safety valve for it. Many in athletics believed that in a boarding school or college setting sports could drain off excessive sexual energy that males might otherwise use in "marauding the refectory like some juvenile version of Grendel" or in sexual escapades with female students, or in antagonistic encounters with non-jocks. A Michigan State football player of the mid-'60s acknowledged that "they (non-jocks) thought we were meatheads and we thought they were gay faggots."[62]

If some sexual exploits proved irrepressible—and became the subjects of knowing winks—coaches were interested in at least relegating them to the off season. Many coaches forbade sex before games in the fear that it would siphon athletic strength. This unofficial doctrine of "dissipation" was an updated version of mid-nineteenth-century health reform belief that linked sexual overindulgence to physical ailment, and in fact made semen the crucial link to vitality. One popular rule of thumb had held that one ounce of semen was equivalent to forty ounces of blood.[63] By the 1960s the doctrine had expanded the possible consequences of dissipation into the psychological realm. In 1971 a memo from a college crew coach told rowers: "This entire question is made more difficult because the norms of society are in flux. What is most important is that you do not develop social relationships which place psychological demands upon you which would limit your performance. It should be understood that the physiological aspects of sexual intercourse have no long term or negative effects, but certainly sexual contact combined with psychological demands limit the performance of an athlete. One should avoid these relationships through the important spring training and racing season."[64]

As the idea of a sexual revolution spread through the youth culture of the sixties like wildfire, sport's adherence to an ideal of restraint seemed absurdly out of touch with the times. Adding to the embarrassment, feminist observers in the '70s made much of the butt-slapping, hugging, and hair-tousling that goes on in male sports, interpreting it as homoeroticism.

The seemingly duplicitous stance of athletes toward sex made them again appear hypocritical. While some observers noted that rock 'n' roll was largely a male domain with the same high-charged connection to sexual conquest, it seemed more open. The wink and the blush that marked sport's response seemed all the more transparent when athletes like Joe Namath bragged of his sexual exploits and when Yankee pitchers Fritz Peterson and Mike Kekich decided, in a highly publicized situation in March 1973, to swap wives and families.

The apparent aspect of pleasure-seeking in the lives of Namath, Kekich, Peterson, and others at least meshed with the devotion of youth to good times. A favorite aphorism of the era, "Make Love, Not War," linked pleasure and politics. Here too, in the opposition of pain and pleasure, expressed in terms of effort versus fun, rock music was more empathetic to the tenor of the times. In 1959 a study of nine high schools showed that adolescent culture was already torn. To be among the "leading crowd" required above all else athletic achievement for boys, personality and good looks for girls. Also highly valued for both, however, was their willingness to "have a good time." In the opinion of investigator James S. Coleman, "A hedonism drains off the energies of most high school students."[65]

While coaches urged young athletes to put effort ahead of fun, rock stars of the '60s embodied hedonism. From the explicit plea of the Beach Boys for "Fun, Fun, Fun" to Martha and the Vandellas' more indirect calls for "Dancing in the Street," rock was awash in pronouncements for fun. One historian read the Beatles as symbolically telling their fans "to kick off their shoes, heed their hormones, and have fun."

A final split between sport and rock was in outlook toward authority. Submission to discipline and internalization of authority (self-discipline) were the foundations of sport's claims to character-building.

Abandoning those qualities was the lynchpin of rock 'n' roll. From Elvis on, rock stars carried reputations as performers willing and able to unravel order, occasionally spurring the rhetoric of hysteria. In 1957 actress Helen Hayes claimed that rock 'n' roll records had brought her son (actor James MacArthur) to the brink of juvenile delinquency. She had cured him, she said, with a dose of Beethoven.[66]

In a 1968 claim that bore directly on authority and order, the *Christian Science Monitor* reported that a San Francisco pest control expert was testing exposure to rock 'n' roll music as a termite deterrent. When exposed to the Steve Miller Band, the termites increased their foraging; "they neglected their family life and kept on eating instead of feeding their larvae and queen as they should have been doing." But, even more remarkably, when exposed to the music of Spooky Tooth, there was even greater agitation and the bugs "appeared in danger of eating themselves out of house and home."[67]

Indeed, though managers, disc jockeys, recording studios, and distributors had a tight hold on the logistical details that could make or break a band, rock musicians seemed to control their own destinies. The whole enterprise of pop music appeared inclusive to youth culture—and independent of adults. And, unlike sports, the intervention required of the gods in forging a rock star seemed to be the gift of luck, not skill. After all, if that voice of Bob Dylan's wasn't Everyman's, whose was it?

The large numbers of baby boomers meant the opposite for sports. Once the province of every boy, sports seemed in the '60s to become more exclusive. In Robert Lipsyte's term, a "varsity syndrome" created an elitist caste that left more and more youth feeling the "unkindest cut."[68] Some youth voluntarily stepped off the competitive treadmill, opting instead for the more esoteric satisfactions of hiking, climbing, or tossing a Frisbee. Others sought isolated outlets such as jogging, marathoning, and eventually triathloning that provided them with opportunities for "personal bests" without the burden of beating others or capitulating to the demands of coaches.

As if rock 'n' roll needed any more ammunition in fighting for the hearts and minds of American youth, it countered the mythology of sports heroism with a timely myth of its own: that of the slain, youthful hero who becomes a god. If the counterculture was in any way an attempt to replace old practices and beliefs with new energies, then it is reasonable to consider that compensatory characters arose as symbols of that new energy. At least one writer proposed that the dominant symbol was that of "The Eternal Child." In Western mythology, these "children" tended to be young male deities who died young but were resurrected to eternal youth.[69] The '60s political arena was rife with them: John and Robert Kennedy, Martin Luther King. Rock produced enough for an all-star band: Jim Morrison, Janis Joplin, Jimi Hendrix.

Some say that their deaths, coupled with the 1969 breakup of the Beatles and the disastrous Rolling Stone concert at the Altamont freeway that year, during which the numbed band members watched Hell's Angels stab a man to death, brought the sixties to a close by exposing the failures and hypocrisy of the counterculture and its music. Still, the tension had been tougher on sport. A few years later, Don McLean would allude to music's ascending importance in youth culture in his cryptic but revealing song, "American Pie." "The halftime air was sweet perfume," he sang, "as sergeants played a marching tune." A few stanzas later his metaphor became more direct: "as the players tried to take the field, the marching band refused to yield."

The younger generations of 1968 are now the older generations. Antagonism between sport and rock music is a distant if not lost memory. In the 1970s and 1980s the two institutions discovered that they had much to gain commercially from an alliance with each other. Looking back, it is easier to see that the seeds for this alliance were always there. Both sport and rock encouraged bodily experience; both were dependent upon the motivations and energy of youth; both once had been disruptive social forces eventually co-opted; both, despite their complex and hybrid origins, had come to be regarded as unique forms of American culture; both were bastions of masculine domination; and both carried important messages. Still, the melding of the two institutions later only served to highlight the real antipathy during the Vietnam era, the hostility itself evidence that sport was making one last stand in defense of old values.

In taking the first step across the gulf between sports and rock 'n' roll, Jose Feliciano brought attention to those messages. Money eventually silted in the gulf, erasing the ideological differences. Rock singers performed the anthem at All-Star games in interpretive styles that clarified through the lens of hindsight just how respectful and melodic Feliciano's rendition had been. Rock stars bought into ownership of professional franchises, and athletes eventually found their way onto the cover of the *Rolling Stone,* rock's Bible. Quite simply, sport surrendered its mythology to the entertainment/celebrity machine. For many, sport is now an act of passive consumption rooted in spectatorship and electronically simulated games. Rock music, on the other hand, has become a showcase for some of sport's muscularity and aggression, a place where buff performers stir the rage of pogo-hopping moshers.

The intervening decades brought Feliciano's career full circle. His popularity in Latin America never waned, his Grammys continued to accumulate, and in the mid-'90s, the man whose license plates still read "LTMYFR" reemerged in America as a star. He appeared in the film *Fargo* and, as the new century began, starred on a national television special with Latin rave Ricky Martin and the also newly resurgent '60s star Santana. More important, Feliciano reconnected with sports, a kind occurrence for someone who still carries a conceit common in males of his generation—that a professional athletic career was a possibility undone only by extraordinary circumstances. "If I hadn't been blind," he says, "I think I'd have been a ballplayer."[70] It took thirty-five years, but the healing hands of time finally finished their work: in October 2003, a sold-out Florida crowd and a large television audience warmly received Jose Feliciano as he sang the national anthem before game five of the National League Championship Series between the Cubs and the Marlins.

CHAPTER TWO

Toil and Trouble: A Parable of Hard Work and Fun

Gable trains as if he's going to row stroke on a slave galley.
—Leo Davis, The Oregonian, *1972*

I'd bang on the wall many times at night in no uncertain terms,
telling Rick to get his ass to bed, shut that music off. He had the
girls in there and they were—I'm pretty sure—smoking dope.
—Wayne Wells, *1972 U.S. Olympic wrestling team*
captain

Even in 1972, at the height of his powers, Dan Gable offered slight evidence of his physical prowess. Just 150 pounds, with black rimmed glasses, slightly rounded shoulders, and sandy red hair—already thinning at age twenty-three—he had a bookish appearance that hid his stature as the most indomitable athlete in the nation's history. A wrestler from wrestling-mad Iowa, Gable's cumulative high school and college record had been 181–1. There had been no one in his Iowa State workout room, including a 420-pound national heavyweight champion, that he feared. In 1971 he had become one of the few American wrestlers to have ever won a world championship. Now, as he prepared for the Olympic Games in Munich, Gable was just one gold medal from immortality.

Rick Sanders was Gable's Olympic teammate, older by nine months. A jaunty 125-pound bantam from Oregon, Sanders had a body that more than a decade of wrestling had sculpted into an odd but functional shape, with forearms that had little taper between elbow and wrist, and squat legs that provided ballast for a head with the one-size-too-large look of caricature. Sanders, too, had won like winning was going out of style. His high school record had been 80–1, with three state championships. He was 103–2 at Portland State, with national collegiate championships in the NAIA, NCAA College Division, and NCAA University Division. He

1968

Official COLLEGIATE---SCHOLASTIC WRESTLING Guide

Rick Sanders
Portland State

$1

Rick Sanders gracing the cover of the 1968 NCAA wrestling guide. *(Photo courtesy of NCAA)*

tacked on five national AAU championships, a Pan Am Games gold, and the first world championship ever won by an American. In 1968, the year he won an Olympic silver medal, he served as the sport's mascot, peering like an innocent choirboy in tights from the cover of the NCAA Wrestling Guide. Now, as he prepared for what would become his final competition in Munich, he had dumped the choirboy look. Sporting long hair, a beard, and a necklace of hand-carved wooden beads, Sanders, too, was just one medal away from immortality, one silver medal from being forever remembered as a slack-ass hippie.

The divisive fury of the Vietnam era put the two wrestlers in a tough spot. While pop culture enticed baby boomers with endless seductions to a life of ease, the nation's elders looked to young athletes for sober assurance that an entire generation had not been lost to hallucinogens, loud music, and an Asian jungle. For those disposed to carrying easy lessons from the tough times, the possibilities attending Gable and Sanders translated to obvious parable.

Gable was deaf to the sirens of pleasure. In the final match of his college career, for yet another national title in 1970, Gable had been upset in a 13–11 thriller by Larry Owings, a brash upstart from the University of Washington who had gone out of his way to compete in Gable's weight class. The following morning's *Des Moines Register* headlined, simply and cruelly: TITLE TO CYCLONES—GABLE FAILS! Stunned by the solitary blemish on his high school and college record, Gable began a seven-hours-a-day, seven-days-a-week regimen that made his body, in the words of writer John Irving, "no more pretty than an axhead, . . . no more elaborate than a hammer."[1] He beat Owings in a rematch, claimed his world championship in 1971, and set his sights on the Munich Olympics.

As Gable was following the unswerving path mapped by his conviction, Sanders was moving through life like mercury on a tabletop. "He could wrestle as hard and fast as anybody who ever lived," Hall of Famer Wayne Baughman told a writer a few years ago. But he also could live as hard and fast as anybody. "Everything looked good to Rick," says '72 Olympic coach Bill Farrell.[2] In a previous era such a hearty appetite might have passed as rakish virtue. In the manly environs of the locker room, wine, women, and song had been winking material for decades; now, however, in the late '60s, to the thinking of many, the new parallels—sex, drugs, and rock 'n' roll—were irredeemable and dangerous components of a worthless youth culture.

Sanders took his fill of all three. His long hair and beard alone caused many to label him "hippie." Ronald Reagan, as California's governor, had in 1966 described a hippie as someone who "dresses like Tarzan, has hair like Jane, and smells like Cheetah." Notre Dame football coach Ara Parseghian was more succinct, once referring to hippies simply as "scum."[3]

To anyone looking to choose sides, the nature of wrestling tilted in Gable's favor. The sport is as old and merciless as the human race. Matches feature barely dressed bodies entangled too intimately for some, and a pageant of disfigurement—crippled knees, crooked noses, and cauliflower ears—that mark it as coarse and vulgar to others. Indeed, wrestling's vocabulary is just a roll call of body parts and hints of what can be done to them: ankle picks, chicken wings, headlocks, bar arms, tight waists, high crotches, cradles, pancakes, and can openers.

The ring is a line painted on a sea of compressed foam; it offers no escape, no ropes to slump against. Matches last six to eight endless minutes (in the '60s and early '70s, international matches went nine). Though rules mute the sport's primitive aspects, a wrestling loss is a humiliating lesson in applied Darwinism. A wrestler who gives in to exhaustion and pain, or has his arms turn suddenly to spaghetti, will be taken apart, his opponent compounding the torture by exposing him as weak, a quitter.

Even ancient and seemingly immutable pastimes, however, were vulnerable to the shifting currents of the sixties, and, for some, the tide of social change carried a measure of approbation for Rick Sanders. The '60s brought two visions—self-sacrifice and self-realization (concepts whose opposition the noted historian and social observer Warren Susman has tracked back to the start of the twentieth century)[4] into notable collision. Whether or not the youth backlash against sacrificial effort lay in subtle pop culture enticements of the '50s and early '60s (Disney's Seven Dwarves, whose happy message was that even work was supposed to be fun; the baby boom television icon Peter Pan, who said sprinkling good thoughts with pixie dust could send one soaring to Neverland—a fancy that may have translated into acceptance of the transportive powers of hallucinogens; the pop music of the Beach Boys, who touted California teen life as "Fun, Fun, Fun"), it is hard to deny that the feel-good slogans of the counterculture—"It's Your Own Thing, Do What You Wanna Do," "If It Feels Good, Do It," and "Make Love, Not War"—owed as much to pleasure-seeking as they did to political philosophy.

One would be hard pressed to create a social profile for predicting one's embrace—or rejection—of the counterculture. Many of its most radical members were collegians from America's affluent suburbs; some, like those who gravitated toward San Francisco's Haight-Ashbury District, were from broken blue-collar homes. Historian Allen Matusow observed, "hippies were only a spectacular exaggeration of tendencies transforming the larger society."[5] Exaggeration or not, conservatives portrayed counter-culture members as spoiled and unmotivated, the products of a consumer culture that encouraged immediate self-gratification in an atmosphere of slackening discipline, child rearing, and educational standards.[6] Neither Gable nor Sanders were any more or less a candidate, by virtue of upbring-ing or demographics, for the counterculture than anyone else. Nonetheless, both would be judged by a society awash in issues brought to the fore by the emergence of the hippie.

Gable was born in 1948, on the cusp of the baby boom, and his child-hood in Waterloo, Iowa, was not one of ease or indulgence. Though his parents, Mack and Katie, oversaw a clean, well-ordered, middle-class household, they drank to the point of fistfighting now and again. In the father's estimation, Dan was the "meanest, orneriest kid alive," and his tendencies were tempered by corporal punishment—Katie occasionally breaking a yardstick over his head, Mack rapping his noggin with a heavy ring.[7] The family dynamics—and Dan's life—changed dramatically in 1964 when his nineteen-year-old sister was raped and murdered in the family home. Mack and Katie wanted to move. Dan insisted they stay, and he took over his sister's room. Thereafter, he poured all of his ener-gies, rage, and attention into wrestling.

Gable's aversion to losing and his capacity for hard work were well established by the time he finished high school. The summer before he enrolled at Iowa State, Gable wrestled a former two-time Big Eight champ on the basement mat of the Gable home. "He beat me so bad that I cried," Gable told *Sports Illustrated.* "Right then I set a goal that I'd work out *at least* once every day." Six years later he was still honoring the pledge.[8]

As Gable's fame began snowballing in the late '60s, media reports scarcely noted his skill or intelligence on the mat. Despite his kinesthetic genius (an *Esquire* profile by Irving noted, "When Dan Gable lays his hands on you, you are in touch with grace"),[9] most accounts focused on one thing: his over-the-top effort. There were rumors that he'd practiced so hard that he had to be removed from the Iowa State wrestling room on a stretcher. A writer asked him about this in recent years and discovered it to be unfounded. Gable's goal had merely been to end a work-out unable to get to his feet. "A couple of times I was so exhausted that I would start crawling towards the door," he said. "Then I'd be good enough to get to my feet. So I never really did do it, but that was my goal."[10]

Even stories aimed at something else eventually circled back to his ceaseless effort. In Ames, Iowa, in the spring of 1972 Gable was arrested for standing outside a keg party with a quarter inch of beer left in a paper cup. When a teammate was also jailed shortly thereafter, he arrived to find Gable using his brief hours in the poky doing pull-ups from a ceiling pipe.[11] In a culture gravitating toward personality, gratification, and fun, it was understandable that many baby boomers saw little point to Gable's dedication. But others did, and to them, both young and old, who believed that America was following the Roman Empire's road to ruin, Gable's regimen looked like exactly the sort of heroic sacrifice needed to put the nation back on track.

Rick Sanders had little pulling him in the direction of heroism. His father, Melvin, a millworker, had an affinity for hard drinking that matched Mack Gable's, but an approach to big dreams that more closely echoed those of Disney's Jiminy Cricket, who told baby boomers that dreams were theirs for a "wish upon a star." Melvin Sanders shot for the stars in an endless succession of implausible schemes that too often ran through the local taverns and eventually led his wife, Anita, to take Rick and older sister Patricia from south central Oregon to Portland.[12] Thereafter, Melvin wandered fitfully through Rick's life, but his big dreams left a lasting impression.

"Peanut" Sanders dreamed of attention and glory. Boys who enter high school weighing less than a hundred pounds know athletics are an unlikely place to find either. Still, for the combative, needy, or gifted—or all three—wrestling can provide entrée to the varsity club. For a rare few, such as Sanders, it becomes more. Wrestling "was in his soul," his sister says. It became, confirms Bobby Douglas, a close friend and now coach at Iowa State, a place where Sanders "had an opportunity to compete and be someone."[13]

With each win over another ninety-eight-pound schoolboy Sanders became more cocksure on the mat, and by the time he took his third high school state title, he was flashing an insouciance rooted in change and unpredictability. During a 1963 nine-match tour of Japan with other

Oregon prep stars, Sanders drew his host's attention as the American team's best, but also its most dangerous: when he asked to stay a little longer in the country, the Japanese told him, "no, go home." Preparing to stage the '64 Olympics in Tokyo, they sensed in Sanders an intrepid spirit—"nothing malicious," assures tour coach Delance Duncan—that alarmed them.[14] They were not specific in their rejection, but the implication was remarkable: they saw the elfin eighteen-year-old as a threat to their meticulous and rigid planning. To Sanders, already cultivating a disdain for tradition, the Japanese attitude was confirmation of what he'd written a few days earlier to a friend. Some of Japan's customs, he'd decided, "are not very practical now days. To put it mildly the Japanese are very resistant to change."[15]

Sanders embraced change. "He was fearless," says Douglas, and during the long hours spent in the wrestling room, Sanders put himself into precarious positions that begged for new approaches.[16] Gable did the same, determined to never find himself surprised on the mat. Surprise delighted Sanders. He learned not just to squirm out of trouble, but to turn it into stunning reversals of fortune. He concocted imaginative, unprovable theories. Don Behm, later one of Sanders's fiercest rivals but closest friends, remembers in particular Sanders's "expansion and contraction theory," a belief Sanders had that his hips worked in tandem through a countervailing tendency to shrink and enlarge.[17]

An Olympic teammate once spotted Sanders running with one foot on the sidewalk and one foot in the gutter. "Why are you running like that?" he asked. "To give my hips more flexibility," Sanders told him. In the years afterward, the teammate asked exercise physiologists about the credibility of Sanders's theory. Nothing to it, they assured him. Nonetheless, Sanders believed, and each new hypothesis stirred him to enthusiastic proclamations. "He'd babble on and on—like little kids will do," remembers Behm. "You couldn't get a word in."[18]

The inventive curiosity pleased Howard Westcott, Sanders's coach at Portland State College. A mathematician with a doctorate from Columbia, Westcott was constantly searching for the angles, balance points, and forces that would tip an opponent. His wrestling room was his laboratory, and he exulted when Sanders began thinking along with him, then started to imagine and refine showstopping moves of his own. "He developed moves never tried before," said Westcott. "He'd accidentally do something, think it was good, and the next thing you know he'd be doing it [regularly]."[19]

Sanders's need to move constantly, to engage an opponent, to put himself at risk was exhilarating to watch. Following a trip to England and Finland as part of the U.S. world team in 1965, Sanders received a letter from the coach, Bill Smith. "Your way of wrestling gives ulcers to people watching," Smith wrote, "but I enjoyed every second of it."[20] In short, Sanders's act had become one of a kind and all that wrestling was ordinarily not—creative, entertaining . . . fun.

Along with teammates and friends Masaru Yatabe and Chuck Seal, Sanders made Portland State a little giant, placing fifth at the 1967 major college tourney. Sanders lost the first match of his college career, ran off 103 straight victories, then—like Gable—dropped the very last—the finals for yet another national championship. Spun down headfirst early in the match, he continued to wrestle, without use of his numbed right hand. He lost 4–2 while attempting to take down his opponent with ten seconds left. One of his detractors says that the truth is somewhat fuller, claiming that Sanders stayed out all night before the match, drinking.[21]

For most athletes this would be a damning accusation. With Sanders it was impossible to gauge the effect because he had by then already folded into the sport all his other interests—food, sex, good times—like pecans into a cake batter. Said Behm: "I watched him take eight ounces of straight rum one day." Sanders's reasoning? Another theory: "It's only eight ounces of weight," he told his friend. "By the time I sober up, I will have lost the six pounds and I won't feel any pain while I'm doing it."[22]

Pulling weight was nearly always a pain. During the '66 trip abroad Sanders was twelve pounds above his limit less than twenty-four hours before competition. A pair of wrestlers from the upper weight classes, annoyed at his irresponsibility, locked him in a sauna while they went to a movie. When Sanders was freed hours later, he crawled from the box limp as a dishrag. Still naked, but armed with a butter knife, he eventually patrolled the hotel hallway in search of the two. The next morning he refused to walk the six blocks to weigh-in; teammates put him in a laundry basket and carried him to the scales, where he refused to stand up. He then went out and nearly upset the world champion. Perhaps the only time that paring weight was tolerable came when he wore a sweat-inducing rubber suit during bouts of lovemaking.[23]

While Sanders managed to stay small, Gable grew into the middle-weight classes. Only once, while Gable was still a high school phenom, had the two found themselves the same size. It was a moment just long enough for one memorable encounter. Before meeting in the finals of a tournament, Sanders approached Gable with some advice: "Bring a baseball bat with you." When Gable asked why, Sanders told him, "You've got me next; you're going to need it." Sanders won, 6–0. As Gable recalls, "I basically needed the bat." By the late '60s they were separated by too many pounds to make a direct rivalry possible. Still, Sanders, aware of Gable's rising fame, kept the needle in. One summer he stopped at Gable's home. Finding the clean-living prodigy out of town, he grabbed Gable's dad, Mack, and went drinking. Then he spent the night in Gable's bed.[24]

Though he'd won their only head-to-head contest, though he'd returned from the '68 Olympics in Mexico City with a silver medal, and though he'd followed that with America's first world championship the following year, Sanders was in Gable's shadow at the end of the decade.

In the next few years leading to Munich, Gable's competitive insularity did little to mute media praise and attention. ABC sent a camera crew to Iowa to record his efforts for what would become a seven minute up-close-and-personal piece to air during the Games. A *Sports Illustrated* feature noted that the Soviets were so impressed with him that they had begun scouring the vast expanse of their republics for a single wrestler who could upend him in the Olympics. Their search, he says, was "the spark that set me on fire again."[25] He continued to drive himself relentlessly; at one point he brought John and Ben Peterson, brothers with Olympic hopes, to work out—and live—for several months in the Gable home.

As Gable eclipsed him, Sanders found new attention by transforming himself into what the press called the "wrestling hippie." Former acquaintances do not agree on how it happened, or on whether Sanders grasped the full implications of his provocation. Some maintain that he never changed from the day they met him. "He was always himself," claims Yatabe. Others say they could sense a new direction. Both camps are probably right: he may not have changed much, but then again he was already equipped by nature to run headlong into the arms of the youth counterculture. Says Behm, "In a way he was a young kid . . . and the things he did were attention-getting devices."[26] They were the kind that would make him a lightning rod in the era's cultural storms.

Amid the splash of large political gestures—an Olympic black power salute, a heavyweight champion's draft resistance, a basketball floor set ablaze to protest university policy—the mere immoderations of a wrestler seem inconsequential. The truth, however, is that the smaller acts of insubordination—a few minutes of curfew tested, sideburns an inch too long, a blazer not worn for a bus trip—committed in the thousands, were just as damaging to sport's ideological foundation. Whether Sanders would have fit everyone's definition of "hippie" or not, the fact is that there were damn few athletes, and virtually none of world-class caliber, who could simultaneously meet the demands of both sport and the surging fun crusades of the counterculture. Sanders gave it a try.

If he hadn't partaken of all of pop culture's enticements to pleasure in his early years, Sanders had, after moving to Portland, smelled what was in the wind. "He drew fascinating people to him," his sister recalls. Some of them, sensing his free spirit and good humor, led him into easy alliance with sex, drugs, and rock 'n' roll.[27] On his own after leaving Portland State, without coach or team to mollify, he exercised his freedom to do as he pleased until it became an addiction—an open invitation to excess as enervating as any narcotic.

Almost overnight, Sanders went from precocious peanut to *enfant terrible*. It would be futile to try to track turning points. One of the lures of hippie existence was its enticement to changing identity so thoroughly and quickly—Janis Joplin, high school ugly duckling turning up at her first reunion as sexy blues queen. You could arise one morning, rinse the Brylcreem out of your hair, comb it with a towel, and climb into a pair of bell bottoms: ready to live life as Someone Else. "Rick was living the life," assures his friend and Olympic teammate Sergio Gonzalez. Appeasing Dionysus, Sanders took his fill of grass, drink, and women. His oversized gym bag became a magician's hat. "We affectionately called him 'Snipe,'" remembers '72 Olympic captain Wayne Wells. "He loved that name. There wasn't anything that he couldn't dig out of that damned ol' bag: sugarless ketchup, wrestling gear, whiskey bottles, marijuana joints." Long before boom boxes appeared on shoulders coast to coast, Sanders began lugging a portable stereo everywhere. Folk rocker John Prine's eponymous first album was a favorite, and Sanders listened over and over to "Illegal Smile," a song whose title was widely interpreted as a reference to marijuana and whose chorus mocked its opponents: "Won't you please tell the man I didn't kill anyone / no, I'm just tryin' to have me some fun."[28]

Fun gave hives to the sport's traditionalists, who regarded good times in the wrestling world the way a cattle rancher regards a plateful of sushi. Gable represented the side of wrestling favored by nearly all of those involved in the sport: the ascetic discipline that punished bodies and denied the pleasures of flesh against flesh. Sanders exalted the sport's hidden delights, the indulgence of tactile sensations. On the mat, he literally embodied fun, a tactic that allowed his ability to be wrongly tainted by the perception that he wasn't trying that hard. This was a cardinal sin at a time when many Americans associated the nation's sudden, humiliating impotence in Vietnam with hippie influence on our soldiers: dope, loud music, but most of all, lack of effort.

Sanders was complicit in promoting the illusion of effortlessness. "Rick always tried to give the impression that he didn't train very hard," says Gonzalez, though he says it was all just "part of his mind games." Baughman, after watching an apparently drunk Sanders appear to guzzle bottle after bottle of beer at a party, caught him—sober as a nun—secretly pouring out the contents on the ground. "I've got to maintain my image," he told Baughman. "You won't tell anyone will you?" John Peterson, one of Gable's training partners, adds: "I think Rick did train hard. He liked the attention he got from acting a little strange . . . [but] there were times when I saw him working out harder than anybody else." Assistant Olympic coach Jim Peckham recalls a day in training camp when the coaches had scheduled a run of the stadium steps: "Ricky Sanders did nothing but complain and moan and groan and whine and bitch." But, when the team finished, everyone came down to the field except Sanders and Gonzalez. "Ricky and Sergio did them again," says Peckham. "Then Sergio dropped out and Sanders did them again."[29]

Those who knew how hard Sanders had worked to become a world champion were puzzled at his wish to have people believe otherwise. Once banished from a camp run by the Christian group Athletes in Action for bringing women and booze into the dorm, Sanders began the 1970s with a series of more public offenses. Following the 1970 World Games in Toronto, he was arrested and fined for marijuana possession. On his way to a dual meet with the Soviets the following year he began running in a plane aisle to lose weight. Asked to stop, he turned belligerent, challenging the stewardesses to throw him off the flight. Though all ended well, with the understanding stews piling blankets on him, the incident earned him another black mark with the sport's higher-ups.[30]

Good thing they didn't know that he had that same year returned West from a tournament on a trip with Gonzalez that would have stood them well with Ken Kesey's Merry Pranksters. During stops Sanders ran barefoot through snowdrifts, perched on top of the sign marking the Continental Divide, rummaged trash cans for empty soda bottles to buy ice cream, walked through four states on his hands at the famous Four Corners landmark, and then dropped peyote buttons at the Grand Canyon. When he found a beaver-gnawed log near a stream, he insisted on finding it a spot in the car and taking it all the way home to Oregon.[31]

Not that he needed to do anything more than have his picture taken to raise the ire of conservative coaches and critics. Wrestling officials in the United States had safeguarded the sport against the insidious encroachment of hippiedom by banning (beginning in 1968) long hair, beards, and moustaches under the guise of hygiene. In 1971 high school referees began carrying into prematch locker rooms rulers to diagnose the afflicted and scissors to effect the cure. International wrestling had no such standards, and in the early '70s Sanders let his beard and hair grow until they wreathed his head with the full size and grandeur of a lion's mane. To keep his anxious hands busy, he carved wooden beads, then strung them together into a necklace. From its center he hung a hand-wrought wooden hash pipe.

Finally, in August of '71, he stepped across the line in the sand when Pennsylvania troopers picked him up hitchhiking along the state turnpike. He was stark naked. Placed in the back of the squad car, Sanders crawled over the seat, got behind the wheel, and began to drive away. But he did it ever so slowly, like a nervous teen inching down the driveway for the first time. The police caught him on foot. He told them that someone had slipped LSD into his coffee. The incident caused him to arrive in Annapolis, Maryland, too late for the tryouts for the 1971 world team. He responded by filing an affidavit that accused the coaches and officials of "arbitrarily" eliminating him from consideration.[32]

The incident saddened America's Olympic coach, Bill Farrell, who was assembling what would become the country's best-ever team. A flex-

Rick Sanders sporting a new look, ca. 1970. *(Photo courtesy of John Hoke)*

ible, compassionate man, Farrell liked Sanders, but he had no tolerance for drug use and little understanding of what seemed to be driving Sanders in such an untoward direction at such a crucial time. Exasperated by the second arrest, in September he wrote Sanders a long, heartfelt plea to do whatever was necessary to remain eligible for the '72 Games. "Some in the Federation do not want you to wrestle again because of the influence on the young wrestler," he wrote. Farrell made it clear he would stand up for Sanders, providing the wrestler curbed himself. In a paragraph of escalating urgency he pleaded: "By changing your ways I mean this. You must stop creating such a bad image. If you want to drink a little, drink in private. Don't tell everyone. If you want to smoke pot, do so in private, don't tell everyone. Stay out of trouble. If you have just one incident between now and June, 1972, there will not be one vote to let you wrestle. Not one. Rick, you have got to stop trying to "shock" everyone. You must stop trying to convince people that you don't care what they think or what they do. You must stop trying to let everyone know that you fight the establishment (whatever that means). Can't you use your good sense and stay clean until the Olympics? I guarantee you, just one more incident, and you will be out."[33]

Sobered, perhaps, by his mother's death in January of '72, Sanders turned down the heat just enough to get by. That spring Farrell mailed all potential Olympians an Athletic Motivation Survey. Sanders didn't send his back and never responded to his invitation to the Olympic camp. When he finally arrived at the team gathering he seemed distant to long-time friend Bob Douglas. "Something was different, something had changed," Douglas says. "I couldn't put my finger on it, but I knew it wasn't the same Rick Sanders that I was very close to."[34]

Gable presented no such mysteries. If anything had changed it was that his zest for work had, impossibly, accelerated. He and the Petersons were insatiable, frustrating a coaching staff that would have preferred they back off a little. "If we had two practices, they'd sneak off and have three," says head coach Farrell. "They'd go off someplace and I couldn't find them." When the U.S. Olympians gathered at the White House for a presidential reception before departing for Germany, Gable and the brothers decided to stay instead in their motel room. There they shoved the beds and mattresses aside and spent the time wrestling on the floor.[35]

Sanders, theretofore "actively disinterested" in politics, according to friend and former professor Earle MacCannell, attended the reception wearing a "Ban the Bomb" button. Behm has vague recall that Sanders also gave Tricia Nixon a brief but impassioned scolding for her father's

Vietnam War policy, though this, he says, could be a product of later mythmaking.[36]

When the U.S. squad landed in Munich, Sanders was in full flight, clearly having the time of his life. He railed in interviews about the stifling effect on sport of Olympic-related publicity and politics and scoffed at an *L.A. Times* reporter who asked about his schedule. "A schedule? I don't have any schedule with what I do with my life . . . Wrestling is my recreation. I get kicks out of seeing what I can do with myself." Asked by another reporter if he checked his appetite for women during competition, he responded similarly. "I don't put them on a schedule," he said, ogling a passing pair of breasts.[37]

Though the coaches and wrestlers drew plaudits for their unity and discipline, Sanders was relentless in his search for kicks. He spent hours in the city's beer gardens, at least once sharing dope with a large gathering of strangers—new friends all. In the Olympic Village, Sanders, Gonzalez, and Behm, who'd gone along as a workout partner, crowded into a small room that quickly became, according to Behm, "a pig sty." Overrun at times with friends and hangers-on—one man spent three days there before it was discovered he was unknown to all three—the partying there had no end. Team captain Wayne Wells, next door, says that Sanders was living out his commitment to sex, drugs, and drink.[38]

When assistant coach Peckham entered Sanders's room a few days before the first competition, he found empty beer bottles littering the floor and Sanders in bed with two women. "Ricky, don't cross me on this," Peckham scolded. "I want those two women out of here now." When he returned the next day, he found that Sanders had followed orders exactly. "If I hadn't seen it, I don't know if I'd believe it," Peckham says, his head still wagging in disbelief twenty-five years later. "He was in bed with two more." Behm and Gonzalez agree that while the tale may be apocryphal, its spirit was pure Sanders.[39]

No small wonder, then, that Farrell says Sanders was, on the eve of the Games, "the center of controversy and discussion." His impudent approach offended some of the others, particularly the Petersons, devout Christians who would end up winning gold and silver medals. "Off the mat, Rick lost," Ben says. "He was a troubled man in the midst of America's hippie movement. Rick was lost in the middle of that. He had no moorings for his life. I wanted to obey God in the scriptures. So when I saw anyone else that didn't . . . there might be tension involved." But, he said, "we were trying to find a way to be in agreement with each other." Most of the time, anyway. Behm says that Sanders's choice of songs during practices struck Ben as "the devil's music" or what brother John later referred to as "wild music." Ben and Sanders battled over the stereo one day, alternately dialing the volume up and down. With each turn Sanders escalated his high-pitched, squeaky needling. "What's the matter—can't take it, can ya, Ben? Can't ya turn the other cheek, Ben?" Peterson's answer was to kick the box across the room, breaking it and ending the devil's work for the day.[40]

If Sanders was the center of the team's attention, it was Gable, the Petersons, Wells, and Taylor, the 420-pound heavyweight, who were drawing the bulk of media interest. The last best hope for Sanders to grab his share would be on the mat. When the past wrestling experience of ABC's head of sports Roone Arledge created the rarity of wrestling matches televised in prime time, Sanders was ready. Announcers Ken Kraft and Frank Gifford loved his act, and their commentary amplified his swaggering reputation. Chuckling, Gifford called Sanders "one of the more interesting characters we have ever seen, and certainly a brilliant wrestler. He's kept everyone around here alert—laughing, checking the crowd out, putting the referee on."[41]

Dominating his first three opponents stoked Sanders's enthusiasm for showy performance. In Westcott's memory, Sanders wore his necklace of beads to mat's edge, removing them only upon the referee's demand and only long enough to wrestle.[42] Current Portland State coach Marlin Grahn, then an enamored spectator, remembers that each time the bantamweight was called to wrestle, the fans in the Ringerhalle scrambled excitedly to claim new seats near his mat.[43] Sanders rewarded them with scintillating wrestling. Against the Italian, Maggiolo, he worked a spectacular cow catcher cradle, inching almost imperceptibly from a position of disadvantage beneath Maggiolo to purchase an instant of possibility. Then, impossibly to the untrained eye, he levered Maggiolo suddenly and irreversibly to his back, folding his opponent's head and rear end together until they nearly touched, the Italian's body rendered as motionless as if it had been dipped in quick-drying cement.

His confidence running high, Sanders commented freely and unflatteringly on Gable. "Gable isn't as relaxed as I am," he told the *Oregonian*. "He wrestles the same way I used to in college—balls out, trying to over-power people. He'll learn, though, and if he stays around, he'll be great." Moving to matters of personality, he chirped, "Sure, our lifestyles are different; so are our wrestling styles. Most Americans don't have style. Me, I'm a cosmopolite. I can wrestle like a Japanese, a Rumanian, or a Russian." Then he added the killing touch: "I used to work hard all the time. But as you get older, you don't work as hard."[44]

Gable may have lacked style in Sanders's eyes, but his first-round bout had brought him his own cachet and lent his quest for gold a new sense of drama. What would finally make 1972 the best showing by an American team in Olympic history was its challenge to the longstanding supremacy of the Soviet Union. For two decades the Soviets had domi-nated on the mats and in the sport's inner circle. They had undue influ-ence both with FILA (Federational Internationale de Lutte Amateur) and with the satellite nations of the Communist bloc. Farrell had warned his wrestlers beforehand: "Just be ready to get screwed and wrestle through it."[45] As American viewers got their first look at Gable, the warning was reified. Handling his Yugoslavian opponent with ease, Gable was sud-denly head butted midway through the match. As blood spurted from a gash above the American's eye, the German referee called time. As a FILA doctor (the only authority for stopping the match on medical grounds) from an Iron Curtain nation advanced toward the mat, Gable's teammates set up a blockade while Farrell wound yards of white gauze round his wrestler's head. The blood momentarily stanched, the doctor bid Gable continue. A short time later, with the blood seeking to ooze through his bandages, Gable pinned the Yugoslav, dispatching the only threat he would have for days. In winning his first five matches Gable allowed not a single point.

Sanders was trying to keep up. Apprising his fourth-round match with favored Hideaki Yanagida, he predicted victory. His confidence stemmed, he explained, from the fact that the Japanese "haven't seen the new offense I have developed." But the Japanese, according to Douglas, "were very much aware of Rick's style," and Yanagida thwarted the American's aggressiveness with caution and speed in the same way that Shigeo Nakata had while beating Sanders for the gold at Mexico City.[46] Yanagida won, 4–2. The gold was gone.

Sanders's subsequent matches gave no hint that he considered it a grievous loss. He pinned an Indian, decisioned a Bulgarian, and then, with the silver medal at stake, pinned Laszlo Klinga of Hungary. Against Klinga, Sanders ran the score to 9–4 in the first period, an exhibition of such effortless invention that Gifford observed, "He's just havin' himself a lot of fun at this point." At 16–5, Gifford empathized with Klinga, telling the audience that the Hungarian was "in with a long-haired buzzsaw."[47]

A few minutes later it became obvious that Sanders's fun had turned to boredom. In the center of the mat he went into an exaggerated "sugar-foot" stance, his right leg hung out on its own, inviting Klinga to grab hold of it. Such baiting was not unusual. Asked about the Maggiolo match in which he had similarly ceded his leg, Sanders had told a reporter, "He didn't have my leg. I had his arm." Now, he lost interest in the leg and in Klinga. His gaze went elsewhere, and Gifford, laughing uneasily, asked Kraft, "What was he looking at?" Peckham, sitting in the corner, knew the answer and it infuriated him: Sanders was watching a match on another mat. Peckham lit into him between periods. "Jesus Kee-rist," he seethed. Worried that embarrassing a Communist bloc wrestler could lead to collusion that might damage the chances of other Americans, Peckham lectured: "You have no right to shame him, Ricky." Sanders, nonplussed, asked the coach what he wanted him to do—pin the Hungarian? Wrestle him in earnest, Peckham said. Sanders returned to the mat and pinned Klinga. He had his second silver.[48]

Still focused on gold, Gable had just one obstacle left. The Soviet search for someone to whip him had settled on Ruslan Ashuraliev. "They went up a weight class and found somebody that they thought was mentally tough enough to pull the weight and be a factor," Gable says.[49] They thought wrong. Though Gable wrestled tentatively, Ashuraliev had no more success than anyone else. The Iowan had simply stored too much away in seven years of training to be undone in nine minutes. Finishing the Olympic tourney unscored upon, Gable won 3–0 for the expected gold. Teammates put him on their shoulders and carried him from the mat, eventually setting him down in a hallway. There, alone with assistant coach Peckham, the universe's hardest working athlete finally revealed the barest hint of what the years of hard work had cost. "Geez, am I tired," he said. "That's OK, Dan," Peckham whispered back. "I won't tell anybody."[50]

Hard-working Dan Gable dominates an opponent on his way to Olympic gold at the 1972 Games.

The inability to reach the top step alongside three of his teammates hurt Sanders more than he let on. Privately, he approached first the Petersons and then Gable with an amazing and humbled proposal: "I want to hang out with you," he told them. The morning after his final match, Gable arose early for his workout—"I wasn't about to change my habits just because I'd won a gold medal"—and, taking Sanders at his word, went to collect his new partner. Sanders looked, says Gable, "like he'd just got in." Gazing up bleary-eyed from his bed, Sanders rolled over, telling the new god of all wrestling, "I think I'll start tomorrow." It was the last time Gable ever saw Sanders.[51]

❖ ❖ ❖

Shortly after the freestyle competition ended, Gable headed for home. "I'll see sights for a couple of days," he told a reporter, "but there isn't much here for me. I can watch Jim Ryun on television."[52] Waterloo, Iowa's hardest working athlete had just buzzed through the world's peak competition untouched. He would be going home a hero.

Sanders was reminded that he would probably be returning as something less. A friend warned him that folks back home were "going to say you didn't train properly and didn't have the right attitude." To which Behm says, "I don't think Rick cared—he never did before."[53] Nonetheless, whether struck by wanderlust or regret, Sanders decided to stay abroad.

Unbeknownst to Gonzalez, after nearly a month in Europe Sanders set out to catch up to his friend, who was by then in Greece. Traveling with the fiancée of Buck Deadrich, another friend and fellow free spirit from the Greco-Roman team, Sanders hitched a ride in Yugoslavia. On a winding road in bad weather, the driver ran headlong into a bus. Rick Sanders and Deadrich's fiancée were killed instantly.

Friends went to Portland to await the body and a funeral. When neither came in timely fashion, old acquaintances read the delay as a personal affront to Sanders and started to stew. Westcott was particularly upset, and former Olympic wrestler Henry Wittenberg railed at the insensitivity of the U.S. Olympic Committee for not intervening.[54] Sanders's stepbrother, Dave Stockner, says—and documents back him up—that the delay owed primarily to the difficulties of dealing with an obtuse Yugoslavian bureaucracy and its demand for cash in exchange for the body. Finally, donations from coaches and wrestlers enabled Portland State to have the remains returned—on a commercial flight, no special honors—and interred near Eagle Creek, Oregon.

Sanders died with $7.50 in his pocket and little of tangible worth in his backpack: parts of his Olympic parade uniform, his wooden beads, a tiny chess set. Eventually, the silver medal, at first thought to be lost, arrived in a diplomatic pouch. It was the only item to which the Yugoslavian government had been unable to assign a value. It merited a simple appraisal: "inestimable."[55]

❖ ❖ ❖

In an era when the young seemed to be gleefully watching the ethics of hard work, frugality, self-control, and postponed gratification swirl down the drain, it was easy to see Sanders and Gable as symbols. It was impossible to disregard Gable's work in assessing his ascendancy. And it was impossible—even for Sanders himself—to ignore the connection between his dissolution and his disappointment. What do the pair look like in retrospect?

Easier to say in Gable's case. He is, after all, still with us. He spent a quarter century after Munich grinding out countless more wins as a coach at the University of Iowa. In all, he won fifteen national titles and twenty-five consecutive Big Ten championships, so many that they blended together until their impact was just as a dull thud: victory was always expected; no crisis ever surprised or debilitated Gable's Hawkeyes.

The years on the mat have had some tangible costs. He has been pained and hobbled by many operations (including two hip replacements). He remained socially insular for many years. "As a competitor," he admits, "whether as an athlete or coach, I always had this way of focusing that kept me from getting close to a lot of people." The emotional suppression kept him from accepting his 1970 loss to Larry Owings. "There was just too much pain there," he admits. Finally, in 1997 he offered sincere compliments to Owings for the first time.[56]

He has, however, had a fulfilling family life. He married and raised four daughters. And he was never an outcast. Despite our tendency to recall the Vietnam era in terms of its *zeitgeist* of upheaval, it is important to remember that Dan Gable, as much as Sanders, was a child of the sixties—a prototype of and model for those oft forgotten ones: those who embraced most of the old virtues, who went in silence to the jungles of southeast Asia, who watched contemptuously as Abbie Hoffman tried to levitate the Pentagon, and kept their hair close cropped so as not to ruin the family portrait. Philip Slater's *The Pursuit of Loneliness* (1970) maintained that those feelings people worked hardest to suppress and spoke loudest to condemn in the '60s were likely those that lay closest to the surface of their own desires. If so, then despite the barriers they built, Gable and Sanders—as well as their supporters and detractors—were just inches apart.

Even years after his death, Sanders continues to yield flamboyant memories. "Rick Sanders stories?" muses Wells. "You could tell 'em forever."[57] In June of 1997, when the remaining wrestlers of 1972 (heavyweight Chris Taylor also died, in 1979) gathered for their first reunion at the Wrestling Hall of Fame induction banquet in Stillwater, Oklahoma, Rick Sanders stories continued to surprise. One told how, after the massacre of Israeli athletes, Sanders had been one of the few wrestlers to attend the stadium memorial. When he found an angry Jim Peckham fuming about man's inhumanity to man, Sanders put his arm around him, kissed him gently on the shoulder, and told him: "Coach, you shouldn't talk like that; it's not good for the soul." John Peterson said that in 1984, while doing Christ's work in eastern Europe, he had run into the Hungarian wrestling coach, the same man that Sanders had pinned in 1972. Peterson asked him if he had a Bible. "Yes, I have one," he replied. "Well, where did you get it?" Peterson asked. "Rick Sanders gave it to me at the '72 Olympics," Klinga told him. Even the unflappable Gable continues to be surprised by Sanders. Read a quote from the *L.A. Times* of 1972, one in which Sanders named him as the only wrestler he wouldn't want to face again, Gable sighed softly. "I was kind of always intimidated by Sanders," he said. "I learned something new today."[58]

He might be more surprised still to know that his attachment to Sanders runs even deeper. In 1968 Gable's future nemesis, Owings, had left a freestyle tournament in Portland triumphant but broke. He'd won his class but had no money to get to Ames, Iowa, for that year's Olympic trials, a crucial steppingstone toward becoming the kind of wrestler who might one day make an NCAA finals. A fellow wrestler—no doubt scraping by himself—recognized Owings's potential and stepped forward with the cash to send him to Iowa: Rick Sanders.[59]

Perhaps the least surprising thing about Sanders was his death. Many who knew him reflect on the inevitability of an early passing, and so they wonder as well about what a longer life might have brought. "He couldn't have coached," muses Behm, "and he'd have kept wrestling—but there are no wrestling bums."[60] That dilemma makes it nearly impossible to imagine Rick Sanders as senior citizen. When he died, his youth—no . . . his being—was trapped forever in the '60s, a tie-dyed bug caught in time's amber. Just as well. It's best we don't see him—in sandals and long, graying ponytail—limping on ruined knees through Portland's Saturday morning bazaar, eating tofu burritos and grooving with the other fifty-something stoners. How should he be remembered, then?

There are many who believe he got what he deserved: two silver medals. Sanders needed fifteen years to gain election to the sport's Hall of Fame in Stillwater, Oklahoma. If he knocked on the doors of the nation's wrestling rooms today, including some in his hometown, more than a few would stay closed.

"There is a kind of cosmic connection between wrestling and life itself," says Iowa State coach Bob Douglas. "You wrestle out of the womb, you struggle when you're dying. Everyday is somewhat of a wrestling match in one way or another."[61] Both Sanders and Gable intuited the connection, even if life itself sometimes appeared to each as a different proposition.

Gable remains confident about the value of hard work. Responding to the decline of collegiate wrestling programs in the 1990s, he has said, "America needs wrestling to survive. I don't mean wrestling, I mean work ethic. We're taking some very important values and letting them slide."[62] It is hard to argue his point when you find that not a single wrestler— not even Gable—made it onto ESPN's list of the twentieth century's top one hundred athletes. Coaches still preach hard work, and many athletes live it, but the byword is talent. Look at highly paid stars who don't run out ground balls, quit on their teammates when the final play is drawn up for someone else, rob fans by failing to fulfill their potential, and you will know Gable's meaning.

Sanders, too, however, had lessons for American sport. At a point in time when fun was seemingly everywhere in youth culture except in organized sports, he was fresh air. Few would concede then or now that the sliver of glory separating silver from gold is really everything. How much virtue was there in the 1996 Nike ad campaign that was contemptuous of Olympic losers (one billboard proclaiming "You Don't Win Silver, You Lose Gold")? We demand more. We suspect a leaden spirit beneath the gold currently gilding our arenas. While too many of our athletes don't seem to be overly committed, we suspect they're not having much fun either.

The people who knew Sanders best, including some he beat, bedeviled, and befuddled, are convinced of his worth. Farrell, who entered the Hall of Fame with Sanders, calls him "the most selfless person I've ever known." Peckham likewise remembers him with affection. Behm, Douglas, Gonzalez, and Yatabe—all of whom command respect in the sport's inner circles—have never wavered in their love.[63]

At Sanders's services, though most of his fellow Olympians did not attend, a large crowd filled Portland's largest funeral home, necessitating loudspeakers for those left outside on the sidewalk. Two women, each believing themselves to be the love of Sanders's life, stepped forward to place a rose on the Olympic flag covering his coffin.

CHAPTER THREE

Ivy League Jeremiad: The Struggle between Winning and Character

We play our games, or watch them contested, with the same tenacious ferocity with which we fight a war in Vietnam and with as little reason or sense. We are taught from the cradle that we have never lost a war and that winning is everything, tying is like kissing your sister and losing is nothing.
—*Leonard Shecter,* The Jocks, *1969*

When the University of Pennsylvania won the Ivy League basketball championship in 1966, throngs of Penn students poured into the streets of Philadelphia, joyously chanting the ubiquitous new mantra of the times, "We're number one, we're number one." Their elation was understandable inasmuch as Quaker athletics had just completed a decade that the student newspaper characterized as "tortuous castration."[1] Just over a year earlier the football team had reached a new low when it lost 55–0 to Princeton in front of a small, miserable *homecoming* crowd—it was the fifth straight week they'd been outscored by the soccer team.

Still, the public gloating over the basketball title made at least one influential Penn alumnus uneasy. He was Jeremiah Ford II, the school's athletic director. Ford recognized that winning was part of athletics, but he believed that sport had an obligation to American values that absolutely could not be compromised in the name of victory, money, or entertainment. In his mind, he and the Ivy League were the final guardians of a dying culture of character, a last hope for victory and honor to coexist. There was not a tougher time to test that hope than in the Vietnam era, a period that increasingly saw winning as "the only thing" and restraint of oneself in its pursuit an area for concession.

Jeremiah Ford II, Penn's ivy-covered athletic director. *(Photo courtesy of University of Pennsylvania Athletic Department)*

To know that Ford was going to be caught in the cultural transformation of the sixties you had only to know that in many ways he was always a citizen of another time. To find Ford's model for athletics you would need to retreat to the English public schools of the mid-1800s. There you could see headmaster Ford's vision: young men housed in intimate association for the purpose of study in the classical academic curriculum. Each day, in venting natural male urges, they would release pent-up aggression in the simulated warfare of game playing. Eventually, the best players in the school would emerge from the masses. Occasionally, they would go out to do battle with the best from other schools and return with the intrinsic rewards and bloodied noses that strenuous competition provide. Of course, they might also return with a heightened sense of school pride. This final recognition was unacceptable to Ford, that is, the "*idee fixe* that athletic results were barometers of university significance."[2]

Many would say that even at his hiring in 1953 Ford's hope of forcing reality to conform to his ideals was folly. An expanding attention to victory, visible in the rise of wire service polls and national collegiate tournaments begun in the 1930s, had become obvious by the 1950s and grown inescapable by the mid-1960s, when schools like Bradley, Duquesne, Loyola of Chicago, Western Kentucky, and Wichita used a handful of basketball recruits to claim Top 10 rankings and new institutional prominence. To Ford such sudden renown was evidence of shortcuts—misplaced priorities and corruption of amateur ideals. Ford found comfort in a place that seemed to have no need for shortcuts. In the Ivy League, he said, "we can hate enough to beat each other but trust enough to schedule each other."[3]

The Ivy Group Agreement, entered into in November 1954, proposed to maintain "the values of the game [football] in the service of higher education."[4] In setting conditions to foster intragroup competition in all sports, Brown, Columbia, Cornell, Dartmouth, Harvard, Penn, Princeton, and Yale agreed that collegiate competition offered "desirable development and recreation for players and a healthy focus of collegiate loyalty." The agreement further mandated that players and coaches "be permitted to enjoy the game as participants in the form of recreational competition rather than as professional performers in public spectacles."[5]

To Ford a professional spirit was defined not only by the presence of money or an overemphasis upon winning, but also by a loss of joy and the abdication of moral authority. He found the idea of recompense for college sport repugnant, and he often denounced the "marketplace mentality" and "bread and circuses" that he saw spreading through college athletics.[6] He preached constantly, perhaps to the point of fixation, on the pitfalls that he thought were inherent in professional games. Ford's contention that one's approach to sport shaped one's approach to life led him to discuss the relationship of athletics to any and every aspect of society, "from Shakespeare to Socrates to Socialism."[7] In fact, upon being asked for comment on John F. Kennedy during the first anniversary of the president's assassination, Ford noted rather obsessively: "I do not think he [Kennedy] was too much in favor of professional athletics. Sure, they were entertaining for the people, but they did not strengthen the national fibre."[8]

Ford had been instrumental in drafting the Ivy Agreement, and many at Penn thought his outspoken passion for its ideals led him to place the conference's sense of moral propriety above his own teams' interests. It was, said one observer, "almost as if he were leaning over backward to make sure Penn didn't win" so that the school would never be suspected of undermining the Ivy spirit.[9]

At the end of the 1950s he made a decision that reinforced that notion. Ford had hired Steve Sebo to coach football at Penn in 1954, following the successful and popular sixteen-year run of George Munger. Sebo's teams lost the first eighteen games they played. Though the Quakers went 11–16 over the next three years, at the end of the 1958 season, Ford, in an uncharacteristic gesture of appeasement to head-hanging alumni, had made the private decision to fire Sebo and had begun a quiet search for a new coach. He secretly hired Rutgers coach John Stiegman—but for the 1960, not the 1959, season. Ford wanted Sebo to close his tenure at Penn with a measure of respectability that might keep him afloat in the coaching job pool.

In a twist of fate nearly too cruel to believe, Sebo led the 1959 squad to the Ivy League championship. As Penn surged from behind to beat Cornell in the season finale, *Philadelphia Inquirer* sportswriter and Penn alumnus Frank Dolson recalled: "I remember looking at him [Ford] when Penn scored the go-ahead touchdown in the second half and [he] was like death warmed over."[10] When Ford, already obligated to Stiegman, fired Sebo in his one surrender to the god of victory, he came away labeled forever as a man who courted defeat.

The tension between Ford's approach and the response of angry alumni had roots in Penn's schizophrenic institutional history and the role of athletics in the school's identity. Penn had long been caught between the state university idea of a school that provides something for everybody and the more exclusionary model of the small liberal arts college. The pull for each was apparent from its beginning, with founder Benjamin Franklin leading the state university crowd and his Anglican aristocrat of a provost, William Smith, standing for the more selective model. This dual identity followed Penn into the twentieth century. Outsiders frequently mistook it for a state school (when Penn's basketball team made the NCAA Final Four in 1979, its supporters found vendors selling Penn State T-shirts outside the arena in Salt Lake City); insiders yearned to rename the school after Franklin.

Compounding this was a troublesome setting. In 1872 the university had moved from a downtown location to its current West Philadelphia site—a nineteenth-century move to the country, as it were. There it was eventually overtaken by the city, cut through and despoiled by thoroughfares, trolley lines, railroad tracks, and factories. Despite the presence of attractive buildings of brick and serpentine the school was, by 1931, according to a later admirer, "a second-rate school in a slum city." As history professor Roy Nichols pointed out: "There were no moonlit nights under the trees. There was no lake. It wasn't sleepy Princeton or historic Harvard."[11]

In the 1930s Penn surged to prominence through sports. Its Council on Athletics constructed Franklin Field (the first double-decked football stadium in the United States), the Palestra (a basketball arena that would attain legendary status), and Hutchinson Gymnasium. To finance the building, the council borrowed $4 million from a bank and, some say, mortgaged its academic soul. The abuses that resulted from Penn's need to fill seats, and the inability of the council to pay off the debt, led the university trustees to bring in a new president, Thomas S. Gates. Gates abolished the council and de-emphasized football.[12] The game rose again, however, in the 1940s, with the team becoming the "Notre Dame of the East" and spawning such performers as Robert Odell, a Heisman Trophy runner-up, and "Concrete" Chuck Bednarik, who became the last of the NFL's two-way players.

The hiring of physicist Gaylord Harnwell as president in 1953 meant yet another reversal of direction. Harnwell sought the balance long absent at Penn. In his first decade he doubled faculty salaries, tripled scholarship aid, boosted research contracts, doubled the university's endowment, and completed forty-five major construction projects. He was, by the early '60s, well on his way to making Penn a "gigantic realization of Thoreau's vision of the noble village of wise men."[13] In practical rather than existential terms, Penn would become to Philadelphia what Harvard was to Boston.

It would be fair to say that for a time Harnwell found nothing troublesome in Ford's allegiance to character rather than victory. The president's 1962 remark at a Varsity Club banquet that "winning half our games is plenty" was typical of his general disinterest in athletics. A close friend says that the president was, in fact, "bored stiff" by sports and positively nonplussed when his Caribbean vacation was interrupted by a phone call requesting his approval for a coach's hiring.[14]

Harnwell refused to intercede after Sebo involuntarily vacated his position as coach of the Ivy League champions and the football team, under John Stiegman, began a new campaign of woe. During successive 3–6 seasons, Stiegman ran one of only three single-wing offenses in the nation. As if to underscore the notion that participation rather than winning was the point, Stiegman adopted, in 1962, a "football for all" approach. He developed three separate teams, named the "red," "blue," and "green," that were meant to be interchangeable. Stiegman declared that any of the three could start. Their record announced that any of the three could lose. At season's end, thirty-eight players (nearly the entire squad if photos are to be believed) received a varsity letter. The football experience bottomed out when a major pastime at the games became throwing open cartons of orange drink from the upper stands of Franklin Field onto freshmen and their dates below. Each week of the 1963 season, a group of students cheered against Penn in the hopes that Stiegman would be fired.[15]

That year Harnwell suddenly began reconsidering the questions: what price victory? what price honor? He decided that it would, in fact, be all right if Penn won more than half of its games. Addressing the football banquet crowd by letter, Harnwell said, "it appears to me and to many of our alumni, students, and friends that over a reasonable period of time we should make a consistently creditable showing with respect to contests won."[16] The next year he fired John Stiegman with one year left on his contract, and he commissioned an Athletic Survey, summoning Yale's

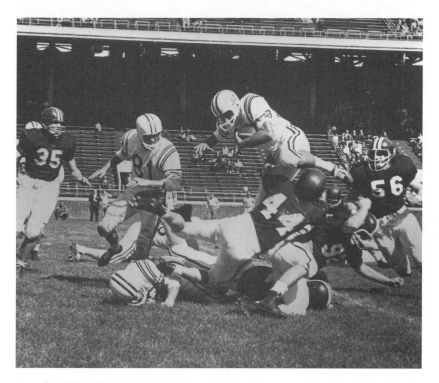

Penn football in the mid-'60s drew few spectators to cavernous Franklin Field. *(Photo courtesy of University of Pennsylvania Athletic Department)*

director of athletics, Bob Kiphuth, to investigate the status and direction of Penn sports. The report acknowledged that "if Pennsylvania cannot maintain a place of equality and respect among its chosen peers, then pride in Pennsylvania is directly and negatively affected." Most of its rhetoric, however, reinforced Ivy policy, noting that athletics "have a social and moral force on a campus which should not be underestimated," and that "academic control of athletics in the Ivy League aims for: stability in a traditionally unstable activity, human and educational values in a field where these values are often ignored, and excellence where excellence counts the most—in the recesses of the athlete's heart and mind."[17]

It was left to Penn to interpret how to maintain equality while not undermining the Ivy concept of excellence. Harnwell's answer was to create the position of Assistant to the President for Athletic Affairs in the summer of 1965 and fill it through the appointment of Dr. Harry Fields, a Philadelphia doctor and former professional wrestler.[18]

Fields reconvened the long-dormant Athletic Council in 1966–67; he solicited faculty support by having professors volunteer to act as "fraters" to all intercollegiate teams in what he termed an "attempt to bring faculty and students closer." He instituted a Career Special Program to provide special academic tutoring to all university students involved in any extracurricular activity. The Office of Admissions, while claiming that "there is no place we can tuck a boy away here," tried to cooperate in admitting a certain number of athletes for each sport.[19] More assistant coaches were hired, a full-time baseball coach was added to the staff to relieve the basketball coach of double duty, and alumni were enlisted in recruiting efforts. The new coaches were young and aggressive. Facilities improved dramatically.

The presence of Fields and his cabinet-level status distressed Jerry Ford. Ford viewed Fields as a creature of those alumni seeking a return to the big time and as an affront to all he stood for. Upon accepting his new position, Fields told the *New York Times,* "we have no intention of violating Ivy rules or leaving the league. It was unfortunate that someone overheard me when I said, 'I am willing to bend the league rules, but I won't break them.'"[20]

Over the next three years, as the influence of Fields broadened, Ford's behavior revealed desperation. He began to stray into enemy territory, even admitting once that "successful teams are an expression of the excellence of the University." He headed a committee that he himself recommended to Harnwell to find an admissions procedure that would make Penn competitive in the Ivy League. The committee eventually decided "that what was good for Harvard ought to be good for Penn."[21] Ford implied that what was good for Harvard was below the ethical standards that he had set for Penn, but he went along with the recommendations nonetheless. Always, however, Ford clung to the belief that because of him, Penn was closer to the Oxford-Cambridge model than the other Ivies and was thus an example to them. His legacy of morality and his fate in the Vietnam era were sealed by his reaction to Penn's 1966 basketball championship.

The 1965–66 Quaker squad, under Coach Jack McCloskey, seemed destined for a spot in the national championship tournament. But the

NCAA had that year set a grade point average of 1.6 (out of a possible 4.0) as the minimum standard for all athletes seeking financial aid, a level that the Ivy League schools, and notably Ford, argued was below the Ivy standard. To accept, they argued, would indicate a differentiation between the scholar and the athlete, a rift antithetical to their stated philosophy of play. Approximately one hundred other schools followed the Ivy decision not to comply, a sign that the Ivies and Ford were not deluded in their belief that they were a compelling example to many other colleges. The previous year the Ivies had refused to obey an NCAA ruling that forbade member schools from entering athletes in Amateur Athletic Union track meets. The NCAA had failed to impose penalties.[22]

The 1.6 controversy was to be different. In late February, both Ford and Yale sent telegrams of conciliation that were unacceptable to the NCAA. Ford had begun his, "While Pennsylvania will not comply with 1.6 legislation . . ." On March 4, with Penn having won the Ivy title, Harnwell received a cordial invitation to the NCAA tournament. All he had to do was refute Ford's earlier telegram. Instead, he wired back support of Ford. In the meantime, anticipating a favorable reply from Harnwell, the NCAA declared Penn eligible.[23] When Penn refused to yield, they sacrificed their treasured tournament spot.

Surprisingly, public reaction was positive. Dolson, writing for the alumni *Gazette,* labeled Ford and Yale's DeLaney Kiphuth "real heroes." The *New York Times* carried an editorial in support, and the *Daily Pennsylvanian,* the student paper, defended the defiance from start to finish. Ford took the latter to be indicative of student attitudes toward athletics, attitudes that "underwent radical change" during his tenure. Believing that he had "dragged the student body 'kicking and screaming' into the Ivy League," Ford said that this support in the 1.6 controversy "made everything worthwhile."[24]

Jeremiah Ford II (a Syracuse University publicist wondered if the athletic director would now be known as Jeremiah Ford 1.6),[25] perhaps thinking the controversy presented him with an advantageous moment to begin a showdown, publicly pressed his case against the type of sport that he believed the hiring of Fields had signaled. In October 1966, he wrote an article for the alumni magazine decrying the win-oriented atmosphere that he thought had made irreversible inroads in the Penn community.[26]

In March 1967 President Harnwell ended Ford's angst by firing him.

"Jerry and I had no differences in philosophy," Harnwell said. "He was dismissed because he failed to maintain a liaison with alumni supporters." Fields also cited the alumni antagonism as the reason for Ford's replacement.[27] Ford had his backers in the resultant mud-slinging match. Dolson sided with him, and the *Daily Pennsylvanian* again rallied to his side. Perhaps it sparked his decision to go out in a blaze of moral furor. When he learned that he was to be removed from his position, Ford called Dolson to his office, pulled the shades "like it was a CIA meeting," and revealed his intentions to unveil a slush fund and spring football practice that had, in his estimation, sunk Penn into a quagmire of moral debasement.[28]

If alumni support really did cost Ford his job, then Harnwell, in directing Penn's massive physical redevelopment, must have thought he needed those alumni for financial support. Such conventional wisdom mirrored the thoughts of Yale alumnus William Buckley, who had written in 1951, "The ultimate sovereignty of the alumni is not only a symbol. It is fact."[29] Bob Brand, a leading student activist at Penn in the sixties, echoed Buckley's sentiment. Ford's firing, said Brand, reflected the reality that universities use "athletics just to get money. We satisfy senile alumni hoping that before they die they'll give us their money." The Student Committee on Undergraduate Education also expressed concern that alumni connections were being given priority over philosophical convictions.[30]

A look at the Penn budget, however, shows some interesting things. Even in its best years, alumni donations constituted a tiny percentage of the university's total operating budget. In 1968–69, when the percentage of alumni donors reached a high of 25 percent, their donations were $2,609,659, a small fraction of the total operating budget of $151,647,000.[31] Furthermore, Penn's alumni donations had risen during its years of athletic woe. In 1962 the university won the American Alumni Council's award for greatest improvement among all independent private universities. Reporting on 1966–67, the alumni *Gazette* noted that Penn was consistently in the nation's top ten in alumni support, presumably referring to past years during which football wins had been scarce. Finally, during the years of Penn's greatest success in terms of victories, 1969–70 through 1971–72, the percentage of alumni donors dropped off steadily, and the total dollar amount of their contributions rose only slightly, actually dipping in 1970–71.[32] This is not to say that alumni support cannot be found in large gifts and endowments for specific building funds. It does, however, give rise to doubts about the connection between alumni giving and athletic prowess.

It seems likely that alumni charity was more heavily influenced by the national economic recession and perhaps alumni disenchantment with student discord, a development more likely to upset the fragile illusions upon which nostalgia rest. For as one writer has opined, "The inevitable dilemma of the alumnus is that his very soul is trapped between two times and between two histories." He hopes that his donation will either reunite the past and present or blot out all but his own special time.[33] That is, he is far less interested in finding his glory here than there.

Whether Ford believed it was alumni dollars most responsible for his demise, or something more complex, the deposed athletic director was crestfallen. Ironically, he had spent but thirty minutes in private conference with Harnwell in his entire fourteen-year stay. Based upon that, Ford had formed a conviction that he and Harnwell viewed sport in an identical light. Despite his paranoid feeling that Harnwell attached to him the "stench" of "flag-bearing alumni, special-pleading faculty members, frenetic press, and hand-wringing administrators" who loved college sport, Ford admitted to "an unrequited admiration" for the integrity and principle of the president.[34]

Ford's reputation had covered Penn while Fields set in place the structure that would bring Penn more victories, and his dismissal aroused the concern of other Ivy League athletic chiefs. Adolph Samorski of Harvard said that Ford, of all the conference's athletic directors, "best understood the principles of the Ivy League." A Yale administrator added, "The loss of Ford is a disaster to us. It's hard to believe this guy was anything but good for the Ivy League."[35] Confirmation that the sentiment was sincere came in a strange twist the summer after his firing, when Ford left Penn but not the Ivy League. Sensing the unsatisfying subjectivity of their rules, Ivy administrators decided to codify them so that interpretation of the Ivy spirit would not be left to chance or caprice. The man they called on to produce the new code was Jerry Ford. It was too late. Penn, as it turned out, had been nearly alone during Ford's tenure in its dedication to an unwritten spirit. The other Ivies had been busily at work for fourteen years revamping it to suit their own needs. In 1967 the Ivy League was ready to abdicate its moral crown for the chance to join the image race and get ahead by winning. The members' desire to codify indicated that the language of morality that had seemed perfectly clear and sufficient to define a spirit in 1954 was inadequate for policing the complexity of ethics in 1967.

Ford's fate as an idealist (in the wake of his dismissal he had written to the other Ivy athletic directors that "Maybe I am what you have always suspected—a reluctant Don Quixote")[36] awaited the broad social tests that placed idealism and pragmatism on opposite sides of a balance scale. Certain initiatives of the post–World War II era had echoed Ford's archaic resistance to the twentieth century's emphasis on relativism, self-indulgence, individualism, and atomism that was made manifest in the 1960s when a group of young theologians reasserted Nietzsche's claim that "God is dead."[37]

The rise in the 1950s of church membership evidenced American concern for plainly stated, community-based moral values. Like the Ivy Agreement, John Kennedy's agenda insisted on purpose through morality—witness the Peace Corps and VISTA. Moral resolve anchored civil rights legislation of the 50s and 60s. Hollywood's 1960s system of rating films comprised a sort of semi-censorship while aiming at definitive standards.[38] President Nixon established a commission on pornography with similar intentions. Such grand and noble public gestures were tough to sell in the unsettled climate of the Vietnam era.

The editors of Penn's alumni *Gazette* noted in 1966: "In our morality, many are becoming more 'cool,' or uncommitted. If life changes swiftly, many think it wise not to get too attached" to any one set of values.[39] The result was a profusion of principles and rampant confusion. When there was little consensus on morality, when tradition was no longer thought to be adequate for transmitting values, image no longer followed naturally from doing the right thing. Rather, it became an important goal to be cultivated and sought after through a flexible strategy. The ambivalence was not about detachment or apathy, it was about the possibility of landing on the losing side.

Ford's firing, like alumni interests, was mired in the deep emotional currents that pitted victory against honor. In past times their opposition had been irksome. In the Vietnam era, they became combustible and lethal. Moral positions became double-edged swords in a divided society

Ford's successor, Fred Shabel, who got along with a loser "as well as Ralph Nader and General Motors." *(Photo courtesy of University of Pennsylvania Athletic Department)*

and, if Ford had caught the edge created by ethical compromise, the other side of the blade awaited Penn's new athletic director, Fred Shabel.

The first non-Penn alumnus ever to be hired for the position, Shabel got along with a loser, according to the student paper, "as well as Ralph Nader and General Motors." For Shabel, the essence of competition was not in participation or even improvement. To him, "that mentality had a conflict in it—because you do keep score—wins and losses." His approach reinforced that of Fields. You can, he said, be aggressive, enthusiastic, hard-driving. You can recruit and still be Ivy "as long as you're not illegal or immoral."[40] He viewed winning as "a cure-all," but he also emphasized from his first days in office that "if there is an Ivy rule, we're not going to break it no matter what the other schools are doing."[41] His view, in an America increasingly attuned to the certainty of winning and increasingly confused about traditional idealist morality, was decidedly pragmatic. He did not demand that the other Ivies bend to his ways. Instead, he took Penn in the direction that he believed the other seven schools had already headed.

The efforts of Fields had already been showing in Ford's last year. Total varsity results for 1966–67 showed Penn with a 138–99–3 record and the freshmen teams with an astounding 126–40–3 mark. Shabel built upon those numbers by finding the university's sources of power and making the connections necessary to use them. He recognized that winning was to be the new yardstick for Ivy athletics. In a world of college athletics where money, prestige, and image were escalating, Shabel took advantage of the fact that the Ivy League, in the words of noted sportswriter Heywood Hale Broun, was treading "a dainty path between amateurism and Notre Dame."[42]

Innuendo trailed Shabel's program, but allegations of clear wrongdoing never surfaced. Driven by extraordinary personal energy and dedication to winning, Shabel turned Penn into the Ivy League's biggest winner. In 1971–72, Quaker varsity teams compiled the best won-loss record in the school's 109 years of intercollegiate competition, 162–60–3. Five teams won Ivy League championships; the heavyweight crew won a national championship. In 1973, Penn had four coaches representing their sports in the high councils of the NCAA.[43]

The new emphasis upon winning came at a time guaranteed to put Shabel in the spotlight. The Vietnam era offered perhaps the highest preoccupation with winning that the country had ever before experienced, perhaps no coincidence in light of the Vietnam War. Most Americans in the mid-'60s, despite mounting numbers of antiwar protests, clung to the hope for an American victory in Vietnam. Public support for the war was still widespread in the winter of 1966 when S.Sgt. Barry Sadler's musical tribute to the U.S. Army's Special Forces, "The Ballad of the Green

Berets," became number one on the *Billboard* music charts, rising conspicuously above the rock 'n' roll fare for five weeks.

When *Life* magazine editorialized in 1966 that "The War Is Worth Winning," they were contradicting President Lyndon B. Johnson, who two years earlier had privately called the Vietnam War "the biggest damn mess I ever saw," before adding, "I don't think it's worth fighting for, and I don't think we can get out."[44] He was, in many respects, playing for a tie. It is more than coincidence that as it became clearer and clearer that the United States would not get out of Vietnam with a win—and maybe without a tie—victory elsewhere in the culture, particularly in sports, seemed to claim greater attention and wield greater clout. The aphorism that "winning isn't everything, it's the only thing," which became attached to Green Bay Packer coach Vince Lombardi, the "when you lose, you die a little" observation of Washington Redskin coach George Allen, and the "defeat is worse than death" proclamation of Minnesota basketball coach Bill Musselman appeared at a time when many Americans desperately wished to see the nation as a winner in the face of an internationally humiliating experience. It is no coincidence, in particular, that more youths quit athletic teams at the same time that the counterculture was urging the United States to pack it in overseas. It was better, it seems, to sit out a contest than to lose it.

The effect that the Vietnam War had on American perceptions of winning became clear when, immediately following the Tet offensive of the Vietcong in January 1968, there was a sudden, massive swing of public opinion against the war. The Tet thrust had convinced many Americans that the war could not be won, and for the first time more people opposed than supported American intervention in Vietnam.[45] Eventually the nonwinning effort became so unpopular that writer Frank Deford observed in 1975, "In the last decade, cheerleader has become a disparaging word. It now conjures up the image of a mindless robot. 'He's a cheerleader for Vietnam' is the particular phrase, I think, that did the most damage."[46]

Cultural preoccupation with winning arose at a time when it could be fed upon by the growing cynicism of the young. Among the visible segment that comprised the counterculture, the stress on competition and winning produced a backlash. Critics denounced modern sport most loudly on the point of competitive zeal undertaken in the name of winning. The attacks were tied of course to other strands of dissent against perceived immoralities, but they produced a conscious attempt by some youth to substitute noncompetitive play such as Frisbee and "New Games" (alternative "sports" that stressed participation and fun rather than winning. They first arose in the late '60s on the West Coast) for traditional sports.[47] As if to confirm the viability of such alternatives, a 1971 Gallup poll revealed that 43 percent of students at sixty colleges had a declining interest in sports, perhaps reflecting a wish to escape competitive environments.[48] At least one corporation, seeking new recruits, took as an article of faith that the counterculture and its anticompetitive message had surpassed the traditional interest among many young people in competition and winning. In 1969 it conceded losing, independence, and lack of effort to the young in this astounding ad in the Penn newspaper:

FAILURE
You'll never get anywhere without it.
Nothing helps a young engineer's career like being given a challenge.
Which is another way of saying *a chance to fail* now and then . . .
Don't get us wrong. We keep our demands reasonable enough so
that our recruits can make their decisions at their own pace. But our
thinking is, a man feels awfully good about even a small decision
when it's *his*.[49]

Nonetheless, there was more to youth culture than the counterculture. To baby boomers raised in competitive situations, sold on the ideal of character-building, and now confronted with the strain on ethics and social responsibility, it was difficult to find a comfortable attitude in the area of "play," and difficult to abandon competition. Pollster Daniel Yankelovich found that in 1970 Americans were fiercely competitive and judged their fulfillment by standards of competitive success. For all the rhetoric of the counterculture, then, it is likely that the great number of young did not renounce the competitive ethic.[50] Indeed, the counterculture, while often ignoring sport and its problems, nonetheless expressed its own goals in competitive terms, as did the civil rights movements for blacks and women. College protestors who laid siege to administration buildings were adamant about not leaving until they had secured victory over the establishment. Two anthems of the civil rights movement expressed their goals in fighting language: "We Shall Overcome" and "We're a Winner." Women's rights took its greatest leap forward in visibility when tennis professional Billie

Jean King routed Bobby Riggs in a 1973 match with a huge national television audience watching in suspense.

Just as the young found it difficult to elude competition, so, too, did they find themselves vulnerable to one of its outgrowths: specialization. Though the Vietnam War served as a large umbrella for general social dissonance, groups dedicated to various reforms showed an inclination for internecine feuds and tended to splinter into smaller enclaves of special interests. Just as strong as the counterculture's quest for a "brotherhood of man" was its admonition to "do your own thing."

In sports, the trend toward specialization had been under way for decades. The Ivy League had resisted it, touting the concept of a well-rounded student. An Ivy athlete trained in the ways of character would become equal measures of Lancelot, Lincoln, and Lindbergh. In 1963 Army coach Earl Blaik, supporting the goal of whole-person development, predicted that two-platoon football—a system that de-emphasized on-field specialists—would return nationally due to Ivy influence. He was wrong. Instead, the Ivy league produced the first of the symbols associated in later years with overspecialization, the soccer-style field-goal kicker. Pete and Charley Gogolak, Hungarian brothers, kicked for Cornell and Princeton in the mid-'60s. In his first game, Pete matched Cornell's field-goal total for the entire decade of the 1950s.[51]

In 1967 Penn produced a startling new admissions document, the McGill Report, that rejected "the concept of a student population composed exclusively or even predominantly of 'well-rounded' individuals."[52] The McGill Report provided explicit and precise guidelines for the admission of athletic talent. The document was death to Jeremiah Ford; in his view, university athletics were obliged to enhance the student. The Ivy Agreement had specifically stated that players were to be "truly representative of the student body and not composed of a group of specially recruited athletes."[53] The new report was a godsend to Harry Fields and Fred Shabel; it meant they could deliberately seek out better athletes who would be obliged to enhance the university.

Almost immediately, the number of black athletes at Penn rose dramatically. In 1968 basketball coach Dick Harter told the student paper: "I don't care what color a ballplayer is, if he's good, I want him. And of course, Negroes get an extra break in the admissions office."[54] Blacks became just the most visible of athletes who, by virtue of their special skills, increasingly stood apart from other students on the Penn campus. To Shabel this was inevitable. He believed that 75 percent of victories came from personnel, 15 percent from coaching, and 10 percent from luck.[55] Recruiting specialized athletes brought Penn the wins they had never dreamed of under Ford. Still, reflecting the uneasiness produced by a culture in flux, the new victory culture at Penn revealed mixed emotions on the part of the school's sportswriters, athletes, and student body.

In the mid-'60s, attention of sportswriters to the "behind-the-scenes" action was in keeping with a national trend to not just report but also examine sport. At the *Daily Pennsylvanian,* sports editor Dan Rottenberg began the trend toward more critical scrutiny during the days of Ford and Stiegman. Rottenberg was highly complimentary to Jerry Ford. While he conceded that athletic alumni hated Ford and that the athletic director was highly sensitive to criticism, he nevertheless praised Ford for his principles and noted as well that Penn tennis and squash teams were among seven Quaker sports that ranked "with the best."[56]

Rottenberg's successors, though they touted winning Penn athletes, became more attuned to their perceived roles as observers, critics, and watchdogs. Following a 1968 Penn-Columbia soccer game in which there were "fists flying more often than the ball," writer Mark Lieberman ventured that Shabel's presence "has made victories the goal of Pennsylvania. This goal can lead to the win-at-any-cost attitude instead of the play-for-the-fun-of-it feeling which should be present." In Lieberman's mind, "the wholesome atmosphere of sports came a bit closer to defeat, even closer to extinction" during the soccer game.[57]

A year later, the paper compared Shabel's stand in a controversy over the participation of Penn athletes in the Maccabiah Games to Ford's handling of the 1.6 crisis and concluded that Shabel's actions constituted the "Rape of the Quaker." Steve Bilsky and Alan Cotler were to have played on the U.S. national basketball team. When it appeared that doing so might again jeopardize Penn's spot in any post-season NCAA tournament, the pair decided not to play. The decision was left to the players, but only after a little arm-twisting by Shabel. Former sports editor Guy Blynn wrote that Shabel lacked guts in the matter.[58] That same year the *Daily Pennsylvanian* conferred upon Shabel the "William Calley, 'I'm Only Following Orders' Award" for building a winning machine at the expense of the Ivy Agreement, a charge that ludicrously tied Shabel to the most egregious acts of war.[59] Finally, in the winter of 1971, at the height of Shabel's and Penn's success, the paper printed a five-part series of unflattering critiques that accused Shabel of sacrificing Ivy principles to winning.[60]

The athletes, as protégés and beneficiaries of the character-building system, and those most susceptible to the wishes of authority, were in a bind. Penn's pre–Athletic Survey pledge to be merely competitive in effect had meant little chance to win. Even the adherents of character-building through participation were hard put to resolve this problem insofar as the *chance* to win was part of its gospel. Harrison Clement Jr., member of the football and track teams in the early '60s, said competitive parity in his time was an illusion. It led, he contended, to a "philosophy of mediocrity" that destroyed the self-esteem of its athletes.[61]

Heavyweight wrestler Bruce Jacobsohn shared Clement's abhorrence to what he termed Penn's "benign neglect." Jacobsohn felt that Harnwell's and Ford's moral commitment had tied the hands of Penn athletes and contributed to a malaise wherein "losing ceases being abhorrent and the whole concept then mires down to some sort of dullness, and the pleasure of winning ceases being as pleasurable because you haven't gambled as much in terms of your own emotional framework."[62]

In the views of Clement and Jacobsohn, then, excellence and losing were mutually exclusive concepts. But athletes weaned on the character-building concept had difficulty casting away its advertised benefits for the mere sake of winning. Jim Riepe, Clement's friend and captain of the 1964 football team, sensed that the institutional effort to win was not maximum, yet still he thought that the experience of the 1–8 1964 season held long-term rewards that outlived the fun of winning: "Character is not built," he said, "when you're on a roll . . . character is built when things get tough . . . I came out of that [bad coach, bad knee, losing] better. It took a couple of years, but I came out of that far, far better in terms of adversity and everything else . . . It was just fun doing it. It was a very significant thing fighting our way through all of those problems and playing."[63]

Despite bitter feelings about the mediocrity he thought Ford imposed, even Clement reflected decades later that "if I hadn't failed as an athlete and had that sense of frustration, self-doubt, I'd have a helluva time coping with some of this stuff [real life problems]."[64] Jerry Ford could not have written a better defense of participation, an argument that sport's character-building process prepared people for the hardships of real life. Of course, the idea that sports could be likened to real life offended many young. In recounting his experience in Vietnam, a disillusioned veteran wondered: "Why didn't our teachers, charged with preparing us for life, ever mention the possibility of Vietnam? Surely they knew that life would offer greater crises than third-and-17 on your own 6-yard line."[65]

In the winter of 1973, while expressing renewed concern for Ivy ethics, the *Daily Pennsylvanian* admitted that it was "the desire of a majority of the Penn community that this school should have the best damn athletic program possible." Almost certainly, the students' moral sense of self was the hostage of the powerful fact of identity-seeking and its manifestation in the widespread quest to order society through numerical rankings—that is, after years at the bottom, many Penn students enjoyed winning. In their regard, Ford's philosophical approach to sport made him a "representative to a theoretical past."[66]

Despite the wish by some to hold onto that past, Ford's vision was irretrievable. When he made his annual report in 1970, Gaylord Harnwell wrote: "We cannot go home again to an era now gone with the wind. For it is the winds of change rather than the breezes of summer that are blowing across our campus and they will undoubtedly grow with intensity with the change of seasons."[67]

In 1962 a fraternity member had told *Holiday* magazine, "We're all disappointed Harvard men." Ten years later the image of Penn was still "vaguely self-effacing and unsure."[68] But the university that Philadelphians regarded as "the school on the hill" had decided that the way to join Harvard, Yale, and Princeton, the "schools in the clouds," leaned more heavily on victory than honor. The shift could be found in the many small acts, words, and deeds that, drop by drop, contributed to the larger deluge.

After a freshmen basketball game in 1969, Penn rooters began chanting "The refs eat shit," a reaction which, according to the *Daily Pennsylvanian* reporter, gave one an idea not of how ill-mannered the crowd was but of "just how atrocious the calls were."[69] The following year Dave Friedl, a player on the 150-pound football team, advised a reporter to "Remember, it isn't a crime to play dirty, but rather to get caught playing dirty."[70] Penn basketball coach Dick Harter had received Christmas cards from every coach in the Ivy League and the Big Five after an 11–14 season. After taking the Quakers to the top ten nationally in 1970–71, he received just two. Such were the costs of victory. In the new atmosphere where winning counted most, John Powers noted in the *Harvard Crimson:* "Yale feels inferior to both Harvard and Princeton, Dartmouth feels inferior to Harvard, Princeton, and Yale, and everyone entirely dislikes Pennsylvania."[71]

CHAPTER FOUR

When Falls the Coliseum: New Perceptions of the Physical

While stands the Coliseum, Rome shall stand;
When falls the Coliseum, Rome shall fall;
And when Rome falls—the world.
    —*Lord Byron,* Childe Harold's Pilgrimage, *Canto IV,*
    Stanza 145

On October 1, 1970, the Phillies and Expos played the final baseball game in Philadelphia's Connie Mack Stadium (née Shibe Park). Early in the evening, the crowd of 31,822 began dismantling the old brick and steel ballpark at Twenty-first and Lehigh. The Phillies handed out facsimile seat slats as remembrances. The fans used the ersatz souvenirs to help hammer apart the real seats, then threw them out onto the field. They tore off the outfield railings and billboards; they ripped the rain tarp to shreds, took hot dogs and beer from vendors, ransacked the dugouts, and ruined the turf. In the eighth inning, five fans got onto the field. Between innings, a boy stole the ball off the mound. In the bullpen, popular Phils pitcher Chris Short evaded a constant hail of wood, beer cans, and bolts. After a fan ran onto the field and grabbed left fielder Ron Stone's arm as he broke for a batted ball, the umps considered calling the game, a possibility that made the edgy players a bit jumpier. First baseman Deron Johnson remarked, "I'm just glad Montreal wasn't beating us 10–1, or we never would have finished the game." When the last out finally came, the fielders ran for their lives. Groundskeepers bravely raced fans to claim the bases. A helicopter hired to ceremoniously transport home plate to its new South Philly home was unable to land. The fans finally returned to their cars, carrying through blocks of urban blight their many souvenirs: rows of seats, clutches of fresh turf, jars of infield dirt, batting helmets, twisted bits of metal—and a restroom urinal.

Fans stripped the advertising from Connie Mack Stadium's fences after the final game in 1970. *(Urban Archives, Temple University, Philadelphia, Pennsylvania)*

The Vietnam era seemed awash in such scenes: community-building/destroying rampages, bacchanalian victory fests, gatherings that delighted, horrified, and defied the senses while blurring the lines between sport and the larger society. They were defining moments for perceptions of sport because they brought attention to two paradoxical agreements that supported the character-building ideology: first, that sport, by virtue of its tamed and judicious use and display of physical prowess, had an important place in the life of American society; and second, that playing fields are marked off as special spaces for special things apart from the real life of society. The physically raucous Vietnam era begged several questions about those assumptions: Were athletes subject to the same rages that seemed to be spoiling modern America? Were arenas sanctuaries or battlefields? And what set the era's outbursts apart from the goalpost-ripping, bonfire-burning, and tickertape-dumping spectacles of earlier decades?

The answers require a reckoning with America's prior regard for physicality. The years between World War II and the Vietnam era had been golden ones for images of American vigor. The most vibrant popular icons of midcentury lore were rugged, hardened, and physically courageous: the cowboy who wandered deserts in Louis L'Amour novels and John Wayne movies; the soldier who had bullets carved from his body without anesthesia, or the tailgunner who went down with the plane; the frontiersman who tamed bears and Indians; and the athlete who overcame debilitating childhood disease to become the world's best. All of them became prototypes for entertainment's leading men. The twenty-three Tarzans that appeared on Hollywood screens between 1940 and 1965 were all muscle, needing few words to assert dominance over all the creatures of the earth. Disney's Davy Crockett used language primarily to embellish his bear-huggin', gator-rasslin' feats. Superman was a newspaper reporter, but his real value to society was in his ability to defy speeding locomotives, bullets, and gravity. For every Brer Rabbit that survived on wit, there was a Mighty Mouse, a Popeye, or a Spiderman ready to thwart foes with supernatural physical gifts.

Goaded by Cold War anxiety and Soviet strength, however, Americans in the late '50s and early '60s confronted the possibility that post–World War II prosperity had resulted in slackening strength that betrayed the examples of their pop culture prototypes. In 1961, Australian mile record holder Herb Elliott denounced the United States and its people as "weak, soft, and synthetic," reinforcing a message that President John Kennedy had sent a few months earlier when he called in *Sports Illustrated* for revitalization of "The Soft American."[1]

For most Americans, questions about the worth and meaning of physical dominance, and consequently sports, really did not have to be addressed until, as with so many other questions, the Vietnam War seemed to demand a new set of answers. In discussing American foreign policy in 1966, Sen. J. William Fulbright noted the existence of two Americas, one quietly self-confident, the other arrogant in the use of power. Conduct of the Vietnam War led Fulbright to conclude that the United States had fallen prey to "a psychological need that nations seem to have in order to prove that they are bigger, better, or stronger than other nations." Implicit in this mentality was the belief that "force is the ultimate proof of superiority."[2] One of the first campaign proclamations of vice presidential hopeful and U.S. Air Force Gen. Curtis LeMay in 1968 underscored this belief. "We ought to bomb Hanoi back to the Stone Age," LeMay announced. The conflict in Vietnam would shake this doctrine of "ultimate proof" to its roots.

Many Americans, particularly the young, derived from the war unsettling images of physical might and its contribution to national, institutional, and individual identities. As news anchors read the daily death tolls, the war brought into focus concern over the prepolitical type of authority that the ritualistic domination of one body over another expressed.[3] President Johnson became sensitive to the implications of the nation's use of might. In July 1965 he told Americans that though the United States would not surrender in Vietnam, neither would he "bluster or bully or flaunt our power." In an astounding assertion from a leader at war, Johnson one week later said that, "We're trying to do the reasonable thing, to say that power and brute force and aggression are not going to prevail."[4]

There was little doubt about Vietnam's life-and-death importance to the young. Busfuls of the committed and blue-collared reported daily to military induction centers. In the first five months of 1968, 40,000 students participated in 221 major demonstrations on 101 campuses. Most were protesting the Vietnam War and what they thought was an establishment belief in "the efficacy of violence and the politics of the deed" as expressed by the likes of LeMay.[5]

For many youths, Vietnam represented a clash over irreconcilable conceptions of life and death, vitality and debilitation. Inasmuch as there was no victory or even end in sight, the war carried for many a sense that *Time* later recalled as one of "meaningless, profligately blasted youth."[6] Because of the bombing of Hiroshima in 1945, wholesale annihilation hung over the baby boom generation like a mushroom cloud. First from missile silos in Siberia or Cuba and then from Vietnam, a distant, impersonal dread threatened them—unseeable, unknowable, unstoppable. As the United States' effort in Vietnam was revealed as weak, ineffectual, and unheroic, as the draft numbers and death count rose dramatically after 1965, the youth movement's major objections to the conflict became generalized arguments regarding the devaluation of human life, the indignity of killing others, and the prevalence in the world of degrading acts of violence.

Parts of popular culture reflected a growing intolerance for physical dominance. Baby boomers had been raised on a diet of television in which violence prevailed in eight of every ten programs, with 7.2 violent actions occurring per hour. The violence depicted frequently stunned, maimed, and killed without much visible distress. Of all shows, cartoons were the most violent.[7] But while violent programming persisted throughout the era, and the nightly news carried the carnage of Vietnam into American homes, other shows began countering the rage. The villain-crushing heroism of television's Superman in the 1950s yielded to the pot-bellied camp of Batman in the 1960s. The violence of this "caped crusader," who made a prime-time splash in 1967, was parodied by the appearance on the television screen of comic book balloons that punctuated each phony punch with words like "Pow," "Bam," and "Kkkrunch."

While a few shows, such as *Combat* (1962–67) and *Dragnet* (1951–59, 1967–70), continued to depict the traditional heroism of soldiers and police, many others poked fun at these things. The very popular *Andy Griffith Show* (1960–68) had a bumbling deputy serving under a sheriff who carried no gun. *McHale's Navy* (1962–66) and *Hogan's Heroes* (1965–71) portrayed American military men not only as unheroic but also as con men and nincompoops. The popular *Gomer Pyle, U.S.M.C.,* one of the country's top-ten rated shows during its 1964–69 run through the heart of the Vietnam era, lampooned America's war machine. Pyle was a gentle country soul from Andy Griffith's fictional Mayberry, North Carolina, who enlisted in the Marine Corps. His ineptness at the skills of war frustrated his gung-ho sergeant but made him a popular figure with audiences. In 1972 *M*A*S*H* began a long run of success by more pointedly criticizing the mentality of war. Set in the Korean War, *M*A*S*H* starred doctors at odds with the senseless brutality of combat.

Sports, after surviving the turn-of-the-century controversy over college football deaths that had stemmed from mass plays like the flying wedge, had become, owing to the facade of character-building, largely exempt from criticism about its brand of physical dominance. A 1964 photo of New York Giant quarterback Y. A. Tittle, kneeling on the turf following a Steeler blitz, blood running down his forehead, became famous. Tittle's blood and mud were taken as emblems of a ferocious and manly struggle. That year *Sports Illustrated* found nothing untoward in titling an article on linebacker Dick Butkus "Brute with a Love of Violence," and nothing undue in boxer Floyd Patterson's promise to "destroy [Cassius] Clay" with "vicious" punching that would "never stop."[8] These merely underlined a 1960 cover that had proclaimed the "violent face of football" as nothing more than the "harsh spirit of a big, tough game" (in 1966 *Life* was still advertising NFL play as the "Controlled Violence of the Pros").[9]

When *Esquire* magazine printed a special section in 1967 on violence, football was, as "a display of total violence and mayhem," the only sport that drew mention.[10] When historian Arthur Schlesinger Jr. published a small book on the violent America of the 1960s, films and television figured in his assessment of "violence as an American way of life," but not sports.[11] Indeed, to the celebrants of sports, violence claimed its victims elsewhere—the thirty-four dead in the Watts riots of 1965, the thirty-three who died in the wake of 1968's assassination of Martin Luther King Jr., the tens of thousands killed in the jungles of Southeast Asia. If *Esquire* and Schlesinger didn't consider sports a significant part of the era's turbulent reckoning with physical mayhem, however, there were many people who could not avoid seeing connections.

On college campuses—the places that claimed to have found a way to reconcile mind and body—sport's role in the era's turmoil was evident. From at least the late nineteenth century, there had been antagonism between campus "jocks" and (choose one) "wets," "nerds," "wimps," "pukes," "geeks," or "eggheads." The dividing line between jock and puke was whether one believed that the core of the college experience was found in the classroom or in the extracurricular activities and associations that reinforced a social hierarchy ruled by athletes, fraternities, and their auxiliaries.

Without a doubt, the separation between jocks and pukes was supported by an awareness of the degree to which physical might—real or implied—granted power to the jocks. Before the Vietnam era, a campus showdown between the man of physical prowess and the man of intellectual cunning would be no contest. Television's *General Electric College*

Bowl, which ran from 1959 to 1970 and pitted college teams in a contest of knowledge, probably offered the only avenue for academic measurement that would have drawn a glimmer of student interest. By and large it was the athletic arena that offered the most visible way to express identity and attain status. As Ohio State assistant football coach John Mummey wryly observed in 1974, "You don't have 87,000 people at a spelling bee."[12]

The successful promotion of and belief in character-building allowed proponents of campus athletics not only to claim that physical skill had a bearing on one's social development, but that it indeed entitled one to rub elbows with the intellectually elite. Conceding publicly to the primacy of education as the goal of a university, adherents of competitive athletics spent decades stretching education's umbrella to cover the playing field. The proof of their success lay in the widespread acceptance of the oxymoron *athletic scholarship.* Only the Ivy League, which never conceded a difference between athletes and all others on campus, found the term distasteful.[13]

The notion of rubbing elbows took a literal turn in the Vietnam era. The assertion that athletes knew how to confine their physical expression to the playing field looked patently false. Often, it was Vietnam policy that proved the catalyst. At many campus political demonstrations in the mid-'60s, the threat of violence between jocks and demonstrators hung daily in the air. At Towson State University near Baltimore, the president used a young and intimidating coaching staff to deter demonstrators from their targets. It was a tactic followed at other schools. In 1965, at Penn, a group of jocks "taunted, grabbed, and hit some students and faculty members who happened to be carrying signs of protest (though) most were content to chant 'Hit 'em again, harder, harder' . . . or to sing the national anthem."[14]

To those actively involved in politics, most jocks seemed unthinking, apolitical, and hence trivial. Not enough athletes seemed, like distance runner and 1964 Olympic gold medallist Billy Mills, to care about larger matters. Mills quit running in 1965. As he explained: "I felt I could not participate in a sport when people were being killed in Vietnam." Or, as Columbia student-author James Kunen put it: "There's no real social value in sports." In describing the 1968 student strike at Columbia, Kunen wrote: "Every so often I get hit with eggs, which a small group of jocks are having good clean fun throwing. Since they have no arguments and no support for their arguments (of which they have none), they have no recourse but to assault us like this and sing fight songs—that's right, fight songs. They are standing there—I beg you to believe this—throwing eggs and singing 'Roar, Lion, Roar' all the while."[15]

To jocks who opposed demonstrations, their involvement was anything but apolitical. Their politics were in opposition to what they perceived as an abdication of authority by a group of "morally flaccid" administrators who were going "to let these turkeys take over their school." For some, the whole question of political associations merely amplified old tensions that sprang from old divisions—jocks versus nerds, doers versus thinkers, people of conviction versus those of ambivalence. Michigan State footballer Phil Hoag saw demonstrators as "just losers, going nowhere, doing nothing." Of course, then, "There was no question that anytime you could punch one, you punched them."[16]

But, while rhetoric and common wisdom said that the nerd, hippie, puke was a pacifist—a physical dropout—in reality, during the Vietnam era, the critics of sport and the military failed to take note of a curious thing happening within their own circles. According to author Theodore Roszak, the linking element among all the young was that of "articulate behavior falling away before the forces of the non-intellective deep."[17]

The counterculture, and those who combed its actions for meaning, saw in the appeal of sex, drugs, and rock 'n' roll an underlying shift from nihilistic destruction to therapeutic physical activity. That meant the development of new physical expressions derived in part from the desire for open experience, the wish to shed technology's omnipresence and return to nature, the quest for personal fulfillment, and the avoidance of destruction as epitomized by the Vietnam War. All could be seen in the prominent themes of popular songs from 1967 to 1971, which emphasized nurturance, universal love, and sensory gratification.[18]

Susan Sontag, a self-proclaimed member of the movement, observed that the counterculture of the young sought to dismantle an old consciousness rather than build a new one. "Hence the anti-intellectualism of the brightest kids," she wrote, "their distrust of books, school; their attraction to non-verbalized experiences like rock [music] and to states, such as that under drugs, which confound verbalizing."[19]

Though sometimes referred to as merely a new substitute for beer, psychedelic drugs struck some analysts as a symbol of the attempt to re-enter the forbidden regions of the body-consciousness and establish a break between the individual and established society.[20] Rock music often accompanied and complemented drug use in its presentation of lyrics, images, and electronic distortion that stressed open experience and experimentation. In Philadelphia, two discotheques, the Trauma and the Electric Factory, catered in the late '60s to the psychedelic crowd, backing deafening music with multiple projections, "hypnotic synesthesia, and kinesthetic lysergia."[21]

Opposition to establishment causes, including the war, was consciously irrational and anti-intellectual. (It was thus highly ironic that for many draft resisters, their escape from the physical threat of war came through their symbolic attachment to the intellectual in the form of their student deferments). Their politics were affective and dramatic.[22] More important, they were physical. As the antiwar movement gained power and physical stature, the countless number of boys who had hung lifeless from a school gym's pull-up bar—beet red with effort and shame—found an outlet that allowed them a taste of the jock's world. Norman Mailer, watching the protestors at the 1967 march on the Pentagon, saw their cheering camaraderie as compensatory behavior for having "never traveled on a high school victory bus."[23] Vice President Agnew sensed the same and was repulsed by the possibilities of his political enemies turning to force. "A society which comes to fear its children is effete," he told college students in 1969. "If my generation doesn't stop cringing, yours will inherit a lawless society where emotion and muscle displace reason."[24]

While the new darlings of the media—political activists like Stokely Carmichael, Mark Rudd, Mario Savio, Abbie Hoffman, and Jerry Rubin—appeared to be men of words, their rhetoric often urged insurgent physical deeds. Indeed, the politics of the counterculture came to be those of threatening confrontation. Demonstrators who placed flowers in the rifle barrels of National Guardsmen outside the 1968 Democratic National Convention in Chicago were as physically provocative as their antagonists, reenacting the childhood ritual of drawing a line in the playground dirt.

Clearly, at the height of the Vietnam era Americans were ambivalent about war and resistant to the trivialization of real killing. Nonetheless, the opposition to violence in theory and the perceived horror of its reality in Vietnam did not prevent segments of the peace movement, some dedicated pacifists, from resorting to violence themselves. It was, psychologist Kenneth Keniston theorized, at the point that the counterculture recognized its own capacity for violent behavior, that it self-destructed.[25] The nonviolent dogmatism of the movement gave way to its affective politics, at times denying the humanity of its adversaries, just as it accused American soldiers of doing to the Vietnamese. Meetings of the leftist Students for a Democratic Society ended in fistfights, black power became linked to the threat promised by Black Panther rifles, protestors at Columbia squared off in physical combat with counterdemonstrators, and the peaceful aura of 1969's Woodstock music festival yielded to the violence of the Rolling Stones' Altamont concert, in which a motorcycle gang stabbed and stomped a spectator to death just a few yards from the performing band members.

The inability of the peace movement to thwart its own internal violence provided practical evidence for scientific research that was, since the turn of the century, preoccupied with the organic stems of human behavior. In the '60s, as social critics continued to shift their analyses from Marxian to Freudian issues, researchers explored the fertile grounds of aggression, violence, destruction, and domination. Elaborating on Freud's 1920s theory of the "death instinct" (the passion to destroy), Robert Ardrey (*African Genesis,* 1961; *The Territorial Imperative,* 1967); Konrad Lorenz (*On Aggression,* 1963), Desmond Morris (*The Naked Ape,* 1967), and I. Eibl-Eibesfeldt (*On Love and Hate,* 1972) all delivered the same basic thesis: man's aggressive behavior as manifested in war, crime, and destructive behavior was due to a genetically programmed instinct seeking discharge. This school of instinctivism became an ideology that soothed fear, assuring men that they were powerless to change their natural tendencies toward violence. Likewise, behaviorism, popularized on campuses in the 1960s by B. F. Skinner, stressed that man's behavior was merely the reaction to social conditioning, a variation on the theme of helplessness.[26] In 1973, Erich Fromm proposed a third option. He stated that there were actually two types of aggression, one programmed by genetics that was defensive and benign, and a second that was malignant and programmed by lust. He believed that the latter was on the rise in the 1960s.[27]

Despite its own inherent contradictions, the counterculture never backed off their attacks on organized sport. To its critics, sports were anti-quated. They were commercial spectacles that had become, as in ancient Rome, an opiate of the masses. The counterculture ridiculed sport as both nonserious—"the worst kind of indulgence in the American cult of the rugged, unique, superior individualist," according to one political radical—and as too serious—childhood games that had lost their play-fulness. Sport was "circus," the thing that distracted the masses from political dissent.[28]

Football absorbed the brunt of the attack. It was to its critics emblem-atic of an imperialistic and bullying society. In deriding intellectual crit-ics of the game, Agnew singled out the chairman of an "avant-garde magazine" who had written that football "makes respectable the most primitive feelings about violence, patriotism, manhood."[29] Michael Oriard, a Notre Dame starter and professional player in the 1960s, has argued persuasively that yardage in football is gained, not possessed, and that the game is not inherently linked to a military ideology.[30] It is a meas-ure, then, of Vietnam's persistent influence that few supporters refuted the counterculture's claims that American football and aggression in Southeast Asia were linked. Other former professional players like Dave Meggyesey and Gene Sauer condemned the sport's brutality. Leftists within the sports world like Jack Scott and Paul Hoch derided Vince Lombardi's use of hatred to motivate players and decried the vicious tem-perament of players like cornerback Jack Tatum, who proudly titled his 1980 autobiography, *They Call Me Assassin.*

Tatum, who played for Ohio State in the late '60s before his profes-sional career, and most football players and fans were unapologetic. *Life,* which had five years earlier pronounced football a "big, tough game," continued to glorify it, applauding the sport's "most violent men" with a December 1971 cover dedicated to "The Suicide Squad."[31] The public acclamation of violence may have been at odds with a great many of the young, but in a time of division, there were a great many more who rejected pacifism as an American goal. Few of Vince Lombardi's many admirers had difficulty with his belief that players needed to "work up a good hatred." When Green Bay's Jerry Kramer published *Instant Replay* in 1968, a best-selling diary of his 1967 season with the Packers, his chap-ter titles made football's connection to war unabashedly clear: "Preliminary Skirmishes," "Basic Training," "Mock Warfare," "Armed

Combat," and "War's End."[32] In fact, professional football had become so popular by decade's end that many believed it had unseated baseball as the national pastime, an eclipse, as one historian put it, of "bunt" by "punt."[33]

For all the attention that football received, there did seem to be something new and contrary going on in the early '70s emergence of a new prototype for the athletic body. Frank Shorter, a long-haired and mustachioed American runner, won the 1972 Olympic marathon in Munich. His victory, seen by tens of millions of television-watching Americans, seemed the fulfillment of promises for fitness made by Dr. Kenneth Cooper in his 1969 groundbreaking book, *Aerobics*. Shorter had the body of a bookworm, and the gentle instincts of a hippie. The nonconfrontational and therapeutic aspects of long-distance running blossomed in the wake of his gold medal. Within a short time, jogging was a craze among baby boomers. Not everybody could have the body of a linebacker, but jogging seemed to offer the promise of health, serenity, and an endless string of "personal bests" to anyone willing to put on a pair of Adidas, Puma, or Nike shoes and hit the streets every day. To run like Shorter, to fulfill individual goals without the need for teammates, changed perceptions of what an athlete looked like and was called on to do and be. He democratized and broadened the concept of "athlete."

As athletes did in fact begin to blend into the larger cultural mix in the late '60s, adopting aspects of counterculture style and sentiment, so, too, they began to move away from the pure muscularity that had separated them from the weak, the jocks from the nerds. In the early '60s they had already begun to search for strength in the unlikeliest of places—that province of the nerds, the mind. And toward the end of the era they were searching in the mystic parts of the brain that had theretofore been the province of the counterculture.

Though coaches and athletes were certainly interested for at least a century in psychological aspects of performance such as motivation, and though Coleman Griffith wrote two books in the 1920s to help coaches improve performance, sports psychology gained academic status in the 1960s. Academicians cite the 1966 publication of *Problem Athletes and How to Handle Them* by Bruce Ogilvie and Thomas Tutko as a touchstone. Some athletes had been well ahead with their own brand of applied research. Olympic shot-putter Parry O'Brien had, in the '50s, used techniques akin to those of Disney's Merlin Jones, a campus brain who, in 1965's "The Monkey's Uncle," had given an academic boost to jocks by hooking electrodes and recorders to their heads while they slept. O'Brien, trying a form of self-hypnosis, recorded pep talks. Then, he said, "I'd put the tape player under my bed, get into a sleepy state and let it all sink into my subconscious." O'Brien had also tried yoga and "from the Hindu principle of ayurveda he acquired 'placidity, sereneness.' He listened to Tibetan bells, to Balinese and Afro-Cuban drumming, all of which, he believed, helped him achieve a warrior's frenzy."[34]

What was surprising in the Vietnam era was that the search for a mental edge wandered from the labs of academe and tradition to the mysticism associated with wiccans, wizards, and witches, to the teachings of Eastern religion and the uncharted areas the counterculture sought with the roadmap of hallucinogens.

Pursuit of the warrior's edge through mind play became the goal of Mike Livingston, the University of California's crew coach. In searching for a blend of "the rational and the secret sources of strength," Livingston advocated approaches like those O'Brien had tried. He thought Eastern religion and yoga could help athletes to "control latent physical powers." Influenced by the writings of Carlos Castaneda, Livingston envisioned the athlete as a warrior "who wins a battle over his inner self." Nort Thornton, the Cal swim coach, "also believed that coaches were fast approaching the outer limits of what they could teach their athletes in terms of strength, endurance and technique." The "real frontier," for Thornton, "was in the area of mental training."[35]

Other athletes, coaches, and writers adopted this focus on inner dialogue, viewing athletic achievement as therapeutic mastery of one's mind rather than domination over another's body. Dr. George Sheehan, the "running doctor," wrote often of the mysteries of joy and self-discovery that rewarded the efforts of long-distance runners. Many jogging enthusiasts believed that their use of Long Slow Distance would lead to the same transformative experiences claimed by those who dropped acid. In 1974, Timothy Gallwey had a hit with *The Inner Game of Tennis*. Like William Murphy's 1970 book, *Golf in the Kingdom,* Gallwey adapted Eugen Herrigel's much earlier *Zen in the Art of Archery* to tennis (and later skiing). The key to them all was "letting go," relaxing one's inhibitory consciousness so that the body could do what it was capable of doing.

But what would come "naturally" to the body once one let go? Was it dehumanizing or simply human to aggress? Was football a sign of an aberrant society or a reflection of human violence harnessed for productive outcome? If the answers didn't come out right, could sport really be a way to build character? The wrong answers flashed in capital letters during the first week of February 1972. University of Minnesota basketball player Corky Taylor, a black man, decked Ohio State center Luke Witte, a white man, with a right hook with thirty-six seconds remaining in a hard-fought game. Apparently contrite, Taylor offered his hand to the fallen Witte. Instead of helping him to his feet, however, Taylor pulled Witte closer and kneed him in the groin.[36] For the next ninety seconds, the home team Minnesota players, including some from the bench, unleashed a no-holds-barred attack, punching and kicking the defenseless Witte and another white teammate into semiconsciousness. Fans poured out of the stands to join the fray, bedlam ensued, and officials terminated the game. Photos of a dazed and battered Witte, blood tracking down his cheeks, accompanied media stories decrying the violent outburst.

As *Sports Illustrated*'s William F. Reed recounted the game, his words slipped sports into the midst of the nation's sore spots—war, civil disorder, activist politics. He noted that Ohio's governor called the attack on Witte a "public mugging." He took Minnesota coach Bill Musselman to task for the message over his players' shower: "Defeat is worse than death because you have to live with defeat." He quoted Witte's father, who, while teaching at Musselman's previous college, had observed that "his players are brutalized and animalized." And throughout Reed used the terms *riot, slaughter,* and *assault and battery* to describe the incident. The fans, he noted, "were motivated to the point of frenzy," and, insidiously tying the incident to things larger, he wrote that "this was a cold, brutal attack, governed by the law of the jungle."[37]

As Ohio State's coach Fred Taylor aptly remarked: "There's more at stake here than basketball games."[38] Indeed, there was. The incident revealed the nation's uneasiness with physical prowess, intimidation, and violence. Like the war, it was an "ugly affair;" like the antiwar demonstrations, it was a "riot;" and like guerilla fighting, it was "governed by the law of the jungle." The *Columbus Citizen-Journal,* while rather reserved in its coverage, echoed the magazine. Sports editor Tom Keys called the

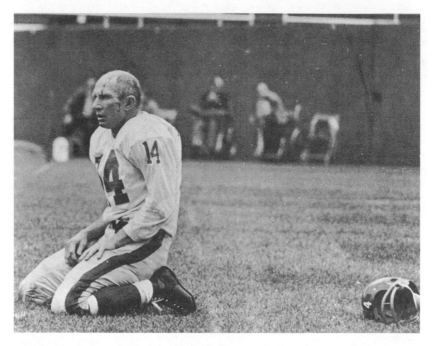

Bloodied but unbowed, New York Giant quarterback Y. A. Tittle was an early '60s emblem of the rugged NFL. *(AP/Wide World Photos)*

incident an "unprovoked assault," an "ambushing," and "brutality so savagely demonstrated." What, Keys asked, "did Bill Musselman, trainer of the Gopher circus, do to settle the animals who play for him?"[39] Sticking to the whole affair was the sour taste of deep racial divisions. In short, sports were no longer a world apart, but rather one more brutal part of a world that seemed to be seething with rage and frustration.

In abandoning their compact to use sport as safety valve, athletes seemed to be fulfilling counterculture claims. In *The Culture of Narcissism* (1974), Christopher Lasch speculated that a fear of excessive competition was tied to an association of competition with boundless, violent aggression that cannot be controlled.[40] When San Francisco Giant pitcher Juan Marichal turned suddenly and viciously on Los Angeles Dodger catcher John Roseboro in August 1965, "swinging his bat like a headsman's ax," the incident had been viewed as an isolated and aberrant incident, which, indeed, it was. Some, like Dodger coach Danny Ozark, ascribed it to the possibility that Marichal was just "a goddam nut."[41]

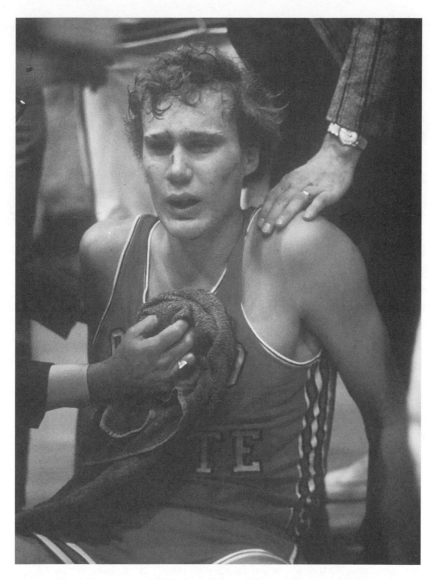

Bleeding from lip, cheek, and eyebrow, Ohio State's Luke Witte was a symbol in 1972 of violence gone overboard. (*Heinz Klutmeier*/Sports Illustrated*)

The reactions to the Ohio State–Minnesota game, however, were different. They hinted that in the course of less than a single decade Americans believed its athletes had lost the ability to mediate between the ferocity needed in sports and the ferocity that was ripping through its cities and the jungles of Vietnam. As if to confirm the loss, the behavior of Ohio State's Woody Hayes seemed to validate social fears that what had once been calculated had become random and uncontrollable. In his prime, Hayes had worn a baseball cap held together by carefully razored threads. When practice would go poorly, he would make a calculated show of his discontent by ripping the hat to shreds. In the late '60s, however, he had begun shredding other things, like sideline down markers, during games, in earnest. Hayes's career came to an end in 1978 when he punched an opposing player who had intercepted an Ohio State pass.

If the players were swept into the chaos and ambiguities of the larger culture, it was no surprise that spectators would fail to honor the sacred space and time of games. In the years before the idea of character-building solidified, both athletes and fans had treated playing fields as nothing special. Ballplayers carried pitchers of beer onto the field in the early professional years, and fans had routinely stood on outfield turf, interfered with play, and sometimes chased umpires while brandishing guns. Between 1880 and the 1960s, however, as definitions of sport moved toward the artificially contrived and away from the naturally derived, so, too, did stadiums and their areas marked off with lime become increasingly regarded by the public as places where real time and space were suspended. The regard created a paradox: as the playing fields became more rarefied, the claims of character-building were that activity there prepared people for the real world.

The possibility that the arena could remain a fantasy place unaffected by the developments outside it ebbed when spectators and athletes decided to allow intrusions from "real life." In 1965, the U.S. Naval Academy suspended its football series with the University of Maryland after Maryland fans capped two years of acrimony by throwing eggs and debris at the visiting midshipmen. During the 1969–70 basketball season, an arena floor was set ablaze in protest of what some regarded as Brigham Young University's racist Mormon policies. South African golfer Gary Player was "doused with soft drinks and verbally abused by protesters in Dayton, Ohio," and black athletes on many campuses boycotted or interrupted athletic events in the name of civil rights.[42] When Tommie Smith and John Carlos raised their black-gloved fists on the Olympic victory podium at the 1968 Olympics, it was clear to the entire nation that athletes saw the arena as open for "real world" business.

Finally, all pretense to specialness vanished during a series of violent fan rampages between 1967 and 1971. On October 1, 1967, the Detroit Tigers lost the pennant with a home loss in the season's last game. Disappointed fans stormed the field and damaged it.

Then, in 1969, the improbable success of the New York Mets sent fans into a frenzy. In successively bolder and more damaging fashion—first when the Mets clinched the pennant, then when they won the divisional playoff series, and finally after triumphing in the World Series—fans claimed Shea Stadium for themselves. After the final out of the Series, the players ran for cover as fans emptied from their seats and tore up 6,500 square feet of sod. They lit red flares and firecrackers, stole all the bases and home plate, chalked on the wooden outfield fence, and trampled through owner Joan Payson's private box. Joe DiMaggio was in attendance. One of the oft-told stories about the Yankee Clipper from the 1950s involved his wife, Marilyn Monroe. Returning from an overseas jaunt during which she had entertained throngs of roaring GIs, she told her husband, "You've never heard anything like it, Joe," to which DiMaggio replied in candid deadpan, "Yes, I have." All the more interesting then to hear his reaction to the aftermath of 1969's clinching Game Five: "I never saw anything like it."[43]

While press reactions avoided criticizing the New York fans, reports again carried language that smudged the lines between sport and civil unrest. Just days after a massive but peaceful march in Washington, D.C., to support a Vietnam War moratorium, Shea was described as a "disaster area," a "battlefield," and a "war zone." *New York Times* columnist George Vecsey likened fans to "extras in a pirate movie, all hot-eyed and eager to plunder." Joseph Durso, also of the *Times,* called it "one of the great, riotous scenes in sports history," but his fellow writer, Robert Lipsyte, thought the scene "too bad, because people are always littering their concrete and ravaging their earth, and it seemed we might have found a better way to celebrate." [44]

The following fall, when Connie Mack Stadium closed, Philadelphia fans showed that they had not found a better way, but had merely perfected it. This was—like antiwar rallies and civil rights marches—a planned moment of collective power. Some people brought in their own tool sets to complement the wooden souvenir slats used by most in disassembling the stadium. The sounds of hammering could be heard

Seats damaged in the fans' final-game rampage. *(Urban Archives, Temple University, Philadelphia, Pennsylvania)*

throughout the game, a sound that the Philadelphia *Bulletin* described as "a percussion symphony only Excedrin could possibly have appreciated."[45]

When the game finally ended, the masses began demolishing the park in earnest. Two hundred policemen (with a reputation for physical confrontation) were present, but according to *Daily News* sports writer Bill Conlin: "The word to cops was cool it. Bust no heads. Arrest only as a last resort." Despite the damage and one stabbing, they made no arrests. A nurse in the first-aid room had begged the Phillies not to give out the souvenir slabs of wood. Their failure to heed her advice left her shaken.

"She had never seen anything as terrible, as frightening, as senseless as this," wrote the *Inquirer*'s Frank Dolson. A quivering Frank Lucchesi, Phils manager, seconded coach Billy DeMars's characterization of the scene as "mob violence." "Never saw anything like it in my life," Lucchesi said. Front office worker and later Phillies owner Bill Giles surveyed the field and asked aloud, "Was this an atom or hydrogen bomb?"[46]

As had been the case with the Ohio State–Minnesota basketball game and the Shea Stadium mayhem, reporters again used language that likened the events to incidents of civil unrest. "It was the greatest day for vandals since the Huns played Rome," the *Inquirer* claimed. Tom Fox of the *Daily News* called it the "rape of a stadium." The closing, he continued, "should have been listed as a homicide." The insinuations of urban violence were not unexpected in Connie Mack's case. The old palace sat in a rough West Philly neighborhood that had kept away fans in the ballpark's final decade. The *Bulletin*'s George Kiseda, in fact, called the stadium baseball's "oldest, dirtiest, and smelliest playground—Skid Row with grass." For him, to see the closing in terms of the tumultuous Vietnam era came naturally. "The last day," he wrote, "was like a Michelangelo Antonioni movie with sound effects by the Joint Chiefs of Staff, choreography by Timothy Leary, LSD, and story by Marshal McLuhan." Conlin was more explicit in drawing parallels to the fractious times: "Nixon and Agnew should send observers every time a city closes down a ball park. It is the one social activity that truly brings Americans together again. A people that learned to destroy together can certainly learn to enjoy together."[47]

When an Ohio State victory celebration took place the next month in Columbus, many partyers would have claimed that "destroy" and "enjoy" were not mutually exclusive. Surveying the mayhem on High Street, a forty-five-year-old housewife enthused, "Oh, I want to come back to school. The kids are having such a good time, I'm glad we came down to see the festivities." A philosophy professor with wife and three children in tow said, "This is a lot of fun as long as the kids don't start smashing things. We wanted our daughter to see the block party so she knows what college is like."[48] The kids did start smashing things.

There was a stabbing, a shooting, and a rape. Store fronts and phone booths were broken. Parking meters were carried off. A man ripped the wiring from a traffic light control box. As the sparks flew, he proclaimed, "It's so cool," before falling off the curb. Kenneth Bader, Ohio State's dean of students said, "I saw a kid beating on a don't walk sign with a metal post and I tried to get him to stop. But he turned around like he was going to hit me so I just let him beat the sign instead." A number of cars were overturned, including one from which the driver was first pulled out and beaten. The *Columbus Citizen-Journal* described the event as a "city-sanctioned victory party," but the actions of the police indicated that this was no different to them than an antiwar disturbance or an inner-city riot.[49]

About 1:00 A.M. a patrol helicopter began training a spotlight on the crowd, estimated at ten thousand (this was in the days before sizing up crowd attendance became a more scientific, though still highly debatable, task. The crowd, in my remembrance and later calculations, was many times larger). Shortly thereafter, police asked the crowd to go home. When a portion of the 100 riot-equipped force, some with bayonets mounted, began to move down the street, it was met with a hailstorm of rocks and bottles. The police finally cleared the area at 5:00 A.M. with the help of tear gas, fire hoses, and wooden pellets. In all, sixty-five arrests were made, scores of injured were treated at University Hospital, and property damage was extensive.[50] A dean at Columbia University had wondered a few years earlier whether a lack of adventure and physical challenge "might have something to do with kids jumping around in the streets these days."[51] Maybe. But maybe there wasn't a lack of physical challenge so much as a disregard for the boundaries that defined appropriate spaces for meeting them. The word from Columbus Safety Director James Hughes left no doubt that sports were a part of the times. "If we can learn anything from Kent State, or Jackson State," he said, "it is that you can't take on an overwhelming crowd with insufficient force."[52]

When Roone Arledge had launched ABC's *Monday Night Football* just a few months earlier that fall, he had hired commentator Howard Cosell with the certainty that Cosell would not hesitate to draw parallels between sport and events outside the stadium (sportswriter Larry Merchant said Cosell made the "world of fun and games sound like the Nuremberg trials"). This was as Arledge wished it: "I'm tired of football being treated like a religion," he said. "The games aren't played in Westminster Abbey."[53] The celebration on High Street in Columbus showed that fans had already gotten the message.

Large-scale violence struck a final time in October 1971 following the

World Series championship of the Pittsburgh Pirates. As 40,000–100,000 (again, estimates varied widely) filled Pittsburgh's streets to celebrate the victory parade, the scene at Columbus repeated itself: bonfires, rock and bottle throwing, overturned cars, widespread property damage, the requisite quote: "I never saw anything like it" (uttered by a motorcycle cop). To this, Pittsburgh added nude dancing and upped the rape total to a dozen. Police ended the "party" with dogs and billy clubs, greeted by chants of "Pigs, pigs, here come the pigs."[54]

Pittsburgh fans and the Pittsburgh media were torn. There were the expected parallels drawn between revelers and "wild, vicious varmints," but there were also some who saw the outbreak of violence as the work of the "lunatic fringe" rather than a collective hysteria. The *Pittsburgh Press* denounced other media reports that described the city as the "last days of Rome" and claimed that there had been neither an "army of hoodlums" nor an "orgy of destruction." In congratulating the homecoming Pirates, reporter Margie Carlin admitted that Pittsburgh did "go a little bit crazy," before adding "and nobody blames them a bit."[55] No one seemed to take note that at the beginning of the decade, when Bill Mazeroski's home run decided the seventh game of the World Series against the Yankees and the city went a little bit crazy, there was nothing "vicious" or "lunatic" about the celebration.

Afterward, such incidents went into sudden decline. When victory sparked eruption in the next few decades, the occasions did not elicit apocalyptic visions or language. It could be that the storm clouds dissipated as quickly as they had gathered. In the week of the Columbus rampage, that city's *Citizen-Journal* ran an editorial by James Reston that declared politics to be in a slump and pretty girls making a campus comeback. That same day the paper printed the results of a survey of Ohio State's 8,000 freshmen. Sixty-two percent of them expressed negative feelings toward student disruptions, 72 percent had positive feelings toward police, and 69 percent opposed the leftist Students for a Democratic Society.[56]

When all the damage was added up, then, what made these incidents noteworthy? What differentiated the celebrations from other times, other parties, other goal-post-toting rampages and bonfires? This: for a short time they seemed a natural part of the era's landscape—not so much a moment of escape as an episode of deep immersion—more like the riots in Watts, the levitation of the Pentagon, and the fiasco at Altamont.

When people began to perceive sport as part of larger social trends, it became implicated—as had the Roman Coliseum—as metaphor for a civilization in decay. The Coliseum—or Flavian Amphitheater—had stood at a central location, a symbol that both masked and revealed the harsh realities of Roman culture. If the Coliseum was a real place, built of stone and sustained by murderous spectacle, then twentieth-century America's coliseum was a symbolic one built of commerce and myth and sustained by the dreams of countless young boys. As long as those dreams carried the positive feelings of good character, the idea of the arena as an unreal place—its physical space protected by ideas—was easier to sustain.

After the '60s—as in the late nineteenth century—it was a place that needed barriers and security details to protect it. Of course, it could be argued that in snatching souvenir patches of turf, seats, and urinals, fans were, in fact, acknowledging the sacred aura of the coliseum and hoping to keep a small piece for themselves—not unlike questing for slivers from the cross. Of course, without the myth of character-building to validate them, souvenirs collected in Sportsworld have become—like Mark McGwire's seventieth home-run ball—commercial items, commodities made more valuable by their notoriety as valued possessions than as symbols of achievement.

If fans were indeed collecting to preserve a part of the past fading from sight, then they were acknowledging the passing of special spaces. The 1970s brought stadium architecture—concrete multipurpose donut fortresses—that set sports apart from urban downtowns but made little attempt to preserve a sense of specialness. In response, the 1980s and 1990s saw a wave of nostalgia for places with "character." Baltimore's Oriole Park at Camden Yards became the model for a wave of retro baseball parks. The Hollywood film *Field of Dreams* (1989) re-endowed America's farmland with the magical qualities that had linked baseball and rural sentiment in public consciousness a century earlier. These locales are evidence of what sociologist Orrin Klapp referred to in the 1960s as modern society's conversion of place into space.[57] The new parks are "pseudo places," sites like Disney World that use cleverly arranged building material to evoke a sense of a "real" place.

As if to underscore the end of the era, a final act of political trespassing in the arena was enacted in the year following the fall of Saigon. In Los Angeles, in the opening month of the 1976 baseball season, a man and his eleven-year-old son ran onto the outfield turf of Dodger Stadium during a game. After putting lighter fluid on an American flag, the man set it ablaze, ostensibly in protest of the treatment of Native Americans. Dodger outfielder Rick Monday grabbed the man and tossed him over the left field bullpen fence. Perhaps certifying the nation's exhaustion with such confrontational drama, the heroic flag rescue did not even get a mention in the *New York Times* or the *Washington Post.*

CHAPTER FIVE

The Greatest: Muhammad Ali's Confounding Character

He is fascinating—attraction and repulsion must be in the same package.
—Norman Mailer, Life, 1971

For many Americans, their first glimpse of the Vietnam era came on February 18, 1964. On that day a group of young men in a Miami Beach fight gym previewed the future of the world. The Beatles, recently landed in the United States for a knockout appearance on the *Ed Sullivan Show,* had come to meet heavyweight fighter Cassius Clay, who failed to show on time. "Where the fuck's Clay?" groused Ringo Starr. "Let's get the fuck out of here," said John Lennon. When Clay finally strode in, he dispelled the gloom. "Hello there, Beatles," he called. "We oughta do some road shows together, we'll get rich." When he tried out one of his running gags, however, the testiness resurfaced. "You guys aren't as stupid as you look," he said. "No," Lennon responded, "but you are."[1]

The edginess finally passed when the five men ran through a series of comical poses for photographers: Clay dusting all four Beatles with a single punch; the singers forming a pyramid in an attempt to get at the boxer's jaw; Clay thumping his chest above the prostrate quartet as they prayed for mercy. As the group departed, Clay turned to *New York Times* writer Robert Lipsyte and wondered out loud, "Who were those little faggots?"

As their influence built week by week, the importance and connection between the five men dawned on some observers in a way they themselves had not understood. Not all thought the alliance was positive. New York columnist Jimmy Cannon wrote famously and contemptuously that: "Clay is part of the Beatle movement. He fits in with the famous singers

Ali delivers a domino punch to the Beatles, February 1964.

no one can hear and the punks riding motorcycles with iron crosses pinned to their leather jackets and Batman and the boys with their long dirty hair and the girls with the unwashed look and the college kids dancing naked at secret proms held in apartments and the revolt of students who get a check from dad every first of the month and the painters who copy the labels off soup cans and the surf bums who refuse to work and the whole pampered style-making cult of the bored young."[2]

Cannon's jumbled rant may have been paranoid, but he was not wrong in recognizing Muhammad Ali as an apocalyptic figure. Throughout the Vietnam era, the boxer upset entrenched notions of sport and character. In most cases, however, he did not merely challenge tradition. Rather, he embodied the tension between new and old by presenting himself as a series of paradoxes, provoking difficult questions to which he offered answers that pleased everyone and no one. Did his popularity, for example, owe to his winning or to his combination of wins and losses? Was his draft resistance cowardice or conviction? Did America want a heavy-weight champ who delivered a heavier wallop with his mouth or his fists? One whose face reflected the peril of the ring or the ability to evade its dangers?

Overarching all of the answers—indeed, framing the questions themselves—was the issue of race. This is understandable because from the late nineteenth century forward the idea of sport as a character builder was intended to elevate and prepare white men as leaders of society. Blacks and women, to the minds of white males, were not going to lead American society in the twentieth century; whatever these lesser beings made of sport—exercise, escape, entertainment—would be for their own lesser reasons.

The color lines that existed in sport into the 1950s had grown from an impeachable but nonetheless widely believed foundation of "scientific" race theory that had, for a century, pinched data on bodies and brains into a shape supporting white assertions of intellectual and moral weakness in blacks. Many whites believed character to be an elusive and unreliable qual-ity among blacks, contending that African heritage imparted even to the economically and socially advantaged a genetic predisposition to bad behavior that might reveal itself at an unfortunate moment. Thus, despite Jesse Owens's rebuke of Hitler, Joe Louis's service in the army, Jackie Robinson's willingness to turn the other cheek, or Wilma Rudolph's defeat of childhood polio, white attitudes toward black athletic success remained reserved.

Young Cassius Clay had overcome some of those reservations, endear-ing himself to Americans as he returned triumphant and irrepressible from the Rome Olympics of 1960. As Lipsyte has remarked, "He was kind of the perfect American ambassador to the world. He was totally lovable."[3] Fighting shortly after his meeting with the Beatles in 1964 Clay "shook up the world" by beating Sonny Liston, the prohibitive favorite, to become the world's heavyweight boxing champion. He shook it harder the next day when he forsook his name (his "slave name," according to him) to become Muhammad Ali. To many whites, claimed onetime Black Panther Eldridge Cleaver, Ali's decision to join the Nation of Islam was a "betrayal." One of the sect's leaders, Malcolm X, explained the fear underlining the betrayal: "They [whites] knew that if people began to identify with Cassius and the type of image he was creating, they were going to have trouble out of these Negroes because they'd have Negroes walking around the street saying, 'I'm the greatest,' and also Negroes who were proud of being black." Black author Wallace Terry later made clear to an interviewer, however, that the change was disturbing to some blacks as well: "You just wanted to say, 'Tell me it ain't true, Muhammad. Tell me you're really Cassius Clay, aren't you?'"[4]

Ali's transformation from Christian to Muslim seemed to some whites much like going from Stepinfetchit to Nat Turner. The change broke a compact that Americans had forged with their black athletes—"be good Negroes and enjoy the fruits of athletic success"—and assured that race would be an explicit issue in all that Ali would touch in the next decade.

Nothing was more explicit—or explosive—than the issue of manliness. Tied as it was to matters of prowess and courage, it was at the dark heart of racial divisions. By the late nineteenth century many white middle-class men believed that a shift from labor of the body to labor of the mind had left Victorian culture "effeminate."[5] Believing that behavior and bonding that reinforce male dominance grew "from a more primitive type of manhood," Thorstein Veblen in 1899 wrote that entering a competitive struggle without ferocity and cunning was "like being a hornless steer."[6] Soon thereafter, Sigmund Freud tied dominance, aggression, and bonding directly to man's primitive sexual drives and suppression of them, and thereby made the relationship between sexuality and behavior apparent.

Rising attention to the rapidly organizing and expanding structure of sports served two ends. Sports provided an antidote to effeminacy, allowing an outlet for dominance and aggression while at the same time promising to dissipate sexual urgency and turn it toward constructive ends. Still, as whites remade manhood, "finding new ways to celebrate men's bodies as healthy, muscular, and powerful," they were required to give attention to both gender and race, two things that, according to historian Gail Bederman, "linked bodies, identities, and power." As Bederman has written, civilization at the turn of the century had become, in the minds of white men, an "explicitly racial concept."[7]

It was a conceit that reinforced ideas of white superiority but simultaneously made the physical prowess of blacks a constant threat. It could be turned on white men and summon the ghosts of Nat Turner, or it could be turned on white women and summon the myth of black sexuality. In the case of black athletes, trouble could come in both ways. So it was that first black heavyweight champion Jack Johnson, as conqueror of white men in the ring and white women in the bedroom, touched off race riots in the wake of his many affronts to white society in the early 1900s.

Owens, Louis, Robinson, and other black athletes at midcentury appeared safer, following the unspoken but central rules of being a "good Negro," which entailed a repression of sexual appetite and public deference to whites. Still, the myth of black sexuality in America was an old— even if often an underground—problem for white males. The image of blacks as promiscuous animals of wanton sexual appetites has been a part of American consciousness for centuries. Eugene Genovese, in his account of American slavery, *Roll, Jordan, Roll,* revealed that the idea of black moral laxity had existed in seventeenth- and eighteenth-century Europe. Before long, he wrote, "Europeans and Americans were hearing lurid tales of giant penises, intercourse with apes, and assorted unspeakable (but much spoken of) transgressions against God and nature."[8] In the 1950s, Lillian Smith, in *Killers of the Dream,* proposed that modern white fears of blacks stemmed from the idea that black men, if not dominated, would go after white women as vengeance for the white humiliation of black female slaves in previous centuries.[9]

As steps were taken at the time of Smith's book to desegregate American society, fear of black sexuality presented itself in several ways. In the South, there was militant resistance to the repeal of Jim Crow laws that broke down the physical separation of the races.[10] One of the stumbling blocks to integrating Baltimore's golf courses and swimming pools in the 1940s was the fear of some parks' board members that those settings would allow black men too near to white women.[11] More subtly, the first serious attempts at rock music censorship came when rhythm and blues, the code name for black music, began to cross over into the white marketplace.

Even in the loftiest of social settings palpable distrust and sexual suspicions were present. Penn's black Rhodes Scholar and basketball star John Wideman told *Look* magazine in 1963: "At college, I've found that there's no cleavage (between the races) beyond the physical fact, although in a way—socially, I suppose—I've often wondered if things would have gone along the same way if I'd had a white girl friend on campus. There's a fine line there, a line that is a kind of threat, something that even in the most liberal circles isn't talked about, and that's the idea of . . . well, probably sex. The actual fact of a Negro-white relationship . . . (means) then there is complete equality, and there's nothing that would actually separate the races anymore. Anything that goes toward that direction creates a tension. And that's a psychological situation that can't be remedied by any amount of constitutional reforms."[12]

As the specter of black militancy loomed in the late '60s, it highlighted the second of white fears—that of black revolt. During a 1968 Columbia University fight about where to build a new gymnasium, Harlem blacks instilled fear among whites by threatening to make the situation a violent one. In June of 1966 *Life* magazine investigated the real possibility of black violence in an article titled "Plotting a War on 'Whitey.'" In San Francisco's hippie haven, Haight-Ashbury, an oft-heard belief among whites was "Spades are programmed for hate."[13]

The possibility that the hate would erupt into confrontation was what made the menacing Sonny Liston—posed in a Santa Claus hat and a scowl for the cover of the December 1963 *Esquire*—"America's worst nightmare." Ali's embrace of his blackness blended both threats: the sexual and the vengeful. Los Angeles sportswriter Jim Murray once said about Ali: "I'd like to borrow his body for just forty-eight hours, there are three guys I'd like to beat up, and four women I'd like to make love to."[14] Murray was often simultaneously funny and astute, so what was the nation to think when he managed with that quip to expose every white man's fears—black physical retribution coupled with the myth of black sexual potency? At best, white America could laugh uneasily.

It might have been easier to know what to think had Ali been more like Liston. Instead, he presented a complex puzzle. He boasted constantly of being "pretty," an assertion counter to traditional manliness, yet one that some blacks saw as the anchor for their claim that "black is beautiful."[15] He often laughed with white reporters, yet he was fully aware of white fear. Before his mid-'70s bout with George Foreman he told the press: "What you white reporters got to remember is, black folks ain't afraid of black folks that way white folks are afraid of black folks."[16] As for sex, those who followed Ali closely in the '60s report that he had a healthy libido that was often gratified. If any of his dalliances included white women, they never came to public light.

Of all the factors that constituted manliness, none were more instrumental in defining Ali and confusing white America as his position as a conscientious objector against the draft. For many young men doubts about the value of military service in Vietnam blossomed in two ways: in a preoccupation with the draft that indicated reluctance to serve in Vietnam and in the consequential guilt over not having served. Males either went to Vietnam and fought or they stayed behind with the knowledge that others less fortunate were fighting.

For most draft-age men the most pressing reason for their dilemma was President Lyndon Johnson's commitment to the war as evidenced in draft numbers. In February 1965 only 3,000 men were called to service. In the next six months the total was 87,300, and the estimate for September through November of that year was 97,050.[17]

In claiming exemption on religious grounds in early 1966 Ali absolved himself of the guilt. Conscientious objection was a stand that insinuated reflection, not cowardice. When he was stripped of his title shortly after refusing induction in May of 1967, thereby forfeiting what would become three years of income, Ali's refusal to serve appeared to be one of indisputable moral conviction. For the millions of Americans who supported the Vietnam War, however, Ali's stance looked more like hustle than moral fortitude. But for all those who perceived the war to be unjust, Ali's RSVP to Uncle Sam's invitation became a shining example, though not one without problems.

For one, not fighting in Vietnam seemed to be turning off the very path that Joe Louis and Jackie Robinson had taken while earning the respect of all Americans. Both had served in the military and, despite Robinson's court-martial, it served their images well. Though a number of black athletes—including Jim Brown, Kareem Abdul-Jabbar, and Bill Russell—supported Ali's decision not to report for induction, Louis and Robinson did not. "I think it's very bad," said Louis. Robinson was more specific: "He's hurting, I think, the morale of a lot of young Negro soldiers over in Vietnam." Wallace Terry, author of *Bloods: An Oral History of the Vietnam War by Black Veterans,* has met many of those black soldiers. He recalled for an interviewer, "Many of them told me that Muhammad Ali had given up being a man when he decided not to be inducted into the armed forces . . . They were absolutely stunned; they were shocked, they were upset, they were angry, they were frustrated, they were bitter. They hated him for it."[18] Ali's refusal also reinforced the bitter feelings that many

Americans felt for athletes who managed to evade combat. The indifferent stance of elite and professional athletes toward military service was certainly not unique, but it was, to many Americans, galling.

A greater puzzle was the irony, apparently unnoticed, that Ali's resistance carried for blacks generally. His membership in the Nation of Islam marked him as a figure whose life was indivisible from his color, and his use of his Islamic ministry as the basis for avoiding war marked him as someone who could not fight on grounds of pacifism. How strange, then, in 1966 when, in a fit of pique at yammering reporters, Ali declared, "Man, I ain't got no quarrel with them Vietcong." As Lipsyte, who spent several years covering Ali for the *New York Times*, has written, the famed comment came from exasperation and may not have accurately (certainly not fully) reflected Ali's draft stance.[19] Nonetheless, antiwar Americans seized upon it as an expression of common sense—rather than religious—opposition. This meant that Ali essentially agreed with those whites who claimed generally that the nation had no legitimate quarrel with North Vietnam. It was also precisely what any black draftee, those fighting the war in disproportionate numbers, could have claimed as well. Oddly enough, many blacks who opposed the war did not lean on this practical argument but stood instead on moral grounds, claiming the draft to be institutional genocide. Even then, however, they did not adopt the same antimilitary attitudes that characterized white student opposition, and they did not, by and large, follow Ali's example.

Ali's draft position was further confounded by this question: why did Ali have no remorse about quarreling with unknowns in the ring—the killing game? It was a paradox that did not escape Congressman Robert Michel of Illinois, who noted on the floor of the House: "Apparently Cassius will fight anyone but the Vietcong." Ali himself openly declared, "There's one hell of a lot of difference in fighting in the ring and going to the War in Vietnam," but the anger in his voice, not any philosophical thinking, lent the claim its sound of conviction.[20]

In an era given to inquiry about the application of might, a pacifist as heavyweight champion of a brutal sport made some sense. In his 1969 work on male bonding, Lionel Tiger proclaimed that "the amalgamation of size, power, dramaturgical savoir faire and dominance" were central to sport's appeal to males.[21] The heavyweight champion was the supreme symbol of dominance. How significant was it, then, that the physical aura of Muhammad Ali was one that stung like a bee and floated like a butterfly, particularly when contrasted to the brutish and violent style of the man he dethroned, Liston?

Before losing to Ali, Liston had dismissed the young boxer's style. "As a fighter," he told newsmen, "I think he should be locked up for impersonating a fighter."[22] But Ali's promotion of a style that featured lightning speed, grace, and an unhittable defense that protected his beauty went over big with the public. Boxing, after all, was not at the height of popular appeal. The deaths of fighters Benny Paret (in the ring in March 1962) and Davey Moore (in March 1963, four days after sustaining injuries in the ring) drew criticism that depicted boxing as an archaic contest in a civilized world. Bob Dylan's scathing indictment, "Who Killed Davey Moore?" badgered the public conscience with an accusatory chorus, "Why, and what's the reason for?" There were, then, public relations payoffs to be reaped from a heavyweight champ for whom boxing seemed a softer exercise. The portrayal of Ali as a dancer ("Fred Astaire," one observer remarked of him regarding his 1966 fight against Cleveland Williams—"just like he was in a jitterbug contest")[23] masked the brutality that is the essence of the fight game and, once in place, obscured the side of Ali that was cruelty. But cruelty and brutality were integral parts of Ali's ring persona, and obscuring them only contributed to his paradoxical nature.

In the ring he was both Brer Rabbit and John Henry. The aspect of his fighting that was sledgehammer showed intermittently, but when it did Ali was revealed as a warrior willing to club and be clubbed. When he fought Joe Frazier for the third time, in 1975, both men stood toe to toe, drawing on power and resources that tested more than their will to win. It also tested their willingness to punish another man, their will to live, and, thus, their willingness to kill. Ali's cousin Coretta Bavers recalled, "He told me the next morning that he was closer to death than he'd ever been."[24] It was a confession he often repeated.

If that contest seemed to smack of valor and nobility, the flip side of the champ's brutality was evident in two earlier fights. In the '60s, at the top of the boxing world, Ali had a range of tools at his disposal. Norman Mailer noted that, at times, Ali "played with punches, was tender with them, laid them on as delicately as you put a postage stamp on an envelope." It was not a style that most heavyweights would have valued.

But, as Mailer observed, Ali's attack also included, "a cruel jab like a base-ball bat held head on into your mouth."[25] In his November 1965 bout with former champion Floyd Patterson, and then a year and a half later against Ernie Terrell, Ali used mostly the latter, his game turning pitiless and sadistic. Angered because both opponents had dismissed his religious conversion (Terrell insisting on calling him "Clay"), Ali laid on punches and words with venom. Against Patterson, a proud black man well past his prime, Ali was relentless. Lipsyte, who recalled the bout as "the ugli-est prizefight I've ever seen," asserted, "You really had the sense that he was just this little boy picking the wings off a butterfly. Floyd was so small; he was bent over with a back spasm; he could barely defend himself, and Ali was taunting him and hitting him. I personally was disgusted." *Life* magazine agreed, calling the fight "a sickening spectacle."[26]

The fight with Terrell was similar, Ali hitting him at will while demanding that Terrell call him by his Muslim name. Ali biographer Thomas Hauser told film documentarians, "Ali went out there to make this a horribly vicious, humiliating experience for Ernie Terrell, and he carried it on long past the time when Terrell was competitive in any way. And it's ugly. It's fifteen rounds of 'What's my name?'"[27]

Perhaps it was just coincidence, but, with the exception of the third Frazier fight, Ali's dark side was most apparent when he was on top. The '60s were full of dynasties—Vince Lombardi's Green Bay Packers, the UCLA basketball Bruins, the Boston Celtics. They were popular anti-dotes in a society forced to witness the impotent American war effort nightly on the network news. But Ali was never more lovable or popular than when he was the underdog, a phenomenon that brought out his Brer Rabbit cunning and again connected him to powerful currents of the Vietnam era. He had risen to prominence after slaying Sonny Liston, the boxer that Ali's trainer, Angelo Dundee, called the "Monster Man." Clay had, many writers agreed, outfoxed Liston, disarming and unnerving him with his loudmouthed bravado, appearing manic nearly to the point of insanity. The mythic significance of the win was not lost on Clay or his admirers. Malcolm X's widow, Betty Shabazz, claimed: "My husband said all he had to do was to put his mind to it—surely if God had seen fit for David to be successful over Goliath, he could be successful over Sonny Liston."[28]

Strangely enough, though the United States was at an impasse against

North Vietnam, antiwar protestors and Ali, through his rhetoric ("I ain't got no quarrel with them Vietcong"), both portrayed America's enemy as an underdog, a tiny force trying to hold on against an overwhelming power. It is ironic, then, that as Ali became ensconced as champion, fought as the favorite with power and a lack of mercy, he increasingly annoyed the establishment but appealed to the counterculture. After he lost his title for refusing induction, his martyrdom appealed to those who opposed the war, but he regained his more widespread popularity only after a loss in the ring reduced him once more to underdog. Following Ali's loss to Ken Norton in 1973, the acerbic Jimmy Cannon had crowed: "He is the guy the hungry kids want to get their hands on. No one appreciated being a winner more than Muhammad Ali. He is a loser now."[29]

He was not one for long. In 1974, when he upset George Foreman to regain the crown, the victory seemed moral vindication and proof positive to his many sympathizers in the draft case that the Vietnam War had been immoral. The war, by then, was more widely held to have been wrongfully fought by the United States, so it is no surprise that Americans generally applauded Ali's reemergence. Strangely, what was most praised was his cunning—the very type of deceit employed by the Vietcong. During the war, American spokesmen went to great pains to point out that the North Vietnamese's guerilla fighting was an immoral way of fighting—comparable to terrorism—and one at odds with American tactics, in which there was "a vested interest in abstaining from such acts."[30] West Point football star and Vietnam combatant Pete Dawkins tried to explain tactfully what he felt was a basic difference between Americans and the North Vietnamese, but he could not disguise a sense of righteousness. "They're not devious people," he told *Life* in 1966. "They're Oriental. Part of their culture is that they attack a problem indirectly—they sneak up on an issue."[31] In adopting his strategy for facing Foreman, Ali decided on an indirect attack. Of course, most Americans missed this irony as they missed, as well, the shabbiness that the cunning camouflaged.

The triumph over George Foreman not only saw many Americans cheering for the reluctant draftee to defeat a man who had proudly waved the American flag in the Olympic ring at Mexico City in 1968, it also delivered a jolt to the concept of worthy opposition. Falling back on an old tendency to demean opponents, Ali had decided on a new tactic for his fight with the huge slugger. Threatening Foreman with a "ghetto-whopper" (because "it's thrown in the ghetto at three o'clock in the morning, which is when me and George are gonna fight"),[32] Ali decided instead that the way to beat Foreman was to slump against the ropes and let Foreman hit him until exhausted. The tactic was brilliant, but smacked of the duplicity that many whites believed characterized both blacks and the Vietnamese. It was clearly reminiscent of Brer Rabbit's Tar Baby tactic, and Ali's label for it, "Rope-a-Dope," and his nickname for Foreman, "The Mummy," were best appreciated by a culture now fixated on victory and fast losing touch with the idea of worthy opposition.

Maybe the least noted but most significant aspect of the Foreman fight was that Ali made victory appear easy. Unlike his fatiguing earlier bouts with Frazier, the "rope-a-dope" seemed to deny the tenet of character-building that demanded hard work. The tactic was, on the one hand, intelligent and clever, in the same way that Paul Newman as Butch Cassidy had been in the immensely popular 1969 film of a Western outlaw fueled by wit and optimism. However, it was also akin to playing possum and, in Ali's case, thus tied to the trickster of black folklore and white suspicions of blacks as naturally gifted—but not hard-working—athletes. The idea that whites were hard workers while blacks were shirkers was one that had been necessarily absent from much of the discourse on sport during the decades prior to integration. The breakdown of segregation following 1954's *Brown v. Board of Education* (the Supreme Court's rescinding of its 1896 approval of the doctrine of "separate but equal" in *Plessy* v. *Ferguson*) released blacks into many fields theretofore closed off, a flood that some southern white gentlemen still refer to despairingly as "The Deluge." Perhaps nowhere did the before-and-after numbers climb more steeply than they did in sports. By the early '60s blacks already constituted percentages of professional teams in numbers disproportionate to their representation in the larger population. More revealing were their inroads in intercollegiate circles, where all manner of ruses had been used for decades to deny opportunities to blacks. The Southeastern Conference was the last major conference to integrate, but when its schools did, the result was explosive. Just seven blacks played sports at four schools in 1966, the initial year of SEC integration. But by 1980, nearly 70 percent of the conference's basketball players were black, as were nearly one-third of its football players and track athletes.[33]

The new prominence of black athletes—and their refusal to

acknowledge sport as a confirmation of "good" American values—dramatically undercut the idea of character-building by calling into question the depth and genuineness of American goodness. Besides Ali, important athletes like Henry Aaron, Arthur Ashe, Jim Brown, John Carlos, Curt Flood, Kareem Abdul-Jabbar, Bob Gibson, Oscar Robertson, Bill Russell, and Tommie Smith pointed out the disparities between sport's claim to being a meritocracy and their own experiences as second-class citizens. Any hope that some whites may have been harboring for a return to old ways was dashed for good in 1966.

The NCAA basketball championship that year was expected to go to the University of Kentucky. Adolph Rupp, Kentucky's curmudgeonly coach, had become college basketball's leader in games won without playing a single black player in his thirty-six years at the helm. As he took his all-white team into the title game in College Park, Maryland, he was opposed for the first time by a starting five that was all black. The underdogs from Texas Western (now the University of Texas at El Paso) stunned Rupp and the nationwide television audience with a 72–65 victory. Afterward, it was impossible to evade the question of black athletic competency, and Kentucky—which had been slow to integrate—accelerated its use of black players.

The sudden rise of the black athlete—refutation of a century of the myth of white superiority—demanded explanation. The most convenient for whites was to acknowledge it as the necessary outcome of a biological physical advantage. As blacks became increasingly visible on Vietnam era playing fields, the nineteenth-century notion of a primitive, physically superior race was recycled and picked up new adherents, even among blacks. Peter Andrews, a basketball player at Penn in the mid-'60s, said that if you took the blacks off of the school's great basketball teams of the late '60s and early '70s, "you got another Dartmouth and Brown."[34]

The most controversial and visible declaration of this possibility came early in January of 1971 when *Sports Illustrated* published Martin Kane's article, "An Assessment of Black Is Best." While granting that "not all the successes of the black man . . . have been entirely due to physical characteristics," Kane nonetheless leaned heavily in that direction, concluding: "Every male black child, however he might be discouraged from a career with a Wall Street brokerage firm, knows he has a sporting chance in baseball, football, boxing, basketball, or track."[35]

If blacks were scientifically certified as natural athletic talents, it was one more reason for some whites to deem them unfit for the character-building club. Character meant hard work, and who could be sure of effort in the face of such God-given talent? The notion that blacks had developed a racially distinct style of play, especially in basketball, that touted individual flamboyance at the expense of teamwork,[36] heightened the portrayal of whites as hard workers—and intelligent—while demeaning blacks as something less.

In the matter of effort, the stereotype of the lazy black lingered in the background of many situations and turned others into hostile confrontations. When Andrews, though the captain, quit the Penn team in the middle of his final season, he felt that coach Dick Harter did not really believe that he had had an earlier injury that affected his play. According to Andrews, Harter merely "thought I had a cavalier attitude."[37] The possibility that white coaches would view black athletes as fakers and laggards may have unwittingly pushed some black athletes toward even greater effort. An unidentified black athlete at Penn told the *Daily Pennsylvanian,* "everything I do is representative of my race. I don't care if I'm the only black athlete playing—I'm pushing just a bit harder than the whites."[38]

Muhammad Ali was supremely gifted with physical skill. No doubt, when it came to character, it was easier for his detractors to see him that way than to acknowledge his intelligence or work ethic. In fact, the press made a good deal of Ali's initial failure to pass the armed services intelligence test, printing samples of the types of simple questions—fractions and the like—that Ali had wrestled with unsuccessfully. "Rope-a-Dope," though widely applauded as shrewd and masterly for an old fighter, nonetheless served to distance Ali from the tenets of character-building. It not only raised entertainment above fair play but also implied an other-worldly sense of self that tapped into another aspect of Vietnam era lore.

It was as poet—in making predictions and then carrying them out—that Ali was at his most perplexing and pleasing. Only Ali the verse maker seemed to know ahead of time what disaster, like "Rope-a-Dope," might befall his opponents. His poetry in and out of the ring put him at odds with sport's alliance with science. Scientifically grounded theories of athletic achievement, begun in the nineteenth century, produced a performance principle that encouraged people to see athletes as mere representations of their conditioning regimens, nutritional supplements, and illicit drugs—that is, athletes as scientifically created performers. Though the performance principle was necessarily at odds with character-building from the outset—character being a subjective, unscientific measure of a person—one of the reasons that character building had become so firmly entrenched in public consciousness was that it was effectively disguised as a scientific quest—a submission of the will in step with the demands of a progressive, modern, scientific, and secular world.

The Vietnam era neither quickened nor slowed interest in the scientific quest for enhanced performance. The increasing use of steroids, weight training, and ergogenic aids were merely new steps in the progression. The sixties were, however, the time that brought science and character into noticeable collision. Ironically, the counterculture, which strove for a more human, less technocratic society, ridiculed what appeared to be human strengths—effort, ethics, discipline—when critiquing sport; likewise, many coaches and administrators who believed wholeheartedly in character-building—and who, like Vince Lombardi, could be highly emotional and volatile—tried to lessen the effects of emotion on performance. Justifying the new use of computers as evaluation tools in 1968, Dallas Cowboy executive Tex Schramm explained, "I thought we had to find a way to judge players without emotion."[39]

Though Martin Kane, the same *Sports Illustrated* writer who would later offer explanation for black athletic superiority, tried to discover the scientific Ali, photographing and timing his punches in 1969 with an Omegascope, and though Ali was tied explicitly to the politics of his time—both of race and war—his charisma and success seemed to come from a mystic place that stood outside of convention and was rooted in emotion. In fact, the ten-page spread of Ali's technique as dissected by the Omegascope was ironically titled "The Art of Ali."[40] In his crowing, soaring, playful ascendancy to pop culture icon, Ali seemed to be, like the Beatles, the rollicking incarnation of another baby boom icon, Peter Pan, whose popularity took wing with the 1960 television airing of a stage production starring actress Mary Martin.

The characteristics of Pan—disdain for the adult world, for the specter of aging, for gender distinction, for rules—were those of the "Eternal Child." According to one observer of popular culture, the myth of this *puer aeternus* ran through sixties counterculture as a symbol or metaphor for favored beliefs and behaviors.[41]

A boxer—subject to so many manly ravages—was unlikely to serve as an Eternal Child, but Clay/Ali fit the bill. He was undeniably playful. Even sitting atop a pile of cash for a *Sports Illustrated* cover, he seemed unfettered by material—or adult—concerns. In his early years his skin was smooth and pretty, his verses elementary and comical. Even after his body had begun to go slack, his demeanor remained boyishly mercurial. As trickster supreme he was impossible to pin down. He wore at one time or another each of the masks that various historians have identified as those that blacks donned to survive slavery: the deferential "Jack," the submissive "Sambo," the ferocious and threatening "Nat." In scheduling his fights from Manila in the Philippines to the African jungles of Zaire, his restless globetrotting made the world his home.

The myth of the Eternal Child also holds that the trickster in that child represents a "powerfully anarchic, anti-authoritarian impulse, a drive to revolt, to disrupt or overturn the existing order."[42] In an age that featured a rejection of old authority and a search for new, Ali was most vivid as a figure who recognized little authority other than his own.

As a fighter Ali supported an entourage of trainers, friends, promoters, advisers, and newsmen. He was, however, beholden to few. His ring decisions became his own, from his need to punish Patterson and Terrell to his slugfest with Frazier to the adoption of "Rope-a-Dope." As trainer Angelo Dundee notes, "I won't kid you. When he went to the ropes, I felt sick."[43]

Outside the ring Ali's self-reliance was the archetype of an entire generation's affair with individualism and independence. When Hollywood filmed his biography, *The Greatest,* in 1977, the song that became the film's centerpiece explained that Ali had rejected heroes early in life, settling on self-dependence and self-love as "The Greatest Love of All." In defending his draft resistance he eschewed complexity. It was simple. "All I did," he said, "was stand up for what I believed." Continuing, he noted that "everything I did was according to my conscience. I wasn't trying to be a leader. I just wanted to be free."[44] Freedom, of course, is the flag-bearer for American claims to greatness, but it is also the spark that ignites debate about the relative merits of anarchy and conformity.

Ali had no qualms about whom he upset. His rejection of authority was both broad and significant. In spurning the army he thumbed his nose at America's most important civil institutions—the government, the military, and the capitalist economy that supported them both. In converting to Islam, he rejected the Christian God. Indeed, in conversation with sportswriter Jerry Izenberg, Ali intimated that Christianity rested on an unforgiving foundation. Asked how he thought his draft problems would be resolved, Ali told the writer, "Who knows; look what they done to sweet baby Jesus."[45]

As it turned out, Ali's identification of himself with Jesus accentuated a final aspect of the Eternal Child, that of "gods who die or are slain and then are resurrected in the spring—so that they become, in effect, undying, immortal, eternally youthful."[46] When boxing's officials stripped Ali of his crown in 1967 they made him that rarest of treasures—the living martyr—and prepared the way for his resurrection and ascension three years later. Ali reveled in his martyrdom. In April of 1968 he posed for the cover of *Esquire,* his beautiful body riddled with arrows.

All of the ways by which Ali became a symbol—unconsciously or not—were instrumental in his largest rejection, that of the entrenched racial hierarchy. His early fight promoters, draft officials, money men, even Christianity's most important figures were white. Ali chafed at this. His public declamations on politics, wars, and religion were evidence that his actions were undertaken deliberately in the spotlight. His separatist yearnings for a black homeland ("We want a country. Why can't we have our own land?"), black pride ("When are we going to wake up as a people and end the lie that white is better than black?"), and black sovereignty ("I will die before I sell out my people for the white man's money")[47] may have derived from his dealings with the Muslim leaders Malcolm X and Elijah Muhammad, but his fame made his stances on civil rights crucial to all of America, particularly to black athletes.

But it was as black athlete that Ali became embroiled in some of his strangest contradictions. When it comes down to it, whatever there was of an actual "athletic revolution" owed more to the actions of black athletes than it did to the indignities expressed by white athletes and sportswriters. It was black players who boycotted the AFL's 1965 All-Star game over an issue of pay; the raised fists of John Carlos and Tommie Smith at the 1968 Olympics forced the nation to acknowledge that

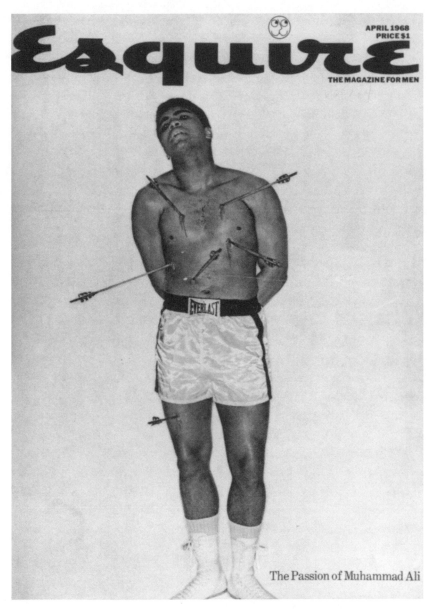

APRIL 1968
PRICE $1

THE MAGAZINE FOR MEN

EVERLAST

The Passion of Muhammad Ali

The martyred Ali on the cover of Esquire, April 1968. *(Photo courtesy of* Esquire Magazine*)*

SportsWorld was not one big happy place; and Curt Flood's decision to challenge the reserve clause would have lost some of its symbolic power had Flood been white. Still, when sociologist Harry Edwards proposed a black boycott of the 1968 Olympics, one of the unconditional demands for shelving the boycott was the restoration of Ali's title. Edwards often repeated his dictum that whites universally exploited black athletes as modern-day gladiators. How strange, then, that Edwards never hesitated to bring all of his influence to bear on restoring Ali to the top of that gladiatorial world. No doubt Edwards saw Ali as a figure who could help transform the arena into something less exploitative, but historically who has created more capital for entrenched sporting interests than the heavy-weight champion of the world?

Even stranger was Ali's own paradoxical contribution to the meaning of race and color: that he, light-skinned and pretty, suspicion of white blood tainting his claims to racial exclusivity, had come to embody the hopes, anger, and venom of so many blacks—had risen to become king of the world not only by beating other blacks but also by humiliating them publicly in the demeaning language used for centuries by whites—by addressing them as "nigger" in the most casual of utterances, by pronouncing them dumb and unworthy,[48] and by pointing out their similarity to apes. If Joe Frazier was, as Ali constantly maintained, a "gorilla" in contrast to his own café au lait look—it was a stern refutation of more than Frazier's countenance. If black was truly beautiful, then how could Frazier be an "ugly gorilla"?

In noting the "intense chords of ambiguity" that Ali struck as a black public figure, writer Gerald Early recently asked if Ali was "a star boxer, or through his genius, the utter undermining of boxing? Was he a militant or the complex unmasking of militancy?"[49] Paradox invites these questions and others. How could the nation countenance such ambiguity in either its heroes or its villains? How could someone so instrumental in undermining traditional notions of character end up idolized decades later as a man of unassailable character? The answer may be that it was the ambiguity itself that made Ali such an enduring and fitting symbol of the Vietnam era. In a competitive, capitalist society Americans find dichotomy and opposition so inescapable that we fall in naturally with those who seem to reconcile them for us. The Vietnam era, so fraught

Ali lights the Olympic flame in Atlanta, 1996. (*Peter Read Miller*/Sports Illustrated*)*

with polar tensions, demanded no less than a contradictory figure of Ali's stature and style.

We were never quite sure what to do with Ali during the time that he strode the world stage, alternately clowning, stinging, mocking, laughing, scorning, and humiliating. As Ali once pointed out: "All kinds of people came to see me. Women came because I was saying, 'I'm so pretty,' and they wanted to look at me. Some white people, they got tired of my bragging. They thought I was arrogant and talked too much, so they came to see someone give the nigger a whuppin'. Longhaired hippies came to my fights because I wouldn't go to Vietnam. And black people, the ones with sense, they were saying, 'Right on, brother; show them honkies.' Everyone in the whole country was talking about me."[50]

By the time Atlanta hosted the 1996 Olympic Games, we were sure what to do with him. His reputation now softened by time, his many controversial stances left largely unchallenged, his swagger undone by Parkinson's syndrome, we handed him the torch that lit the stadium flame. It was a mighty moment of symbolic reconciliation—of black and white, old and young, amateur and pro. Ali had indeed become the seeming essence of an America more whole than it had been a quarter century earlier.

His magic, once performed solely in the ring, is now a handful of tricks—a disappearing handkerchief, a levitation illusion—that he uses to entertain the people that still trail in his wake. He is generous with his time and his person. He signs Muslim tracts by the thousands for free. Still, Ali retains an edge, an unknowableness that can be unsettling. By turns he is the comic, his lips pulled back tight against his teeth in a parody of anger, and the militant. Looking over a group of four white men waiting to be immortalized by posing with the champ for a photo, Ali calls them "four vanillas" to his "chocolate." Giving the up and down to another middle-aged white man who has waited two decades to be introduced to the "greatest of all time," Ali labels him the "Great White Dope." In both cases, Ali smiles. It is charming, but not convincingly warm.

Did history shape the man or the man history? Anytime you have to ask the question, you can be sure that it is neither, but rather both. If the biggest issues of his times were the Vietnam War and civil rights, no figure who meant more to each survived to the new millennium. Of the countless athletes who came through the era, none were more representative of the issues related to sport's character-building capacities.

It is probably no coincidence that character-building as the paradigm for sport was eclipsed at the same time that blacks took over the highest levels of play. The idea that blacks and whites were distinct races owed much to Ali. In selecting an identity as "black" rather than "Negro," by adopting separatist leanings after converting to Islam, and by making color matter on his very large stage, Ali reinforced the polarity of the times. What could be further apart, after all, than black and white? Everything in between mattered little. In 1972, Three Dog Night topped the charts with "Black and White," a song that claimed dichotomy and featured it in lyrics open to the possibility of both segregation and integration: "a child is black, a child is white / Together we learn to read and write." By the time that Paul McCartney and Stevie Wonder's 1982 duet, "Ebony and Ivory," similarly conveyed the idea that the races could produce harmony but were nonetheless as different as night and day, it was clear that desegregation and integration meant quite different things.

The idea of racial exclusivity has resurfaced often in the ensuing decades. When Hall of Fame running back O.J. Simpson stood trial for murder in 1995, many whites recirculated the possibility that Simpson was evidence of the atavistic violence still lurking in angry black men, ready to be directed at white women. The questionnaire for his prospective jurors included the queries: "If you are not currently a fan, have you in the past ever been a fan of the USC Trojans football team?" and "Does playing sports build an individual's character?" What became clear in the divisive debate over his trial and its meaning was that most Americans had come to believe that color, money, and celebrity were the decisive factors—not lessons from the gridiron. In December of 1997 *Sports Illustrated* asked "What Ever Happened to the White Athlete?" The question came twenty-nine years after the magazine's series on the plight of the black athlete, three decades during which the idea of race had become more pronounced.

Much of American sport at the turn of the century owes at least something to Ali's legacy. His collaboration with Howard Cosell embodied the transition from black-and-white to color television. His insistence on being seen prepared the public for the image-wary likes of Andre Agassi,

Dennis Rodman, and Hollywood's *Rudy.* The poetry and the monologues delivered to Terrell and Patterson legitimized and accelerated trash talking. And, against all odds, his most enduring legacy—that of conviction—means that we still take seriously the idea of sports and character.

CHAPTER SIX

Terrapin Soup: Challenging Authority

I have in mind the fact that in the New Left weekly rating of the people's enemies the institution known as Football Coach ranks high in the top ten—not far behind the Joint Chiefs of Staff, General Motors, the CIA, the FBI, John Wayne, and yours truly.
—Vice President Spiro Agnew, 1971

The image [of Apollo driving the invading centaurs from Olympia] is a potent one, for it recalls what must always be a fearful experience in the life of any civilization: the experience of radical disjuncture, the clash of irreconcilable conceptions of life.
—Theodore Roszak, The Greening of America, *1968*

To claim that Bob Ward should have known the centaurs were outside his door in 1969 is like saying that the makers of Butch Wax should have seen the Beatles coming or that Sonny Liston should have seen Clay's right fist on the way. True, these were surprises in a way that Ward's troubles were not, but Ward's world had always been at a remove from large concerns, seemingly immune to both the revolutionary and the small, cumulative forces of social change. Indeed, as the head football coach at the University of Maryland, Ward was Apollo, and, even after he knew the centaurs were threatening, he was unafraid and unforgiving.

Ward's world collapsed like a jostled soufflé in March of 1969 when 120 of his football players decided he should not be their coach—and then forced him out. There were explicit charges: abusive behavior, inability to "relate," technical ineptitude. Related results had seemed obvious: two wins in two seasons, contempt for the press, a disparity between the celebration of what Ward had been as player and the disappointment in what Ward had become as coach. Above all, though, Ward simply hadn't known—or hadn't cared—how close he was standing to the Vietnam era's anti-authoritarian fire. Lit by American youth, fed by a complex of events and beliefs, it had burnt its way through a number of institutions before finally reaching sports and Ward's beloved game.

The 1960s had brought a steady stream of challenges to authorities in organized sports, so Ward was not alone. The control exercised by coaches antagonized many baby boomers, and as Agnew maintained, the football coach seemed to be a figure particularly despised among leftists. Dee Andros at Oregon State nearly lost his job in 1969 over a player's right to a "neat moustache"; Lloyd Eaton was attacked at the University of Wyoming that year for alleged racism; Woody Hayes was ridiculed throughout the decade for running Ohio State football like a military regiment. Still, when *Sports Illustrated* used a three-part presentation in 1969 to recognize and examine the plight of "The Desperate Coach," Bob Ward was one of the featured cases.

The coach could be forgiven for getting singed. It had never happened to him before. "You thought twice before you tried to burn Bobby Ward," a friend advised a reporter. It was apparent, in the wake of his forced resignation, that Ward could never have imagined that he and any group of football players could experience radical disjuncture or irreconcilable conceptions of life. In genuine puzzlement, Ward had asked a friend, "Don't they understand what it takes to win?"[1]

As a player, Bob Ward had known what it took. The son of an Elizabeth, New Jersey, policeman, Ward had grown into an oak hard football player, the result of an unshakable mental resolve that served him well when he went off to play at Maryland in the late 1940s. A 185 pounder who stayed on the field for sixty minutes, playing both offense and defense, he was a dwarf amid fellow linemen. His determination, fight, and blink-of-the-eye quickness made him a giant. Teams assigned two— and sometimes three—players to try to block him. He was the captain, the Most Valuable Player, and a two-time All-American on some of the best football teams that Maryland ever produced.

Given the background and stature of most coaches in the mid-1950s, Ward seemed well equipped to become one when his playing career ended at the 1952 Sugar Bowl. Whether they were the epitomes of the rising corporate masters described in William Whyte's influential *Organization Man* (1957), reflections of the conformist '50s, reliable guides in an

Bob Ward and the Terrapin coaching staff. *(Photo courtesy of University of Maryland)*

increasingly chaotic and unknowable modern world, or simply father figures, coaches—and football coaches in particular—had followed the
mythic trail of Knute Rockne to become society's trusted tutors of young
men. Assuming infallibility in matters of character, they wielded the
power of tyrants, beneficent and otherwise. When Bob Ward became an
assistant coach at his alma mater, under head coach Jim Tatum, he had
little trouble dealing with players he had stood beside the previous season. There was no loss of confidence in the lessons he'd learned and those
he now wanted to pass on—and no opposition to them from the players.

Ward flourished in his five years on the Maryland sidelines, as did
the team. In 1953, though defeated 7–0 in the Orange Bowl, the Terps
were voted national champions. In 1957 Ward moved to Iowa State for
another five years before the legendary Bud Wilkinson offered him a job
as one of his assistants at Oklahoma University. Oklahoma was part of
America's heartland, but it was isolated from a good deal of the social tur-
bulence that, by the mid-'60s, was commonplace on college campuses on
the coasts. Because of the state's conservatism and the unwavering power
of Wilkinson (he would become a member of Congress after leaving
coaching), football at Oklahoma was a particularly unaffected arena. In

1966 Ward moved on to an outpost where the spirit of the times was even more remote. Working for Tom Cahill, Ward became the defensive coordinator of a fine Army team.

The insularity of the West Point appointment may have done him a disservice. Ward later told writer Mark Carp that he was made to coach at West Point, a place where demands for orderliness and discipline mirrored Ward's own compulsions.[2] When Maryland called Ward home the next year to become the head coach, he returned, vowing to give his new squad "the same zest for the game I had when I played."[3] But much had changed in the ten years since he'd left College Park. With little time to recruit or select assistant coaches to replace the talented group that had left in recent years (including future head coaches of note: Dick McPherson, Sam Rutigliano, and Lou Saban, who had preceded Ward as head coach), Ward's Terrapins suffered all season. They lost all nine games, including a humiliating defeat at the hands of Oklahoma on national television. Outscored during the season, 231–46, the team was the worst at Maryland since 1892. Still, when the student newspaper, the *Diamondback,* summarized the season it was uncritical of Ward. Calling them a team "only a mother could love," the paper reported: "Like 22 ugly ducklings, the Terp football team of 1967 took the field and, week after monotonous week, got the hell beat out of it. The Marquis de Sade could not have asked for more."[4] "It was a nightmare," Ward admitted. "By the end of the season we were all numb."[5] Some of the players who had come to the program prior to Ward's arrival thought talent was not the question and, indeed, a handful of them had pro careers or pro tryouts. Either way, the problems went beyond talent and assistant coaches. They also had much to do with the culture's shifting attitude toward authority.

Working at Oklahoma, and then West Point, had not prepared Ward for anything other than blind obedience from his players. Football players at those places accepted the doctrine of coaches as truth and internalized it as their own. At West Point there was also tolerance of corporal lessons, the laying on of hands accepted as a method of teaching and punishment. In that regard army cadets shared a system of learning with many football players who, across the decades, had taken instructions for an aggressive game from hands-on coaches who found the parallels between football and war to be helpful and motivational.

In 1967, however, while West Point graduates expected their lives to encompass war, many college students—and some football players—took a dimmer view of analogies between military battle and sport. What college students had in greater abundance than philosophical differences about the Vietnam War or physical aggression on or off the playing fields, however, was conviction that it was they—and not their elders—who should decide about such matters.

The roots of the conviction are elusive, though already in the Vietnam era television was being singled out for blame. In the view of several social observers, television messages could be serious and insidious. Jeff Greenfield was convinced that in the world of children's programming that had entertained the baby boom generation, the villain was always a grown-up in authority. And Columbia University activist-author-student James Simon Kunen claimed to have drawn his philosophy of law from television actor Fess Parker in his popular Disney television portrayal of Davy Crockett. Parker/Crockett advised people to decide what you think is right and then go ahead and do it. Wrote Kunen: "Walt Disney really bagged that one; the old fascist inadvertently created a whole generation of radicals."[6]

So it was that when Bob Ward ran his first drills as a head coach in the spring of 1967, he ran into immediate trouble. Described by one player as "the roughest I've ever been through," the drills caused resentment, as did the coach's use of physical threats and physical reprimands. According to one player Ward once threatened to knock his teeth out. Another player, Nick George, after leaving the team that spring following a disagreement about whether he was too injured to practice, told a student reporter that Ward hit and kicked players. Ward denied the charge, telling the *Diamondback:* "I don't hit players. I don't—at least not maliciously."[7] There was a lot riding on that last word. Ward thought his intentions were the primary issue. The players thought the acts themselves were paramount, their very commission an indication of a fundamental lack of respect from the coach. "From my perspective," says Ernie Torain, who played his senior year under Ward, "you couldn't be kicking and pushing and hitting players."[8]

Physicality had served a generation of coaches well and made some— Bear Bryant, Vince Lombardi, Darrell Royal—into revered figures. But even entrenched coaches found themselves challenged on the use of force by players of the baby boom generation. Dave Meggyesey left an all-pro career behind to write *Out of Their League,* a 1971 book that labeled both his professional coaches and those at Syracuse University as uncaring authoritarians who used physical intimidation to punish players; Royal's University of Texas program was blistered for the same things by Gary Shaw in *Meat on the Hoof.* Shaw and Meggyesey may have been both more outraged and more literate than some of their fellows, but they were part of a generation that had absorbed, along with locker-room slogans, a sense of rights while coming of age.

The idea of rights was prominent in post–World War II America. The drives for gender and racial equality were "rights" movements. The migration of masses to the suburbs, the single ownership of homes, cars, phones, and televisions were all part of a push toward privatization and atomization in American culture that reinforced the autonomy of the individual. World War II had committed people to the communal effort and sacrifices necessary to win the war. That done, they reasserted the individualism of American pioneering lore. By and large they did so within the framework of existing social structures. The family had perhaps become more mobile, smaller, and more relaxed in intrafamilial relationships, but it was the family nonetheless. Schools, churches, and political structures looked the same and stood for values recognizable to the great majority of people. The baby boomers, however, turned the subtle wishes for individual autonomy into direct challenges to authority and social stability.

The quest to undo authority by the young was so unsettling and so conducive to media hype that few people recognized that the Vietnam era was a time that promoted both the rejection of *and* the search for authority. The search was, according to historian Peter Clecak, a natural reaction to a world of growing scientific complexity that relentlessly multiplied an individual's ignorance of most matters. When social complexity outran the ability of simple structures to contain it, popular culture produced reliable narrators in the form of authority figures such as Green Bay Packers coach Vince Lombardi, whose simple certainties "came to seem an attractive relief from actual complexities."[9]

Lombardi's appeal also came from his apparent ability to wring perfection from his young charges. From the Massachusetts Bay colony— the "City on a hill"—to the Declaration of Independence and the

Constitution—menus for perfection—to beer commercials that ask us "Who says you can't have it all?" perfectibility has beckoned to Americans for centuries. Historian William Leuchtenburg proposed that John F. Kennedy, through his "heroic poses, his urgent rhetoric, his appeal to idealism and the nation's great traditions . . . inadvertently helped arouse among millions a dormant desire to perfect America."[10] If so, Lombardi's Packers were emblems of the desire. They became world champions in part by running perfectly executed sweeps. A rival coach admitted that, "You know what that damn team is going to do on just about every play. But you can't stop them."[11] Many baby boomers straggled home from sports practices in the dark, the victims of junior and senior high school coaches who, parroting Lombardi, told their players, "We're going to stay here all night if we have to—until you get it right."

To those on the older side of the generation gap, the segment of the young who identified with the counterculture seemed to be incapable of getting anything right. A number of researchers pointed out that most of the younger generation never experienced directly the ballyhooed rebellion of the '60s. Most had not gone to college, smoked pot, engaged in premarital sexual relations, or demonstrated against the war.[12] But those who did captured the nation's attention and drew the wrath of the previous generations. Just why the threat should have seemed so powerful is open to conjecture.

In clinging to the most obvious ideals and denying the confusion, the elders were, according to some critics, trying to reaffirm what was missing from their own lives, not just from those of their children. "No one," claimed Philip Slater in *The Pursuit of Loneliness,* "likes to admit that they have spent their lives in a foolish, evil, or crazy manner . . . When their children cry for peace or social justice they say 'don't talk dirty' or 'get a haircut.' This is a way of saying, 'There is nothing important or disturbing going on here.'" It was a desperate attempt to view the world as unchanging.[13] It led to a hypersensitivity to criticism and was expressed in a directive to the antiwar protestors to "love America or leave it."

The exaggerated hostility that hippies tended to arouse also suggested to Slater that their lifestyle was highly seductive to middle America. His theory held that issues about which a society feels strongly draw equal measures of emphasis and suppression. These opposing forces are much more equally balanced than society's participants like to recognize—were this not true there would be no need for suppression.[14] Similarly, in the struggle to build our own identities and esteem, according to Thomas Cottle in *Time's Children,* we tend to render homogeneous any groups of people we see as being different from ourselves.[15] This, based as it was in the '60s on radically conflicting styles and appearances, helped to mask the deeper unity of drives and needs that seemingly opposing groups shared.[16] In adopting the long hair and loud costuming that they did, the counterculture gave members of the older culture easily recognizable differences with which to construct barriers between the two. Indeed, one student of the phenomenon said that the counterculture conjured the "image of a game preserve which has been set up by the animals. Somehow they are safe within the borders of their community."[17] As if to illustrate both the apparent differences and underlying sameness, journalist Hunter Thompson in 1967 described the Gray Line bus decision to add "Hippieland" to its San Francisco tour. Billed as "'the only foreign tour within the continental limits of the U.S.,'" it was an immediate hit "with tourists who thought the Haight-Ashbury was a human zoo. The only sour note was struck by the occasional hippy who would run alongside the bus, holding up a mirror."[18]

But football players were not part of the counterculture. In many ways the enmity between college football players and hippies was even more pronounced than that between hippies and the older generations. A football player might have stopped the Haight-Ashbury bus, gotten off, and busted both hippie and mirror. On most campuses, the gap between "jocks" and "pukes" was a given. Many students assumed athletes were unthinkingly conservative. At the University of Maryland, Dave Bourdon, a writer for the *Diamondback,* ridiculed the footballers in an April 1968 column titled "Those Dumb Animals." Bourdon divided Terp athletes into two categories: "the dumb jocks" and "those who are afraid to speak." The blame for the latter, according to Bourdon, was the coaches, "most of whom would suffer a grand mal seizure if one of their boys spoke out on some topic."[19]

In the winter of '69 Bourdon would be forced to reassess his position when it turned out that Maryland's football players were more in tune with currents of college behavior than he thought. If permissive parenting and an abundance of material wealth drove the baby boomer quest for individualism, as some contended,[20] the most visible products were college students. A 1969 study of 3,100 men found that self-direction was more highly prized by men of higher social class occupations (most often held by college graduates), whereas those in lower class positions were more likely to value conformity to external authority.[21]

As institutions entrusted with fostering the proper balance between questioning inquiry and civilized acceptance of order, universities received much of the attention and criticism when the balance seemed upset. A dean at the University of Toronto had noted in 1966 that many people "have turned to the universities . . . in hope of finding, through them, a renewed or substitute authority in life."[22] They were looking in the wrong places. At college after college, students sought to usurp administrative power. Angry alumni, parents, and trustees were outraged, calling demonstrators at one university "a rabble of malcontent outlaws," "numbingly stupid and crashingly irrelevant," "psychopathic cases," "un-American undesirables," and "scum."[23]

At Columbia in 1968, the enmity that resulted in the school's closing swelled from a disinclination to even acknowledge the student protestors. Dean Herbert Deane remarked: "Whether students vote 'yes' or 'no' on a given issue means as much to me as if they were to tell me they like strawberries."[24] Coaches were inclined not only to similarly disregard the voices of their athletes, but in fact to use them for their own ends. During the Columbia crisis, and during many other student demonstrations in the latter half of the decade, some coaches encouraged their charges to confront and discourage protestors. Coaches did this, not because they felt the right, but because they felt the great obligation that athletics shouldered in providing stability in a changing culture. Vic Rowen, the football coach at San Francisco State University said: "We're the last chance for the preservation of dignity on campus and I say that without trying to be heroic or corny."[25]

It was ultimately a question of dignity, or a gap between perceptions of it, that sparked Bob Ward's downfall. The 1968–69 season, Ward's second, though better than his first by two victories, was still miserable. Twice he ran onto the field to question calls by what he believed were biased officials; his talented quarterback often sat out with injury; and his relations with the student and local press deteriorated markedly.

Dave Bourdon, the author of the previous year's condemnation of football players as "dumb animals," had become the *Diamondback*'s sports

Athletes were among those who actively opposed the attempts of "pukes" to take over Columbia's administration building in 1968. (*Photo courtesy of* Columbia Daily Spectator*)*

editor before the 1968 season. By the first week of October—one week before Ward's first victory as a head coach—Bourdon was no longer welcome at the coach's weekly press luncheon. According to Bourdon, Ward was upset "because I had the audacity to suggest his blockbuster offense use a screen pass."[26]

To Ward, Bourdon was symptomatic of something he did not like, though he did not fully realize what it was: a shifting of authority that would eventually grant outsized credibility and influence to the media. Ward believed that playing the game rather than writing about it fostered expertise and, obviously, the kind of respect for authority that sports participation demanded. He thought student writers should be more closely supervised. "They don't show any respect for anyone," he charged. "I think it's a crime that student newspapers can write the kind of stuff they write, not only about me but about the president of the University, too. Our society is really going down the drain."[27] He was particularly contemptuous of Bourdon and his fellow *Diamondback* staffers. After his resignation, he told *Sports Illustrated* that among those responsible for forcing it were: "a couple of pip-squeak cub newspaper guys who don't know what football's all about. It happens. Some little sawed-off guy, 5 feet 5, 135 pounds, he can't help it, God made him that way, but he can't play, so he gets on the campus newspaper and all of a sudden he's got power he never thought of having. That's what it's all about on campuses today, power, whether it's in qualified hands or not, and when boys see other boys getting it they want it, too. They just copy what the rest of the kids are doing. They're like sheep."[28] Mark Carp, one of the *Diamondback* writers, admits that he can understand some of Ward's irritation. "Here I am," he remembers, "I'm twenty something, and I've got all this power, or at least perceived power. I can write these things and 'blah, blah, blah' and people read 'em and 'Hey, I'm pretty special,' so in that respect part of this was, in effect, my chance to take a shot at authority."[29]

Ward was not alone in noting the irony of authority rejection among youth. That is, it frequently begged the question of whether it was truly autonomous challenge or merely a different shade of conformity. Upon taking office early in the decade, one university president remarked that, "You don't have to teach people to conform; they'll take care of that themselves."[30] When Bob Ward's players finally revolted in the winter of 1969, they reached a consensus so extensive that it can, at least in retrospect, be taken for just the type of sheeplike conformity of which the coach spoke.

The events of what came to be known as the "Great Football Rebellion" became recognizable on February 25, 1969. On that day Ward made his first appearance at informal agility drills. In the *Diamondback*'s retelling, a player stated that Ward "comes out and smacks a couple guys around and we all say, 'Here he goes again. Nothing's changed.'" Late that night a meeting took place and a petition circulated, on which 113 names would eventually appear, requesting Ward's dismissal.

The players and the newspaper were adamant that the outcry was the outcome of four things: physical abuses against players; verbal belittling of players and assistant coaches; fear tactics, including the threat of lost scholarships; and technical ineptitude.[31] Of the last of those no one could be sure. The *Diamondback* had, in fact, agreed prior to the '68 season that the Terps' lack of talent merited sympathy for Ward. "He did indeed inherit a bad team. Very bad. He also had an unbelievable amount of bad luck," Bourdon wrote.[32]

The first three were not, in Ward's mind, grounds for grievance. "When we went on the field, I got pretty mean with them. Not mean, but aggressive—grab 'em, slap 'em on the helmet, that kind of thing, things if you don't know what football is all about, you can't understand." They were things Ward was convinced "it takes to win." His proof was Army, where, he said, "they responded. We won eight games and Tom Cahill was named the Coach of the Year. But at Maryland they didn't want to fight for it."[33]

The players' ability to define what they wanted to fight for—or over— was advanced, ironically, by Ward's initial decision to move the players into the top two floors of one campus dormitory. The student paper decried the displacement of regular students, but the closeness meant, in Ward's words, that "when they did rebel they were all together, right where I put them, and every night it was like a convention for the gripers."[34]

The griping may have been about Ward's physical and emotional intimidation, but it was also about the restrictions—social and academic—that Ward's dormitory plan entailed. "Maryland had a history of athletes flunking out," he noted. "I cracked down on many things. I wanted them to keep their rooms presentable, to go to class." He ordered a coach-monitored study period every night. For a time he imposed a curfew on some of the team. "I know the ones who were in trouble griped about all the restrictions," he said, "but the point is, if anybody was interested in their academic welfare it was me."[35]

The morning following the petition signing, the team decided to hold another meeting in lieu of practice. By then a handful of ringleaders had emerged. Charlie Hoffman, a little-used 260-pound, nonscholarship player was one. "He only played in a few games," Ward complained to the press. Bruce Olecki, a six-foot-three 235-pound one-time letterman but second-stringer under Ward, was another. "Ten days before that grievance meeting," Ward told *Sports Illustrated,* "we had our football banquet. Olecki didn't get a letter and I heard he was fuming about that." The *Diamondback* additionally cited Ralph Sonntag, a six-foot-three 242-pound starter as a leader.[36] It is probably no coincidence that all three were tackles. Ward's method of imparting technique often found him, in khakis and T-shirt, demonstrating a move in nose-to-nose contact with a lineman in full gear. It was at such moments that frustration and physical proximity could lead to the lessons of a hard slap to the helmet.

In Ward's mind, there was a small core of "bad apples with bad attitudes" behind his trouble. "Some of the guys who were in that group that night hadn't been on the team for a year and a half," he claimed. "They'd quit or they'd been run off."[37] Ward believed that most of his squad understood his goals and tactics. After defeating North Carolina for his first victory the previous fall, the coach had asserted: "The big thing that makes it worthwhile is that I know the boys are with me in my aims."[38] The team had also surprised Ward during the '68 season with a cake on his birthday.[39] Most convincing to Ward was a *Diamondback* writer's assessment the week before the revolt that no more than a dozen players were considering leaving the team before spring drills.[40]

When the players met on the afternoon of the twenty-sixth, they were already wary of public perceptions. They arrived in suits and ties. One admitted that, "We don't want to hurt the school or administration. We're not a protest group."[41] But, of course, they were. It did not matter whether they shared the antiwar convictions of many on campus, because by 1969 the politics of social change were becoming secondary to the politics of personal liberation, and these, it seemed, the Terp players understood as well as any of their fellow students. They may have understood better. Challenging authority took many forms in the Vietnam era, and some collegians were not particular about the causes. At Maryland, in the winter of 1969, defiance encompassed nude streaking and—on the same night—both a panty raid and a massive sit-in at the president's house.

The rebellious players were, for the most part, careful and deliberate, though Olecki, believing Maryland's governor, Marvin Mandel, had an interest in Terrapin athletics, phoned the capitol and spoke with Secretary of State Blair Lee. Lee described Olecki as unhappy but somewhat incoherent.[42] Mandel claimed to have no jurisdiction in the matter, and so the fate of Bob Ward rested in the hands of his players and an old ally.

Jim Kehoe had been Maryland's track and field coach for more than twenty years. Bob Ward had thrown the javelin for him. The two shared a philosophy on the value of sports ("it plays a very positive part or has a very positive place in the total educational picture," Kehoe told a Maryland English class in the mid-'70s), and particularly discipline, in building character ("I believe totally in discipline. I believe totally in authority.").[43] On February 10 Kehoe had become Maryland's acting athletic director. His official term would not begin until July 1, but he was granted the immediate authority to fire and hire. The power came just in time to make his first task the unenviable one of handling the "Great Football Rebellion."

Alerted to the February 26 meeting, Kehoe left track practice early. Though he first tried to dissuade the players from a revolt, he was persuaded to sit down with several players that evening. The grievances he heard convinced him to meet later with the full squad. "I'm going to sit them down, close the door, and go on from there," he said. "I want to find out who's unhappy and why."[44]

The meeting was scheduled for Monday, March 3. The night before, the team convened again. Art Staggs, a black freshman, said he could not complain about Ward, and at least two other blacks left the meeting in disgust. Freshmen were not eligible for varsity play in 1969 and the separation between them and upperclassmen was pronounced. The irony was that many black athletes in the late '60s were particularly sensitive to the idea of rights. Ernie Torain had marched in Washington for civil rights. "There was more than just an athlete involved" in dealing with Bob Ward, he remembers. There was an aware and articulate activist as well.[45]

Following the meeting, the *Diamondback* pronounced the team only "shakily coherent."[46] One of the mysteries of human relations is how revolution spreads from the fervid faith of the few to capture the more generalized disenchantment of the many. UCLA basketball star Bill Walton, an athlete whose political convictions ran deep in the Vietnam era, has said, "When everybody thinks the same, nobody thinks."[47] He meant it as an indictment of the old jock, conservative message embraced by people like Bob Ward. But it could have applied just as readily to Ward's players, who suddenly seemed without dissent or personal nuance when it came to their coach. The Terps' punter, Billy Van Heusen, who went on to kick professionally for Denver, ascribed the phenomenon to inevitability. "I thought the players would act eventually," he said within a few months of the revolt. "It only takes time for one out of every three to take the initiative and stand up for himself." Torain, who opposed Ward's "dictatorial style," also thought the situation had an air of inevitability. "Nobody was talking to people like that in those days," he says.[48]

By the following evening, energized perhaps by the presence of television cameras and reporters (photos were allowed before the room was closed to the press) and surely riding an adrenaline boost induced by their coming confrontation with Ward, the 120 players had affected an air of solidarity that shook the coach. According to the *Diamondback,* players said he was surprised to see the whole team there. When he noticed three former players, he had them removed. Charlie Hoffman opened with a team statement. For the next ninety minutes other players rose to speak, reiterating their tales of physical and verbal abuse and their claims of communication problems. Though Kehoe granted Ward five minutes to rebut each speaker, the coach sat silently through them all. The confrontation ended when the soft-spoken Staggs rose and asked Ward in genuine wonder, "Coach, how can you want to stay here when nobody wants to play for you?"[49]

For Ward, the question was a bewildering one. The issue was not one of preference but of necessity. "This is a moral thing with me," he told the *Washington Post.* "I'm trying to help these boys. I want to make gentlemen out of them." Van Heusen claimed the coach wanted more. "He wanted everyone to be like himself—an All-American."[50] But even Ward's status as an All-American had become a matter of interpretation and debate. "He was an overachiever as a player," Torain says. "He was a small guy who played guard or something—made All-America or something like that."[51] In the eyes of some players, Ward had been an All-American through effort. As effort became a more precious commodity in the '60s, however, many of the young viewed talent as a more admirable route to success.

Some people say that Bob Ward would not have been vulnerable if his team had been winning. The thinking is that in programs where success was measured only in victories, personal autonomy was a less formidable obstacle than in losing programs. In the words of one athletic director: "they'll dive on loose balls, they'll play your defense, they'll wear a blazer on the road, and they'll shave, 'cause if you win, they have no choice. But if they're losing, they're gonna jerk your chain on some of those Mickey Mouse rules."[52]

To an extent, the argument is a valid one. Winning might have stalled the revolt or quashed it entirely. Nonetheless, the contention is speculative. Even in the win-oriented Vietnam era, victory was not a guarantee of security. Winning did not save the job of Woody Hayes at Ohio State after he punched an opposing player in 1978; it did not save Frank Kush the next year at Arizona State after more than two decades of grabbing hold of facemasks and rattling helmeted heads; and it did not save Lloyd Eaton at the University of Wyoming after he was accused of racist treatment of blacks in 1969. Most notably it did not save the job of Jim Owens at the University of Washington. Featured as another of *Sports Illustrated*'s "Desperate Coaches," Owens was fired in 1969 for failure to relate properly to his black athletes. Though he was coming off a 3–5–2 season, he had taken the Huskies to the Rose Bowl in 1959, 1960, and 1964. Asked if winning would have altered the players' perceptions of Bob Ward, Torain answered flatly: "No."[53]

Ironically, Ward's players eventually damned him for wanting to win too much, and Bourdon singled out Ward's obsession with victory as a "common sports personality trait" that Ward had in "an unnatural abundance."[54] In fact, allusions to the idea of personality kept surfacing in the speech of players. Before the showdown players remarkably went on record as saying they agreed 100 percent with Ward's academic and conditioning programs, as well as his restrictions on conduct, appearance, and dress. But, according to their statement to the press, there were two issues causing irremediable friction: a personality conflict ("His personality instills no desire to win or be coached by him") and his technical ability, of which a 2–17 record was cited as prima facie evidence.[55]

On March 5, after a long meeting with Kehoe, Ward resigned. The players, described by press and Kehoe alike as courteous and dignified, presented this formal statement: "We would like to express once again that in no way was our action related to any other campus disorder here or at any other school in the country. We have and always will respect Mr. Bob Ward for his athletic accomplishments at the University of Maryland and we are sorry that the personality conflict between us and Mr. Ward existed and that an understanding could not be reached."[56]

It would be as unfair to attribute frivolous or superficial behavior to the players as it would be to attribute an ounce of insincerity to Bob Ward. Doubtless, the players disappointed Ward daily, and doubtless he crossed a line in dealing with them. Kehoe, who would later tell a group of undergraduates that, "Frankly, [in matters of standards] I support the coach," also told them that "any coach that isn't consistent with a reasonable I think position is going to find himself in trouble." When *Sports Illustrated* sought Kehoe's take on what had brought down his "Desperate Coach," he told them that coaches with a "rigid perspective" could no longer thrive in a college environment where "kids are so much smarter" and "more aware than they were 20 years ago."[57]

Ward, Kehoe, and the mutinous players were trapped in a unique time. Ward would have been more likely to survive a decade earlier. His authority would have been ironclad, his claims to building character unquestioned. Even in 1969, alumni, university presidents, and parents besieged Kehoe, admonishing him not to cede to the "student radicals." As he told the *Diamondback*, "I've been chastised as someone who has no respect for authority and as one who let the hippies overthrow the coach."[58] It was a common stance that the mainstream took in combating what felt like damaging change. When head coach Dee Andros withstood the challenge of some of his Oregon State players over issues of personal appearance in 1968, a supporter wrote him, "Students have to abide by rules or the country will go down." When the faculty senate reproved the coach's rules of conduct, Andros likened it to "giving the hippies the license to walk naked at graduation."[59]

Ward's fellow football coaches were stunned at his downfall. Penn State's Joe Paterno, while admitting that he did not know the specifics, thought the American Football Coaches Association should investigate. "I don't think it's a good thing for a squad to fire a coach," he told *Sports Illustrated*. "As an association, we ought to know what happened."[60] When the AFCA Board of Trustees met that June, its director, Bill Murray, reported that Maryland had turned down an investigation request. Also on the meeting's agenda was a general discussion of "the problems of football coaches as they relate to militants and student groups." By the following January, Murray and South Carolina coach Paul Dietzel had convinced Maryland to cooperate, had visited the campus, and prepared a written report, which they decided could not be made public at the time.[61]

For all their assurances that their quest was not a protest, the players did see the situation as a confrontation to be won, not a problem to be assuaged with compromise. Speaking under grant of anonymity, a prominent player from the team remembers feeling that "you weren't going to tell these kids anything." Ward says that a former player later told him that it "was terrible what we did." In the heat of the moment, however, some of them were joyous in anticipation of triumph. They could not, according to Bourdon's account, "keep themselves from admitting that they were about to successfully pull one off." Approaching the ballyhooed conflict, another had predicted that "Ward will be 2–18 before the meeting is over."[62] Ward had, then, scored an unhappy victory of sorts. His team had become united and single-minded against a common opponent.

Kehoe, recognized as a fair man who wanted the situation resolved as equitably as possible, acknowledged that the situation set a dangerous precedent. Upon taking the job, he had admitted that he was "actively seeking to get the press on his side" and was "profoundly aware that this medium can make or break him in his new role." He apparently conducted a successful courtship because one week after Ward's departure, Kehoe fired without backlash Terp basketball coach Frank Fellows to make room for Lefty Driesell. In a strange twist that demonstrated just how polarized and unforgiving the era was, Fellows was bounced, in part, because he was not Bob Ward manic. According to the *Diamondback*, "niceness" was Fellows's "tragic flaw." He never "got mad enough," the article stated. The paper that had wondered whether Bob Ward was too mean to win now asked in headlines: "Fellows: Too Nice to Be a Winner?"[63]

The snowball effect that Kehoe and Paterno feared appeared initially to be gathering force. Forty-seven of the Oregon State football players who were unhappy with coach Andros quit before making it to the 1969 season; one day after Fellows was fired, the varsity basketball players at the University of Virginia expressed dissatisfaction with their coach. Most coaches did not lose their jobs, however. Instead, they adapted to the realization that players and the media had gained new power. The Brown University *Alumni Monthly* wrote in 1971: "This is the era of the anti-hero . . . If a coach tried to pull the old 'win one for the Gipper' routine in the scintillating seventies his players would probably reply: 'Get serious.'"[64]

The seeds of individual rebellion that flowered in the Vietnam era, causing athletes to reject authority, had already been unearthed in the writings of some 1950s thinkers. David Riesman, in *The Lonely Crowd* (1950), blamed advertising, television, and suburbia as influences on what he termed *other-directedness*. Vance Packard's *Hidden Persuaders* (1957) accused the ad men of coercing individuals. William Whyte (*The Organization Man,* 1957) and C. Wright Mills (*The Power Elite,* 1959) added to the claims of individual helplessness in a world where people were manipulated by a social structure beyond their control. Reaction against such restraints would seem inevitable, and it seems quite logical that the Vietnam era, with its countercultural emphasis on "doing your own thing" evinced such backlash.

In the athletic arena, coaches searched for the right mix between character and winning, between individual identity and collective aspirations. The quest of athletes to escape authority in the Vietnam era made the undertaking difficult. Though athletes had a great stake in supporting the authority that granted them privilege, ultimately they too wrestled with the issues that formed the broader youth consciousness. According to Torain, Ward "was setting himself up as the ultimate authority for all your time except for going to class."[65] The time had passed for coaches with that kind of power.

Because most Americans prior to the '60s had accepted sport as a powerful symbol of national character, gestures within athletics for autonomy were particularly visible and disruptive events. It was, in fact, the confusion over the proper limits of authority and autonomy that gave substance and form to all of the other conflicts that took place between supporters of character-building and those challenging them in the Vietnam era. When issues of morality, manliness, physical prowess, or effort were involved, it was the parameters of authority that were debated. Players were not to be told how to look and act manly, not to be told how much effort to expend, not to be told what was moral and what was not, how soft they were physically, or what constituted intellectual relevance.

Since the Vietnam era, unquestioning discipline has belonged to an outdated perception of character. Coaches consider all-out effort, devotion to discipline, and capitulation to authority only within the context of maintaining a winning program. Players have assumed the power to decline plays not designed for them (Scottie Pippen's notorious sit-down at the end of a crucial playoff game in the mid-'90s) and to have coaches replaced who do not match their own visions of how a game should be played (Doug Collins ousted at Michael Jordan's behest; Paul Westphal at Magic Johnson's urging). In a reversal of the situation that undid Bob Ward, basketball pro Latrell Sprewell choked his coach in 1998. After a bout of public outrage, however, Sprewell regained acclaim with a new team, while the coach eventually lost his job.

In reducing the authority of coaches, disgruntled Vietnam era athletes did gain a voice against arbitrary and abusive practices, but they also paved the way for the intrusion of new commanders. Howard Cosell was the first member of the new media to hold himself up as an expert on all matters great and small. By the turn of the century, the anchorpersons of the widely popular ESPN Sportscenter presented themselves both during broadcasts and during commercials for the show as entertainers and stars on an equal footing with the players and coaches they covered. A smirking, desultory tone marked much of their commentary, inviting consumers to regard the impossible skills of elite athletes as overregarded and too often failing.

Additionally, perhaps in anticipation of the day when players would seize autonomy, undertrained coaches and doting parents assumed outsized control of the nation's increasingly organized children's games. "In fact," wrote *Sports Illustrated*'s William Nack and Lester Munson in the first year of the new century, "the fields and arenas of youth sports in North America have become places where a kind of psychosis has at times prevailed, with parents and coaches screaming and swearing at kids, the officials or each other, and fights breaking out among adults."[66]

Six months after Bob Ward left College Park, 400,000 youth met for the Woodstock Music Festival in upstate New York. As those in attendance smoked dope, rolled in the mud, waded naked in ponds, made love in the open, and listened to rock music that gave voice to all of their political and aesthetic hopes, the "Woodstock Nation" seemed finally to have found a way to turn the world upside down. In early modern Europe, the "world turned upside down" had been a common theme of the rituals of carnival, a way of allowing for symbolic inversions of age, sex, and status in societies that were rigidly hierarchical in everyday life. Sport and games had been a primary feature of carnival, one of the arenas for acting out antagonisms toward authorities.[67] On college campuses to the mid-nineteenth century, sport had likewise been rowdy, sometimes bloody, sometimes rebellious escape from the restrictive academic life. For the next hundred years, however, sport and its character-building mythology had cemented authority. In overthrowing their coach, the Maryland football team was a step ahead of the Woodstock counterculture.

In fact, the irony of the two situations was this: in exiling Bob Ward, the Terps had become the kind of protestors they had spent their brief adulthood renouncing; on the other hand, in applauding the low incidence of trouble at Woodstock, the counterculture was exhibiting exactly the kind of socialized civility their parents and coaches had hoped to instill.

Perhaps the greatest irony was that Bob Ward did not leave coaching. He became a valuable assistant coach with three teams in the Canadian Football League, winning Grey Cups with both the Ottawa Rough Riders and the Montreal Alouettes. Eventually, he became a scout in the National Football League while running a liquor store in Annapolis, Maryland. He lives there now—in a gated community. He still looks fit and redwood hard. Saw off a leg and you could count the seventy plus rings. He'd probably reattach it with string and thumb tacks and go on his way. But his two years as head coach at Maryland left a scar. Roger Kahn, author of *The Boys of Summer,* wrote, "With years a man comes to distrust memory. The mind is a dreadful sentimentalizer, forgetting old hangovers and ancient catastrophes. We truly like the past because we know how it comes out. The wars are done. The loves are told." Bob Ward might not agree. He survived, but the world of sport he once ruled did not.

CHAPTER SEVEN

The Bad News Bears: Hollywood Presents the End of the Era

[Paramount's release of The Bad News Bears is] . . . bound to prompt a lot of boring theses about what competition means in the American system.
—Vincent Canby, New York Times, *1976*

There had never been another moment like it on the big screen: a gaggle of triumphant ballplayers—young boys in Yankee pinstripes, one holding a championship trophy as large as an office water cooler—offer their gritty underdog opponents postgame condolences and apologize for the rough treatment they've dealt them all season. As the winners begin to take their leave, the losing shortstop calls out to them: "Hey, Yankees." As the ballplayers and theater audiences turn their attention back to young Tanner Boyle, waiting for his obligatory, "Thanks, we think you're swell guys, too," the feisty blond bantam settles on a different message: "You can take your apology," he tells the Yankees, "and your trophy—and shove it straight up your ass." The gratifying possibility sets off a raucous celebration of beer swigging and head dousing for the losers and a resounding swell of Bizet's "Waltz of the Toreadors" for theater patrons.

For all that the Vietnam era delivered in the way of fights for players' rights, Olympic boycotts, stripped heavyweight titles, and intergender battles, it was this moment—the closing scene in 1976's *The Bad News Bears*—when it was apparent that we had gone through the looking glass, fallen down one hole and pulled ourselves up through another into a new world of American sport.

Both the strangeness and the familiarity of this new world were conveyed in the surreal reaction of reviewers and ad men who treated the film, for the most part, like a slightly saucier rendition of a Disney production. "For pure nutty escapism," read one advertising blurb, "don't miss *The Bad News Bears*." *Variety's Film Reviews* thought the film offered no more than "gentle social commentary." "The script is thin," pronounced the *Washington Post,* "and the ending shaky." Gentle? Shaky? A ten-year-old ballplayer tells his opponents to shove a championship trophy up their asses. That's shaky? No, them's fightin' words, and the failure to herald *The Bad News Bears* as the most subversive sports film ever made was evidence of a reluctance to acknowledge that the fight had been lost, that the film induced a collective detachment that proved Vincent Canby dead wrong. The *Bears* prompted waves of laughter but no theses or outrage. While the nation was distracted by a war, a presidential resignation, and deep civil unrest, its organized sports had begun to steer a new course. Perhaps it wasn't obvious because the "revolution" had been as much a product of changing perceptions and attitudes as it had been of conscious deeds. Featuring few self-proclaimed leaders, it was a bloodless coup against the status quo that was drowned out by the noise from Vietnam, television, and the myriad other social forces of change, and disguised by the new cosmetics of long hair, double knit uniforms, flaring sideburns, and artificial playing fields.

Before the Vietnam era, Hollywood had consciously connected the dots for film viewers, drawing a straight line between sports and old-fashioned American values. Biographical pictures (bio-pics) of the 1930s, 1940s, and 1950s repeatedly exalted hard work, toughness blended with compassion, achievement as a standard of success, and utter respect for authority. Whether the athlete portrayed was Babe Ruth, Jim Thorpe, or Monty Stratton, the formula scarcely changed. Even lighthearted fare such as *Angels in the Outfield* (1951) or *Tall Story* (1960) presented the fate of athletes and teams as an extension of unimpeachable national character. The issue of character was so pronounced that the verisimilitude of sports scenes was secondary; thus, the unbecoming sights of Anthony Perkins trying to dribble, Ronald Reagan trying to throw like Grover Cleveland Alexander, or William Bendix trying to hit like Babe Ruth.

The change in Hollywood's portrayal of sport was rooted in the cultural upheaval of the '60s. It was a decade in which it became clear that there would be no more Pat O'Briens as Rockne, no more future presidents masquerading as the Gipper. Baseball, in particular, went into celluloid retreat. Save for two forgettable 1962 efforts featuring Roger Maris and Mickey Mantle, Hollywood produced not a single baseball film in the decade—and only one, *Bang the Drum Slowly* (1973), an antiheroic film, in the entire Vietnam era. The void not only confirmed that Joe DiMaggio was missing (which Simon and Garfunkel had already made clear), it also made it apparent that no one was looking for him. He certainly was not in hiding with the Bad News Bears. From their beer-guzzling coach to their foulmouthed shortstop to their juvenile delinquent hitting star, the Bears were heroes that only a society that had lost its sense of moral infallibility could love.

Inasmuch as films are not reality (and most viewers are fully conscious that they are not), it seems wise not to attach too much cultural significance to film themes. Commercial releases have always traded in the kind of broad strokes that lend themselves to easy interpretation. You can find metaphor anywhere if you're creative in your search, and the chaos and flamboyance associated with the Vietnam era made looking for its cultural footprints seductive. Other movies of the time—*All the President's Men* (1976) or *American Graffiti* (1973), for instance—could be commentaries on lost innocence. *Bonnie and Clyde* (1967), *Butch Cassidy and the Sundance Kid* (1969), *Dog Day Afternoon* (1975), and *One Flew Over the Cuckoo's Nest* (1975) all took a turn at slapping around authority. Was *Jaws* (1975) merely metaphor for those big American corporations eating good American individuals? Overdrawn analysis, perhaps, but the fact that films are made with the intention of returning profits means that their projections of ideas and ideals are expected to resonate with the American public. The fact that *The Bad News Bears* was one of Hollywood's top money producers for 1976 (challenging *All the President's Men* for the top-grossing spot for six consecutive weeks following their simultaneous release),[1] then, is evidence that its frontal assaults on sports did not offend many viewers.

The plot of *The Bad News Bears* was uncomplicated. A city councilman, threatening litigation, has forced a youth league to accept a new team so that his son will have a place to play. He hires Morris Buttermaker (Walter Matthau), a former minor league pitcher turned swimming pool cleaner and drunk, to coach the Bears. Buttermaker lands Chico's Bail Bonds as the team's sponsor, after which he and his collection of inept kids sink quickly into the league basement. Eventually he lures Amanda Whurlitzer (Tatum O'Neal) and Kelly Leak (Jackie Earle Haley) to the team. The talented pair fuel the Bears' ascent to second place and a championship game with the Yankees. Coach Roy Turner (Vic Morrow) has made the Yankees a perennial winner, employing the relentless drive for perfectibility associated with the likes of Vince Lombardi. Director Michael Ritchie and screenwriter Bill Lancaster (actor Burt's son) have set up the Yankees as the mean-spirited symbol of organized sport gone rancid, and the audience awaits the expected triumph of the big-hearted underdogs. On the verge of victory, however, Buttermaker has a sudden revelation about the costs and meaning of winning. He inserts the team's worst players and the championship is lost by a run, thereby setting the stage for the trophy presentation scene. The audience is left in the unfamiliar position of cheering not only for a loser, but for a team of misfits.

The Bears offered the first film portrait of a new culture that no longer believed sport and good character were synonymous terms. Prior to the long stretch of bio-pics there had been films that gently lampooned one aspect of sport or another, usually related to the college scene: the inflated status of campus heroes (*College,* 1927), a ruthless coach (*The College Coach,* 1933), or the power of alcohol, gambling, or hangers-on to undermine the contests (*We Went to College,* 1936; *The Big Game,* 1936; *Cowboy Quarterback,* 1939). In these, sport's basic goodness always came to the fore; defective character was always mended. Boxing films, of course, portrayed fighters as thugs, pawns, and broken men, but boxing was always an exception to the bio-pic formula. The unsavory underside of society was linked to professional boxing in the 1930s and 1940s, and character in the ring was always at the mercy of unconscionable mobsters and managers. Similarly, a number of films revolved around corruption at the race track.

Ritchie's version of sport was far bolder and more insidious. He had used sport as a subject before (his *Downhill Racer* of 1969, however, confined its tension to that between a coach and a free-thinking Olympic skier), and he would later return to it twice more. A year after *Bad News Bears, Semi-Tough* made light of the corrupted lives of pro football players; in 1986, *Wildcats* milked laughs from the then-absurd premise of a young woman coaching a high school football team.

In making *The Bad News Bears,* Ritchie and Lancaster took a double risk, deciding to indict the nation's sporting character not only through its national game but through the kids that play it. It is true that the game's claim to being the national pastime had been dissolving since the early '60s in the rise of pro football's popularity, perhaps a contributing factor to why no baseball films were shot between 1962 and 1973. Whether because of decaying parks in inner-city slums, a lack of scoring, a proliferation of competing recreations, or something more complex and subconscious related to the era's zeitgeist, attendance at major league games had largely plateaued between 1962 and 1968 and then risen in the half decade afterward primarily because of the addition of expansion teams. Furthermore, Little League baseball was no longer the sole province of American boys. Teams from Japan, and especially Taiwan, dominated the annual World Series.

Baseball's loss of luster did not dissuade Ritchie from using the game to stand the character-building mythology of sport on end. By using instantly recognizable conventions and characters, while at the same time reversing the old canons of sport, the film created an anomaly—a team that was both underdog and bully, innocence and corruption, beacon and decoy—in short, a wonderful portrait of an institution in flux.

The Bears comprised a pack of stereotypes known to anyone who had ever been near a youth league game: the slothful, pudgy catcher (Engleberg, played by Gary Cavagnaro), the Napoleonic shortstop (Tanner, Christopher Barnes), the brainy nerd (Ogilvie, Alfred Lutter), the fleet black outfielder (Ahmad, Erin Blunt), the timid, snot-nosed lamb stuck in right field (Lupus, Quinn Smith). Not a single one had the virtuous bearing of "Chip Hilton" or "Bronc Burnett," fictional athletic literary figures whose heroics ran through multi-title sets that were popular among boys in the 1940s and 1950s (but faded dramatically in the Vietnam era). Flawed as they were, the Bears upset the bio-pic formula by mowing down the stems of sport's character-building ideology one by one.

First, the film subverted the concept of victory with honor. Once the bio-pic asserted itself in the 1940s, sports films dared not end on a discordant note. They all featured some act that blended victory with integrity, the overcoming of hardship being the whole point of the victory (and the film itself). If a subject was not naturally an underdog, filmmakers contrived drama by emphasizing their hurdles: Babe Ruth's childhood abandonment, Knute Rockne's disadvantage as an immigrant; Jimmy Piersall, driven to the edge of insanity by his driven father. *The Bad News Bears* contained no such contrivances. The shortcomings of each player were fodder for laughter and ridicule rather than obstacles to be conquered. Engleberg stays fat, soiling a ball with chocolate in the early going, consuming both bars and wrappers later on. Ogilvie remains bookish, hoping at his moment of heroic calling not to become a hero but to be summoned back to the bench; Lupus has snot on his nose from start to finish; and the Mexican brothers (Joe and Miguel Agilar, played by Jaime Escobedo and George Gonzales) understand not a word more of English at end than at beginning. Jewish pitcher Rudi Stein (David Pollock), so horrible that Buttermaker recruits a girl to replace him, is still bouncing pitches ten feet from home plate in the championship game. In the end, the team not only loses—they don't even get better. Still, their attitude toward victory is remarkable. They want to win; they just don't care how, an attitude that should have brought them disfavor from viewers.

Underdogs, after all, from the time of David and Goliath forward, have occupied a special niche in Western cultural lore, often because of their special moral standing. The underdog is more than just the predicted loser. Real underdogs—win or lose—force their opponents to treat them as worthy opponents, thereby elevating the contest, making it more meaningful. Real underdogs thus possess an aura of moral superiority and they reach their victories via an honorable route. The Bears have no special sense of moral uplift or worthiness. Their first victory comes by way of forfeit, an occasion they celebrate with as much gusto as they would have a game-winning homerun.

The string of wins that catapults them into the championship game comes through Buttermaker's success in using ballet lessons to bribe Amanda to pitch and in using Amanda as bait for reeling in the town's best athlete and most incorrigible juvenile delinquent, Kelly. The latter, first seen lighting Buttermaker's cigar and ripping up the field on his motorcycle, is particularly potent in exposing character-building as little more than facade. When he trades in his leather jacket and bad ways for a baseball uniform and the good feelings of team camaraderie, Leak is a declaration that character is not something developed through years spent in sport's crucible, but merely an act—something that requires little more than a change of clothing.

One of the reasons audiences prefer the Bears to their championship opponents, however, is that the Yankees are an even more distasteful team.

The Bears reject the homilies of sport, but the Yankees overconform to them. Roy Turner, their coach, warns them ominously before the big game that if they lose, they're going to have to live with the humiliation the rest of their lives. That Americans would find this pressurized version of sport to be unsavory was understandable. In the same week that the film first showed in theaters, the *Los Angeles Times* proclaimed a need for "more joy in sports." Asserting that sports had become hurdles rather than fun, Dr. Jean Barrett, a sports psychologist at the University of California at Fullerton, told the *Times,* "American children are exposed to the 'win-at-all-costs' syndrome" earlier than they're capable of handling.[2] In some ways, the championship game in *Bears* and its high stakes replicated the Vietnam War, muddling the sense of rights and wrongs (Lt. William Calley's final appeals of his guilty verdict for misconduct in Vietnam were rejected the week of the film's release), the value of victory, and the means of obtaining it. Why were we rooting for the Bears?

If victory with honor had become a debatable quest, so too had the demand for maximum effort. Did the Bears try hard? When the going got tough, did the tough get going? No. They cared little for effort. Having lost their first game by more than twenty runs, the first thing they decided to undertake as a team was a mass resignation. Did they see the difference in victory and victory hard-earned? No, but why should they have? In the Bears' world, talent and luck were just as desirable as effort and achievement. Two gifted players carried them to success. An improbable catch in right field by the timid Lupus is the climactic emotional moment of the film. It is, however, a celebratory moment built on luck—Lupus has not in any way transformed his skills, and no one would expect him to catch the next hundred balls hit his way. In the championship game, the Bears reach the very edge of victory when the timid Stein, under orders from Buttermaker, leans into a pitch and is hit, and the Yankee pitcher cannot find the strike zone against the cowering and weak-hitting Miguel and Ogilvie, walking both.

As well as shunning effort, the Bears seem to have little regard for the sense of special time and space that sports had enjoyed prior to the Vietnam era. While the film's adults tender to the kids' field with loving care and celebrate the season's opening with an awe-inspiring pizza custom-topped to look like a baseball diamond, the Bears have no such reverence. Buttermaker leaves the pitcher's mound scattered with empty beer cans, and both Leak and the councilman's son wheel their cycles across the field. For Tanner, in particular, the diamond is just another place to fight. He trips opponents, throws his glove at them, kicks an opponent in the groin during a bench-clearing brawl, and scraps with several teammates.

It is Tanner and his lack of restraint who also draws attention to the film's examination of diversity and, in particular, gender. In a speech prescient of the Atlanta Braves' John Rocker's 1999 tirade against segments of the American public he found objectionable, the Bears' loudmouthed shortstop denounces his teammates as "a bunch of Jews, spics, niggers, pansies, and a booger-eating moron." When Amanda appears for her first practice, he repeats his roll call, his eyes narrowing into a hateful squint as he adds with contempt, "and now a girl." The notion of character and sport had for eight decades been reserved for white males. *The Bad News Bears* made it clear that sport's taxonomy of race and gender was changing.

Amanda is the league's best pitcher. Her appearance came close on the heels of lawsuits that imposed girls on Little League baseball for the first time since its founding in 1936. Carolyn King of Ypsilanti, Michigan, outplayed many boys in 1973 to win a centerfield spot in the local Little League. When Little League tried to force her out through the organization's ban on females, she filed suit. The Ypsilanti City Council supported King and threatened the local league with loss of city facilities and resources. Little League responded by revoking the charter of the Ypsilanti entry. That summer the fight moved east when members of the National Organization for Women picketed the Little League World Series in Williamsport, Pennsylvania. In November the New Jersey Civil Rights Division ruled in favor of girls playing Little League ball, a ruling sustained by a three-judge panel of the appellate division of superior court.[3] In *The Bad News Bears,* Amanda, a precocious curveballer, finds little opposition from her teammates or the league. Ritchie and Lancaster have used a girl in this spot deliberately, but, beyond Tanner's initial outburst, supplied the Bears with little sense of offense at her intrusion.

It may be that Americans, with only Billie Jean King's 1973 tennis victory over aged Bobby Riggs to absorb, did not yet see the ways in which gender would figure in reshaping their games. Though the women's movement had made some noticeable strides in the '60s, in the mid-'70s women in sport were still only a few years removed from the "Play Days" atmosphere that had governed many of their competitive situations for decades (women from college teams would be re-teamed with players from other colleges and after a bit of play would sit down to drink tea, eat cookies, and socialize with their new pals). Title IX of the 1972 Educational Amendments Act, in demanding equity in funding and opportunity for females in sport, set the foundation for intercollegiate and interscholastic rivalries that would, by the turn of the century, become as fierce as those staged by the men.

Of course, some people were already asserting that men had no special claim on physical aggressiveness. The *Los Angeles Times* observed in the debut week of *The Bad News Bears* that girls were joining city gangs in rising numbers. Girls who became locked into gang culture were "really tough," it claimed. A policeman added that, "They are as violent as boys—maybe more."[4] Until numerous lawsuits and interpretations of the Supreme Court forced adherence to Title IX, however, most American men paid scant attention to the rising capabilities of female athletes.

The same cannot be said of the participation of blacks following integration in the 1950s and '60s. Black athletes represented, by the end of the '60s, a substantial portion of America's finest baseball, football, and basketball players. Their incursions into a formerly white province did not sit well with displaced whites. Rather than mirror the hopeful sentiment of 1971's *Brian's Song*, in which a black and white teammate use sport to assuage racial tension, Ritchie and Lancaster chose to emphasize the division that integration stirred. Their lone black player, Ahmad, is fast, but he is athletically inept. Humiliated at his incompetence he strips off his uniform and climbs a tree, a stereotypical image that may have been unintentional. When the coach follows him up the tree to offer soothing reassurance, Ahmad tells him, "Don't give me any of your honky bullshit, Buttermaker." A fine moment for racial harmony and trust.

The Mexicans are outsiders as well. Handicapped by the language barrier and Buttermaker's disinterest in what they are saying, Joe and Miguel Agilar are two more representatives of baseball's future rather than its past. Latinos were a growing presence in the major leagues during the Vietnam era, but the press and public expected little of them in the way of good character. When Giant pitcher Juan Marichal hit Dodger catcher John Roseboro over the head with his bat in 1965, the incident was widely considered an oddity that had sprung, at least in part, from an athlete who had missed schooling in the lessons of American character-building. In fact, just a few weeks prior to the attack, *Sports Illustrated* had run an article on baseball's new wave of Latin Americans, pointing out that "to the dismay of American baseball men, Latins sometimes play with a reckless individuality." Translated, it meant that they were not team players. Pitcher Al McBean admitted that "they call us temperamental and we are."[5]

Many reviewers saw *Bad News Bears* as an indictment of overzealous adults coaching youth teams. Indeed, both Buttermaker and Turner are guilty of abuses in pursuit of victory. But from the outset, the Bears are a reflection of youth aspirations of the '60s. They are what anthropologist Margaret Mead labeled prefigurative—youths shaping adults. They are what radical sport sociologist Jack Scott had recommended in his 1971 book, *The Athletic Revolution:* a team in which the coach's wishes are subordinate to those of the players. Whether it is Lupus mixing martinis for his coach or the team refusing to wear athletic supporters by tossing them back in Buttermaker's face, the precocious and unapologetic kids are—as many adults complained in the '60s—running the show.

Part of the era's tension between young and old grew out of the sheer size of the baby boom, which had forced the young to paradoxically undertake their quests for individual self-fulfillment in groups and coalitions. They were "counted and grouped together in classrooms, teams, and packs" to ease the strain of their numbers.[6] In this way they learned the merits of togetherness. But they were also raised on schoolbooks that presented the appeal of the rugged individual and raised in an era when— possibly as a backlash against the corporate and technological powers that exerted increasing control over their lives—Americans were "beginning to appreciate how rich and dangerous each one of us is."[7] So trained, they faced a dilemma: only by direct and personal competition with their classmates could they gain a measure of individual recognition. The fact that their great numbers made individual achievement more difficult added a new layer of Darwinian stress to baby boomers' identity quests and led to an eventual collective demand for individual rights.

Whether by numbers alone, or by the more likely confluence of numbers and special attitudes, the influence of the baby boomers became so pervasive that author Thomas Cottle wondered in 1971: "Do we perhaps make young people bigger than life by writing about them and laying on them the wit and elegance as well as the blandness and foolishness of our own perceptions of them?" Whether by wit or foolishness, the young were willing to act on impulses and unformed understanding to a degree that surprised their elders.[8] The inability of parents to dismiss the ideas of their children led to a pronounced, if somewhat skewed, notion of the young as aberrant and uncontrollable.

The appearance of a "generation gap" became one of the accepted tenets of youth culture, if not an acceptable explanation for all social tension.[9] At times, it seemed the young were distrustful of their elders merely because they were older. Mario Savio, while leading the movement for free speech at the University of California at Berkeley in 1964, helped to popularize the slogan that identified the precise dividing line for judgment: "never trust anyone over thirty."

In some ways those over thirty had, in fact, been contributing to the split between young and old. One of the most insidious aspects of the character-building ideal had been its demand that children's sport heel to adult supervision. In the twentieth century, the playground movement, then interscholastic athletics, then Little League baseball, Golden Gloves boxing, Pop Warner football, and pee wee soccer had brought restrictive, sometimes stultifying, adult values to what had once been areas of free play. As the '60s seemed to get away from adults, those involved in running junior sports tried to keep a disciplinary hold on the young.

In the case of both Roy Turner and Morris Buttermaker, their efforts failed. The film's affronts to authority are numerous and loud, shocking refutations to a concept widely believed prior to the sixties: that youths are innocent, empty vessels waiting to be filled and nurtured by the values of well-meaning adults. In fact, Buttermaker is a self-admitted "asshole," and the players know it. When he tries to steer Amanda's social life, she reacts angrily. "Who do you think you are?" she hollers at him. Purple with rage, he responds, "Your goddamned manager, that's who." He expects the truism to end the discussion, and in the 1950s it would have. Amanda deflates it with a dismissive, "Big Wow." Other players ignore Buttermaker's instructions; Tanner derisively orders him off the field— referring to him as "Buttercrud"—and at a crucial moment Leak snatches his bat from Buttermaker and spits out the word *coach* like it was a bad-tasting bug. After a home run Leak ignores the manager's glad-handing attempts at congratulations.

In the end, though the Bears have skewered most of what Americans had held dear a scant decade before, though *Variety's Film Reviews* had noticed its glorification of duplicity (it comprised "that deadly vicarious manipulation of people that later can lead to matters of national disgrace"),[10] the film was widely regarded as a "feel good" enterprise. Ritchie himself admitted it was "the kind of movie I hope will make the audience feel good at the end."[11] What made it appealing was the change of heart undergone by Buttermaker near the end of the game against the Yankees. He renounces the importance of victory at any cost by pulling his stars in favor of the team's more spasmatic and hopeless cases. The gesture played well with movie audiences, though not with the Bears themselves. They wanted to win, and after Tanner has told the Yankees where to put their trophy, the usually fainthearted Timmy Lupus hurls a beer bottle at them and warns them to "wait 'til next year." As the camera pulls back on the final Bacchanalian scene—as parents hug their precious little losers and swap beers with them—the star-spangled banner slowly comes into view, waving on the left, the kids celebrating on the right, both announcing that, "This, folks, is your new landscape of American sport."

While the public laughed at the Bears, they apparently did so thinking they were mere parody rather than a reflection of large truths or foreboding omens of what sport would actually look like in the absence of a character-building mythology. In retrospect, *The Bad News Bears* appears to express a reality that critics and proponents of sports alike were really afraid of—that stripped down to its barest humanity, devoid of its protective facade, sports might not be such a noble pursuit after all, much less an institution that ought to stand for national temperament or capacity.

The irreverent *Slapshot,* which laughed at hockey violence and small-town America, followed a year later, but in the quarter century following *Bad News Bears* sports films reverted to places where sport and good character could coexist once more. If such a thing could not be accomplished in actual arenas, then at least it was still a possibility in movie theaters.

Recent polls of critics and the public have seen *The Bad News Bears* settle far down the list of America's favorite sports films.[12] Though the title has become cliché and fodder for headline writers dealing with bears, bad news, or anything that rhymes with either, the film's messages escaped scrutiny; maybe that is nothing more than an indication of how blind the country has been in recognizing the roots of much of its disgust with the state of organized American sport as it entered the twenty-first century.

Without question, Hollywood has chosen not to revisit the surly attitude of the *Bears*. After the relative drought of the Vietnam era, the sports film—and particularly the baseball film—has again become a Hollywood staple. Beginning with *Rocky,* which acted as a bicentennial counterweight to the *Bears,* the industry has produced a steady flow of pictures built around sports. They are not merely duplicates of the older bio-pics. One change *The Bad News Bears* induced was an insistence on greater athletic authenticity. The Bears' frightening ineptitude signaled that character sketches were no longer the only focus for an audience.

Something larger of the '60s rubbed off as well. The same therapeutic ethos that sparked the jogging boom made it onto the screen. Sport is now useful for individual transformation—for recovering from one's own traumas and becoming whole. In other words, unlike in old bio-pics, characters no longer use sport to assimilate into the grand adventure of being an American, they now use it to carve out an identity separate from other Americans. Characters are more complex and their obstacles now are often personal flaws rather than hurdles of social circumstance, but the message is the same: sport is a virtuous, productive endeavor.

Sometimes this idea is presented in contradiction of the film's very content. *Eight Men Out* (1988) and *Field of Dreams* (1989), both of which chose the scandalous Black Sox as prime figures, explore loss of character, second chances, and personal redemption while glossing over tough truths. In the first, "Shoeless" Joe Jackson becomes a sympathetic hero, though there is no mention of the fact that he kept the $5,000 gamblers paid him in 1919. In *Field of Dreams,* the fictional black writer Terence Mann delivers a sermon connecting baseball to "all that was once good and could be again" while conveniently ignoring that the Iowa cornfield and the national pastime he is watching are again filled with nothing but white ballplayers (the film also delivers the irony of Burt Lancaster, as Moonlight Graham, helping to restore the good reputation of sport that his screenwriting son tarnished in the *Bears*).

Sports films seldom end with loss or disillusion. In *Bull Durham* (1988), the end of an over-the-hill minor league catcher's career is rewarded, not like many are—with a job selling things out of a car trunk. He gets instead a lifetime of baseball as vocation and a beautiful wife who contemplates the sport as religion. *The Natural* (1984) rewrites the tragic ending of Bernard Malamud's 1952 novel—wherein Roy Hobbs strikes out—so that he can instead set off a firestorm with a gargantuan home run. Even films that set out to expose some of the nastier aspects of modern sport—*The Program* (1993), *Rudy* (1993), *The Replacements* (2000), *Blue Chips* (1994)—outline abuses but ultimately cede to the healing power of sports. Only *Cobb* (1994), which spent most of its time on the subject as aging millionaire rather than as young ballplayer, does not proclaim sport's redemptive might. It paid a price, faring poorly at the box office.

If adult sports films came to fear too much realism, subsequent youth films treated the themes of the *Bears* as leprous. A 1997 documentary on sports on the silver screen offered *The Bad News Bears* as the forerunner of *Mighty Ducks* (1992), *The Sandlot* (1993), and *Little Giants* (1994).[13] Those films, plus others (*Ladybugs,* 1992; *The Karate Kid,* 1984; *Little Big League,* 1994) all feature the underdog format of *Bears,* but they all rely heavily on good character and victory as the only real equalizers for one's lack of talent, wrong gender, or timorous bearing. In short, they are nothing at all like *The Bad News Bears.*

The film voted "best sports film" in the *USA Today* poll was 1986's *Hoosiers.* Not surprisingly, it is the one that came closest to transporting viewers back to a pre-Vietnam period and place of lost innocence. Based on a true story, it told the tale of a tiny Indiana town's high school basketball team that overcomes insurmountable odds to win the state title in the early 1950s. Though it suffered a number of contradictions of its own, it appeared to stress all of the aspects of character and value that modern sport seemed to have ceded in the name of dollars, image, and media hype in post-sixties culture.

To most viewers, it seems, *The Bad News Bears* and the world it portrayed are best forgotten or passed off as lightweight fare. Not coincidentally, that is the same way that many Americans have chosen to remember the Vietnam era—the chaos and division best pigeonholed as a time of temporary lunacy, the quests to turn America into something better regarded as naive and fleeting in their outcomes. Sports films continue to portray heroics that defy the reality of our times perhaps because the reality seems rooted in a complexity that offers no hope of solution.

Fans, athletes, and the media all decry the developments that Simon and Garfunkel hinted at in "Mrs. Robinson" and that *The Bad News Bears* made explicit. In the Bears' defiance of Morris Buttermaker, we see the firing of coaches at the urging of athletes. The displacement of Rudi Stein by Amanda Whurlitzer prefigured the literal displacement of some males and their sports by females via legal interpretations of Title IX. The failures and natural talents of Ahmad surface in the ongoing debate about the differences between white and black athletes. The trophy presentation scene is the first moment in which we are prepared to concede that big games often exist more for the super-hyped after-moment than for their playing; victory is clearly divorced from honor; the hilarity of Chico's Bail Bonds as the Bears' sponsor has become the not-so-funny corporate labeling of everything in the sports world not nailed down; and in Tanner's soliloquies on his teammates we see more than John Rocker—we see the idea of diversity—America's beloved "melting pot"—as division.

We should not expect Hollywood to be particularly worried about these things. History teaches complexities, but reducing problems to their simplest terms is a condition more comfortable to many Americans. It is a predisposition that has allowed the film industry to thrive on the presentation of illusions and to blur the line between character and personality.

As historian Warren Susman noted in 1973, traits of character shift across time and a new culture of personality was displacing an older culture of character as early as 1900. Sociologist David Riesman saw the shift toward pleasing others already complete by midcentury. In other words, character as Joe DiMaggio and Mickey Mantle were thought to have it was already wavering in their own times (in the moments after his death in 2000, DiMaggio was already being flogged as a son of a bitch), though it was still closer as an ideal. As Susman observed, in the nineteenth-century terms such as *citizenship, duty, democracy, work, conquest, honor, reputation, morals, manners, integrity,* and *manhood* were those frequently related to the idea of character. From early in the twentieth century, however, the idea of personality began supplanting that of character, and the terms most often associated with the new idea were *fascinating, stunning, attractive, magnetic, glowing, masterful, creative, dominant,* and *forceful.*[14] Not surprisingly, film deals more easily with personality than character.

Nonetheless, since giving the nation a dose of reality in *The Bad News Bears,* Hollywood has dished out personality that looks and sounds like character. Claims to sport's inherent goodness rely on compelling stories, and as those stories have ceded in post–Vietnam era culture to accounts that have more to do with things other than character (finance, technology, solitary performance), the public is most likely to find those stories on film.

Remarking on West Point hero Pete Dawkins in 1972, Frank Deford wrote: "There is real comfort to be had waking up one fine, polluted, polarized morning and discovering that there is still a Biltmore clock and a YMCA and a Pete Dawkins. Perhaps each morning one last hero should be assigned to stand under the Biltmore clock so we can hear the ticks from the good old times, when peace and prosperity were both lit up at this end of the tunnel and the only shaggy-haired perverts were the four who were making noise in a Liverpool cellar."[15] The last heroes now are on the screen, not under the Biltmore clock. While projecting personalities two stories high, films continue to profit from portraying the ghosts of athletes like DiMaggio and Dawkins, apparitions of character blown away a quarter century ago by incredible winds of change.

Epilogue

*Even Americans who lived through the '60s and remember them
with respect are likely, in some recesses of memory, to be deeply
afraid of them. I know I am.*
　　　　　—*Nick Bromell,* Tomorrow Never Knows, *2000*

I think nostalgia is actually Latin for "return to pain."
　　　　　—*Eric Clapton*

It takes a certain fearlessness to be truly nostalgic for the sixties. A
great number of Americans are pained indeed by remembrance of the
Vietnam era and pine instead for the illusion of the happy days that preceded it. Even many in the generation that came of age amid the turmoil
seemed, in the quarter century after the fall of Saigon, desperate to get
back to the garden: the heartland, the pastoral green fields of dreams, as
if there they could rediscover an America that the '60s had wiped from
the history books.

Of course, those mythical fields never really existed, and in ignoring
the '60s when confronting our dissatisfaction with the state of organized
sports at the turn of the century, we are running from a past. What we
are dismissing or avoiding is the realization that many baby boomers—
in some cases, against all probabilities—once wrestled in sports with the
same sense of oppression, of limits, and of corruption that led a great
number of young people to the counterculture. It is the same sense that
came through in rock 'n' roll, a sense of the sixties—the frightful possibility of revolution.

Of course, if a revolution did overthrow our way of sports—undid
character-building, that is—shouldn't the American public be aware of
it? That depends on the nature of revolution. Is it possible to overthrow
an institution that has no location other than the mind? Can a revolution take place without clearly acknowledged leaders, goals, or direction?
Can people—even those consciously opposed to it—take part in it

nonetheless? Can a dominant idea cede to confusion rather than dia-
metrical opposition? Can a revolution be so quiet that no one heard it?
If a revolution is a turning, not a jettisoning, then yes. Perhaps the
counterculture and all the protests of the time never came close to estab-
lishing new ideals, but the efforts certainly compromised the old ones.
How many were truly committed to change? "Enough," answered notorious activist, Abbie Hoffman.

American sports are different because of the 1960s. Perceptions may
not be all, but during the Vietnam War years they seemed to be reified as
powerful images of reality. The media presented and promoted a chaotic
picture of the world that made it appear, in the words of a popular 1970
song, as "a ball of confusion." For some, it appeared to truly be upside
down. Clearly it was a unique period of assault on American tradition.
Organized sports programs were especially susceptible to the rhetoric of
divergence and confusion as they brought into proximity a new generation, old institutions, and a theoretical—sometimes theatrical—spirit of
inquiry.

By 1960 the concept of Victorian character was outdated already as
reality. By 1975 it had been stretched to its thinnest as an ideal. In the
process of identifying a new paradigm, however, social and psychological
conflicts can remain unresolved. Outdated ideals are kept around as salve.
So it has been with character-building. It's great salve, but it is no longer
the true measure of how we assess athletics and athletes. The critiques of
traditional manliness produced a democratized idea of gender—not only
in how men look and act, but in how women must be accounted for.
Authority has been spread around; if athletes still have too little of it, they
have nonetheless made coaches respond to their feelings. Talent and personality are equal to effort in taking the measure of an athlete's worth.
Physical talent is split off from the intellect in ever more apparent ways.
And the priority of winning has made honor a secondary consideration.

Because of these changes, people no longer trust sport to be the surest
carrier of good character. Still, because it was for so long, the idea that it
still can be has lingered in the collective American mind. Character-
building still gets a lot of lip service. But people expect athletes to find
trouble now; they expect Congress and government to step in and legis-
late collegiate athletic policy; they expect laboratories to sort out and
police the implications of performance-enhancing drugs; and they expect

Nike and the other giant commercial sponsors of sport to supply the slogans by which sport is conducted.

In the end, American society did not come unglued in the '60s, but our sports were transformed. Right now, organized sport serves a plurality of gods—the god of winning, the god of money, the god of mesomorphs and Lycra shorts, the god of celebrity, and, yes, sometimes the god of heroic-sacrificial-inspirational good character. It serves them because the conditions of the Vietnam era peeled away the facade of character-building. How much did it peel away? Enough.

Notes

INTRODUCTION

1. *Ohio State Lantern,* 23 November 1970, 1.

2. Robert Lipsyte, *SportsWorld: An American Dreamland* (New York: Quadrangle, 1975), x.

3. Landon Y. Jones, *Great Expectations: America and the Baby Boom Generation* (New York: Ballantine Books, 1980), 3. Jones believes that a generation is the primary agent of social change and that the impact of a generation is directly related to its size.

4. Kenneth Keniston, *Youth and Dissent: The Rise of a New Opposition* (New York: Harcourt, Brace Jovanovich, 1971), 7, 38.

5. Todd Gitlin, *The Sixties: Years of Hope, Days of Rage* (New York: Bantam Books, 1987), 213–14.

6. Thomas Hauser, *Muhammad Ali: His Life and Times* (New York: Simon and Schuster, 1991), 224.

7. *Baltimore Sun,* 12 November 1988, 3A.

8. James Kunen, "Merrily, Merrily, Merrily, Merrily . . . ," *Sports Illustrated* 30 (16 June 1969): 52.

9. Speech of Vice President Spiro T. Agnew to the First Annual Vince Lombardi Award Dinner, 21 January 1971, Houston, Tex., in John R. Coyne Jr., *The Impudent Snobs: Agnew v. the Intellectual Establishment* (New Rochelle, N.Y.: Arlington House, 1972), 446.

10. Morris Dickstein, *Gates of Eden: American Culture in the Sixties* (New York: Basic Books, 1977), 257.

11. Jacques Barzun, *Clio and the Doctors: Psycho-History, Quanto-History, and History* (Chicago: University of Chicago Press, 1974), 13.

12. Rob Hiaasen, "Taking Home Nixon Tapes Is a Tricky Task," *Baltimore Sun,* 21 April 2001, D2.

13. Robert Lipsyte, "A Besieged and Beloved Guru's Worthwhile Lessons," *New York Times,* 13 February 2000, sect. 8, 9.

CHAPTER ONE: A STAR-SPANGLED COLLISION

1. Jose Feliciano, Personal Interview, 25 January 1995.

2. I should point out that I heard the anthem on live television. Even as an eighteen-year-old, I thought the performance was shocking. My current

assessment of the rendition as gentle and beautiful is by no means shared by many older colleagues for whom I have played it in recent years. Some have left the room in mid song.

3.   Ernie Harwell, *Tuned to Baseball* (South Bend, Ind.: Diamond Communications, 1986), 121–28; *Washington Post,* 8 October 1968, D2; *St. Louis Post-Dispatch,* 8 October 1968, 11A; Ed Wilkes, "Star-Spangled Goof," *St. Louis Post-Dispatch,* 8 October 1968, 1C; Barbara Stanton, "Storm Rages Over Series Anthem," *Detroit Free Press,* 8 October, 1968, 1; Ernie Harwell, Personal Interview, March 1989.

4.   Andrew J. Edelstein, *The Pop Sixties* (New York: World Almanac Publications, 1985), 31.

5.   Howard Senzel, *Baseball and the Cold War* (New York: Harcourt Brace Jovanovich, 1977), 269–70.

6.   Harwell, Personal Interview; Harwell, *Tuned to Baseball,* 125, 126.

7.   Stanton, "Storm Rages Over Series Anthem," 1.

8.   Ibid.

9.   *New York Times,* 8 October 1968, 54; *Los Angeles Times,* 8 October 1968, 1.

10.   *Detroit Free Press,* 8 October 1968, 1, 8A.

11.   *St. Louis Post-Dispatch,* 8 October 1968, 11A.

12.   Feliciano, Personal Interview.

13.   Harwell, *Tuned to Baseball,* 126.

14.   Homer Hickam, *Rocket Boys* (New York: Delta, Random House, 1998), 28–29.

15.   Derek Taylor, *It Was Twenty Years Ago Today* (New York: Simon and Schuster, 1987), 18.

16.   Matusow, *The Unraveling of America: A History of Liberalism in the 1960's* (New York: Harper and Row, 1984), 294; Philip Norman, *Shout! The Beatles in Their Generation* (New York: Fireside, Simon and Schuster, 1981), 293.

17.   Rex Weiner and Deanne Stillman, *Woodstock Census: The Nationwide Survey of the Sixties Generation* (New York: Viking Press, 1979), 242–44.

18.   Norman, *Shout!* 225.

19.   Greil Marcus, *Mystery Train: Images of America in Rock and Roll Music,* 3d rev. ed. (New York: E. P. Dutton, 1975), 18.

20.   Tom Carson, "Rocket to Russia," in *Stranded,* ed. Greil Marcus (New York: Alfred A. Knopf, 1979), 109.

21.   Marcus, *Mystery Train,* 98.

22.   Grant Wahl, "Men on a Mission," *Sports Illustrated* 86 (24 February 1997): 9.

23. At the Los Angeles Olympics of 1984, during the self-conscious "rejuvenation" of America plugged by the Reagan administration, the nation had little trouble with the lack of worthy opposition, chanting "U!S!A! U!S!A! through seventeen days of competition boycotted by the Soviet bloc nations.

24. Nicholas Schaffner, *The Beatles Forever* (Harrisburg, Pa.: Cameron House, 1977), 15.

25. *Daily Pennsylvanian,* 11 February 1964, 1; 12 February 1964, 1.

26. Gail Bederman, *Manliness and Civilization: A Cultural History of Gender and Race in the United States, 1880–1917* (Chicago: University of Chicago Press, 1995), 25.

27. Jon Savage, *England's Dreaming: Anarchy, Sex Pistols, Punk Rock and Beyond* (New York: St. Martin's Press, 1992), 5.

28. George Gipe, *The Great American Sports Book* (Garden City, N.Y.: Dolphin, Doubleday, 1978), 488.

29. Paul Hoch, *Rip Off the Big Game: The Exploitation of Sports by the Power Elite* (Garden City, N.Y.: Anchor Books, Doubleday, 1972), 192. For a discussion of coaches and the long-hair issue, see John Underwood's three-part series, "The Desperate Coach," *Sports Illustrated* 31 (25 August 1969): 66–76; (1 September 1969): 20–27; (8 September 1969): 28–40.

30. Robert Odell, Personal Interview, 30 July 1985.

31. *The 1969 Official National Collegiate Athletic Association Wrestling Guide,* ed. Charles Parker (Phoenix: College Athletics Publishing Service, 1967), 2; *1970 Official NCAA Wrestling Guide,* 7; *1972 Official NCAA Wrestling Guide,* WR-8.

32. *Fields of Fire: Sports in the 60s,* prod. by George Roy, directed and written by Steven Stern, Home Box Office in association with Black Canyon Productions, 1995.

33. Joe Namath, "The Joe Namath I Know," as told to Larry King, *Esquire* (December 1968): 108; *Sports Illustrated* 34 (15 March 1971): 14.

34. John Wooden, Personal Interview, 1 May 1997.

35. *Daily Pennsylvanian,* 11 February 1964, 1.

36. *The Playboy Interviews with John Lennon and Yoko Ono,* conducted by David Sheff, ed. G. Barry Golson (New York: Berkley Books, 1981), 105.

37. Allen Ginsberg, "Yes, I Remember It Well," *Rolling Stone* 415 (16 February 1984), 22.

38. James Simon Kunen, *The Strawberry Statement: Notes of a College Revolutionary* (New York: Random House, 1968), 77; Kunen, James, Personal Interview, 11 January 1995; Steve McGarry, "The Diary of Rock and Pop," syndicated cartoon, n.d., n.p.

39. Underwood, "The Desperate Coach" (25 August 1969): 74.

40.   Dan Rottenberg, "'The Brave New-Lonely Crowd,'" *Daily Pennsylvanian,* 14 February 1964, 8.

41.   See Peter M. Stearns, *Be a Man! Males in Modern Society* (New York: Holmes and Meier Publishers, 1979), and Melvin L. Adelman, "Manliness and Sport: A Review of the Recent Literature" (paper presented at the Tenth Annual Convention of the North American Society for Sport History, Kansas State University, Manhattan, Kans., May 1982), for studies of conceptions of manliness. For the development of ideas about manliness in the Victorian age, see Gail Bederman's *Manliness and Civilization.*

42.   Richard G. Sipes, "War, Sports, and Aggression: An Empirical Test of Two Rival Theories," *American Anthropologist* 75 (1973): 65.

43.   John J. Leary, "The Reality of Dreams: Images of National Power and Mission in American Film" (Ph.D. diss., University of Maryland, 1981).

44.   *Daily Pennsylvanian,* 19 February 1968, 3.

45.   Bob Hoffman, "Manhood and the Movement," *Daily Pennsylvanian,* 20 March 1970, 4.

46.   Lance Morrow, "A Bloody Rite of Passage," *Time* 125 (15 April 1985): 24.

47.   Gene Davis Personal Interview, 9 December 1997; Wayne Wells, Personal Interview, 14 January 1998; Ben Peterson, Personal Interview, 22 January 1998.

48.   *Fields of Fire,* HBO, 1995.

49.   Gipe, *The Great American Sports Book,* 488.

50.   *Life* 61 (9 December 1966): 46; Lawrence M. Baskir and William A. Strauss, *Chance and Circumstance: The Draft, the War and the Vietnam Generation* (New York: Alfred A. Knopf, 1978), 48–49.

51.   Phil Hoag, Personal Interview, 20 February 1997.

52.   Baskir and Strauss, *Chance and Circumstance,* 68–69.

53.   Pete Hamill, cited in Joel Whitburn, *The Billboard Book of Top 40 Hits, 1955 to Present* (New York: Billboard Publications, 1983), 231.

54.   Gary C. Burns, "Utopia and Dystopia in Popular Song Lyrics: Rhetorical Visions in the United States, 1963–1972" (Ph.D. diss., Northwestern University, 1981).

55.   Alice Echols, *Scars of Sweet Paradise: The Life and Times of Janis Joplin* (New York: Henry Holt and Co., 1999), 108–9.

56.   *Fields of Fire,* HBO, 1995.

57.   For a discussion of the existential dread that seemed to paradoxically oppress white, middle-class teens, see Jerry Farber, *The Student as Nigger* (New

York: Pocket Books, 1969) and Nick Bromell, *Tomorrow Never Knows: Rock and Psychedelics in the 1960s* (Chicago: University of Chicago Press, 2000).

58. Norbert Elias and Eric Dunning, "The Quest for Excitement in Unexciting Societies," cited in Allen Guttmann, *From Ritual to Record: The Nature of Modern Sports* (New York: Columbia University Press, 1978), 132–33; Marsha Wolfenstein, "Fun Morality," in *Culture and Commitment, 1929–1945,* ed. with an intro. and notes by Warren Susman (New York: George Braziller, 1973), 84–91.

59. Quoted in Godfrey Hodgson, *America in Our Time* (New York: Vintage Books, Random House, 1976), 312.

60. Quoted in Richard Harrington, "Rock with a Capital R and a PG-13," *Washington Post,* 15 September 1985, H-5.

61. *Daily Pennsylvanian,* 8 November 1968, 3.

62. Jeremiah Ford II to author, 21 April 1985; Hoag, Personal Interview.

63. James C. Whorton, *Crusaders for Fitness: The History of American Health Reformers* (Princeton, N.J.: Princeton University Press, 1982), 93.

64. Kim Story, Tom Wolfe, Albertito Fernandez, letter to the editor, *Daily Pennsylvanian,* 5 February 1971, 4. The letter writers were quoting from the memo that a rower had shown to them.

65. James S. Coleman, "Academic Achievement and the Structure of Competition," *Harvard Educational Review* 29 (fall 1959): 337.

66. Nick Tosches, *Country: The Biggest Music in America* (New York: Stein and Day, 1977), 97.

67. *Christian Science Monitor,* 9 October 1968, 3.

68. Robert Lipsyte, "Varsity Syndrome: The Unkindest Cut," *Annals of the American Academy* 445 (September 1979): 15–23.

69. Harold Shecter, "The Myth of the Eternal Child in Sixties America," *The Popular Culture Reader,* ed. Jack Nachbar, Deborah Weiser, John L. Wright (Bowling Green, Ohio: Bowling Green University Press, 1978), 64–78.

70. Feliciano, Personal Interview.

CHAPTER TWO: TOIL AND TROUBLE

1. Nolan Zavoral, *A Season on the Mat: Dan Gable and the Pursuit of Perfection* (New York: Simon and Schuster, 1998), 10; John Irving, "Gorgeous Dan," *Esquire* 79 (April 1973): 109.

2. Mike Gerald, "Sanders Set Standard as U.S. First World Champ," *Amateur Wrestling News* (7 November 1997): 33; Bill Farrell, Personal Interview, 2 December 1997.

3. Todd Gitlin, *The Sixties,* 217; Underwood, "The Desperate Coach" (1 September 1969): 22.

4. Warren Susman, "'Personality' and the Making of Twentieth-Century Culture," in *Culture as History,* ed. Warren I. Susman (New York: Pantheon, 1984), 216–17.

5. Matusow, *The Unraveling of America: A History of Liberalism in the 1960's* (New York: Harper and Row, 1984), 306.

6. Clecak, *America's Quest for the Ideal Self: Dissent and Fulfillment in the '60's and '70's,* 26–27.

7. Herman Weiskopf, "A Kid Who Doesn't Kid Around," *Sports Illustrated* 36 (19 June 1972): 38; Zavoral, *A Season on the Mat,* 63–64.

8. Weiskopf, "A Kid Who Doesn't Kid Around," 38.

9. Irving, "Gorgeous Dan," 221.

10. Zavoral, *A Season on the Mat,* 10.

11. Irving, "Gorgeous Dan," 220.

12. David Stockner, Personal interview, October 1998.

13. Bobby Douglas, Personal Interview, 19 November, 1998.

14. Delance Duncan, Personal Interview, 9 October, 1998.

15. Rick Sanders to "People—and Georgie," in "Rick Sanders Scrapbook," property of David Stockner, Eagle Creek, Oreg.

16. Douglas, Personal Interview.

17. Don Behm, Personal Interview, 22 October 1998.

18. John Peterson, Personal Interview, 25 November 1997; Behm, Personal Interview.

19. From obituary from untitled, undated newspaper article in "Rick Sanders Scrapbook"; also the *Oregonian,* 20 October 1972, 3M.

20. Bill Smith to Rick Sanders (n.d.) in "Rick Sanders Scrapbook."

21. Personal Interview, interviewee anonymity requested.

22. Behm, Personal Interview.

23. Wayne Baughman, *Wrestling—On and Off the Mat* (Colorado Springs: Wayne Baughman, 1987), 31–32; Larry Kristoff, Personal Interview, 21 October 1998; Masaru Yatabe, Personal Interview, 30 November 1998.

24. Dan Gable, Personal Interview, 22 January 1998.

25. Ibid.

26. Yatabe, Behm, Personal Interviews.

27. Patricia Rogers, Personal Interview, 16 October 1998.

28. Sergio Gonzalez, Personal Interview, 27 August 1997; Wayne Wells, Personal Interview, 14 January 1998.

29. Gonzalez, John Peterson, Personal Interviews; Jim Peckham, Personal Interview, 26 November 1997; Baughman, *Wrestling—On and Off the Mat,* 32.

30. Newspaper article, n.d., in "Rick Sanders Scrapbook."

31. Gonzalez, Personal Interview.

32. Ibid.; "Request for Criminal Record Check," Pennsylvania State Police, 28 April 1999; Affidavit copy in "Rick Sanders Scrapbook."

33. Bill Farrell to Rick Sanders, "Rick Sanders Scrapbook."

34. Douglas, Personal Interview.

35. Bill Farrell, John Peterson, Personal Interviews.

36. Earle MacCannell, Personal Interview, 14 November 1998; Behm, Personal Interview.

37. *Washington Post,* quoting Dwight Chapin of *Los Angeles Times,* 30 August 1972; Leo Davis, *Oregonian,* n.d., from "Rick Sanders Scrapbook."

38. Behm, Wells, Personal Interviews.

39. Peckham, Personal Interview.

40. Farrell, Personal Interview; Ben Peterson, Personal Interview, 22 January 1998; John Peterson, Personal Interview; Behm, Personal Interview.

41. ABC videotape of Olympic wrestling competition, 1972.

42. *Oregonian,* 29 October 1972, 9.

43. Marlin Grahn, Personal Interview, 14 November 1998.

44. Leo Davis, *Oregonian,* 30 August 1972, from "Rick Sanders Scrapbook.

45. Wells, Personal Interview.

46. Davis, *Oregonian,* 30 August 1972, from "Rick Sanders Scrapbook"; Douglas, Personal Interview.

47. ABC videotape.

48. ABC videotape; Peckham, Personal Interview.

49. Gable, Personal Interview.

50. Peckham, Personal Interview.

51. Gable, Personal Interview.

52. Maury White, "Golden Day for Gable, Peterson," *Des Moines Register,* n.d., clipping in Iowa State University Sports Information file.

53. Gonzalez, Behm, Personal Interviews.

54. Marty Twersky, article in *New York Times,* reprinted in *Oregonian,* 29 October 1972, 3M, 9M.

55. "Inventory of Effects," included in letter from Thomas R. Hudson, U.S. Embassy, Yugoslavia, to David Stockner in "Rick Sanders Scrapbook."

56. Gable, Personal Interview.

57. Wells, Personal Interview.

58. Peckham; Peterson, John; Gable, Personal Interviews.

59. Michael Gerald, *Owings! A Decade of Immortality* (Medford, Oreg.: n.p., 1982), 10–11.

60. Behm, Personal Interview.

61. Douglas, Personal Interview.

62. Gable, Personal Interview.

63. Farrell, Personal Interview.

CHAPTER THREE: IVY LEAGUE JEREMIAD

1. *Daily Pennsylvanian,* 6 February 1970, 6.

2. Jeremiah Ford II to author, 21 April 1985.

3. Ford, "Not Just Entertaining Sideshows," *Pennsylvania Gazette* 65 (October 1966): 30.

4. The schools that made up the Ivy League had scheduled each other for decades. The presidents of the eight schools had signed the Intercollegiate Agreement in 1945 to set standards for football. In May 1952 the presidents formalized the Ivy Group Agreement that set policy for football. The 1954 agreement extended the policy to include all sports.

5. *Toward an Ivy Group Handbook,* 1967, 2, Personal Files of Jeremiah Ford II, Jasper, Ark.

6. Jeremiah Ford, "Not Just Entertaining Sideshows," 27–31. John Wideman, who captained Penn's basketball team in the mid-60s before going on to a distinguished writing career, said that Ford even discouraged him from accepting payment to write an article on his personal life for one of the major Philadelphia daily newspapers. John Wideman, Personal Interview, 15 January 1986.

7. Dan Rottenberg, "Penn Is People," *Daily Pennsylvanian,* 10 August 1963, 25.

8. *Daily Pennsylvanian,* 23 November 1964, 4.

9. Rev. Stanley E. Johnson, Personal Interview, 10 December 1984.

10. Frank Dolson, Personal Interview, 10 January 1985.

11. Alfred Bester, "The University of Pennsylvania," *Holiday* 32 (November 1962): 174.

12. Dan Rottenberg, "When the House of Drexel Ruled," *Philadelphia Inquirer,* 26 June 1979, 11A.

13. "Old Ben's New Penn, *Time* 82 (23 August 1963): 58; Bester, "University of Pennsylvania, 172.

14. *Daily Pennsylvanian,* 25 September 1962, 3; Johnson, Personal Interview. Johnson was with Harnwell at the time of the call.

15. *Daily Pennsylvanian,* 18 September 1962, 8; 12 December 1962, 5, 8; 25 September 1963, 8; *The Record,* University of Pennsylvania yearbook, 1963.

16. *Daily Pennsylvanian,* 6 December 1963, 1; Johnson, Personal Interview.

17. Peter Eglick and John Riley, "The Athletic Budget: Penn Pays the Price," *Daily Pennsylvanian,* 19 January 1971, 3; Robert M. Rhodes, "Jerry Ford Out; Penn Seeks a 'New Personality,'" *Pennsylvania Gazette* 65 (April 1967): 33.

18. *Daily Pennsylvanian,* 10 September 1965, 8.

19. University of Pennsylvania, *The Almanac* 13 (February 1967): 1; Harry Fields to *Pennsylvania Gazette* 65 (October 1966): 4; *Daily Pennsylvanian,* 18 April 1966, 8; Mark Lieberman, "Penn Recruiting Needs New Look," *Daily Pennsylvanian,* 14 March 1967, 8.

20. Robert M. Rhodes, "Jerry Ford Out; Penn Seeks a New Personality," *Pennsylvania Gazette* 65 (April 1967): 35.

21. Kenny Grossman, "New Lease on Sports?" *Daily Pennsylvanian,* 9 March 1965, 3; Jeremiah Ford II to author, 21 April 1985.

22. *Daily Pennsylvanian,* 18 January 1966, 1.

23. Ibid., 2 February 1966, 1; 7 March 1966, 1.

24. Frank Dolson, "Sports," *Pennsylvania Gazette* 64 (April 1966): 38; for defense see *Daily Pennsylvanian,* 18 January 1966, 1; 19 January 1966, 3; and Bob Rottenberg's column, 6; 7 March 1966, 1, 2, 6; Jeremiah Ford II to author, 4 March 1985.

25. Dolson, "Sports," 38.

26. Jeremiah Ford II, "Not Just Entertaining Sideshows," 27–31.

27. *Daily Pennsylvanian,* 3 April 1967, 1; Larry Krohn, "Fields Terms Ford 'Unpopular,' Denies Existence of a Slush Fund," *Daily Pennsylvanian,* 31 March 1967, 1.

28. Rhodes, "Jerry Ford Out," 34; Larry Krohn, "The Weightman Hall Crises," *Daily Pennsylvanian,* 31 March 1967, 12; Frank Dolson, Personal Interview.

29. William F. Buckley Jr., *God and Man at Yale: The Superstitions of Academic Freedom* (Chicago: Henry Regnery Co., 1951), 117.

30. Mike Adler, "Ethics and Good Athletics," *Daily Pennsylvanian,* 10 April 1967, 4; *Daily Pennsylvanian,* 7 April 1967, 1.

31. "Alumni Contribution Report," *Pennsylvania Gazette* 68 (October

1969): 23; University of Pennsylvania Financial Report, 1968–69, 23.

32.   *Daily Pennsylvanian,* 2 October 1962, 1; *Pennsylvania Gazette* 67 (September 1968): 47; "Alumni Giving Reports," *Pennsylvania Gazette* 68 (October 1969): 23; 69 (October 1970): n.p.; 70 (October 1971): n.p.; 71 (November 1972): n.p.

33.   Thomas J. Cottle, *Time's Children: Impressions of Youth,* with a foreword by David Reisman (Boston: Little, Brown and Co., 1971), 278.

34.   Jeremiah Ford II to author, 4 March 1985.

35.   Gordon S. White Jr., "Dismissal of Ford Stirs Ivy Storm," *New York Times,* 4 April 1967, 52.

36.   Ibid., 52.

37.   See John A. T. Robinson, "The End of Theism?" 325–35, and William Hamilton, "The Death of God Theologies Today," 337–52, both in *America in the 60's: Cultural Authorities in Transition,* ed. with an intro. by Ronald Lora (New York: John Wiley and Sons, 1974).

38.   See Robert Sklar, *Movie-Made America: A Cultural History of American Movies* (New York: Vintage Books, Random House, 1975), 294–300.

39.   "To Keep Pace with America," *Pennsylvania Gazette* 64 (April 1966): n.p.

40.   Marvin Dash, "Shabel Takes Gamble, Hopes for Big Payoff," *Daily Pennsylvanian,* 7 December 1970, 8; Fred Shabel, Personal Interview, 11 October 1985.

41.   Krohn, "Shabel Wins Over Alumni," 8.

42.   *Daily Pennsylvanian,* 25 August 1967, 43; 8 February 1973, 1.

43.   University of Pennsylvania, Department of Intercollegiate Athletics, *Annual Reports,* 1971–72, 1; Dave Chandler, "Fred Shabel: Question for the Sages," *Daily Pennsylvanian,* 7 February 1973, 8.

44.   *Life* 60 (25 February 1966); *Baltimore Sun,* 15 February 1997, 6A.

45.   Godfrey Hodgson, *America in Our Time* (New York: Vintage Books, Random House), 384.

46.   *Sports Illustrated* 42 (26 May 1975): 8.

47.   For the most pointed among many critics, see Paul Hoch, *Rip Off the Big Game: The Exploitation of Sports by the Power Elite;* Dave Meggyesy, *Out of Their League* (Berkeley, Calif.: Ramparts Press, 1970); Jack Scott, *The Athletic Revolution* (New York: Free Press, 1971); and Gary Shaw, *Meat on the Hoof: The Hidden World of Texas Football* (New York: St. Martin's Press, 1972). For a description of the noncompetitive "New Games," see *The New Games Book,*

ed. Andrew Fluegelman (Garden City, N.Y.: Dolphin, Doubleday, 1976).

48.   George Gipe, *Great American Sports Book* (Garden City, N.Y.: Dolphin, Doubleday, 1978), 494.

49.   *Daily Pennsylvanian,* 17 January 1969, 9.

50.   Daniel Yankelovich, *New Rules: Searching for Self-Fulfillment in a World Turned Upside Down* (New York: Random House, 1981), xvi. William F. Buckley Jr., "Reflections on the Phenomenon," *Esquire* 82 (October 1974): 125–28, and Shaw, *Meat on the Hoof,* 233, also believed that a universal appetite for competition was present in all elements of society, including the counterculture.

51.   Pete Gogolak, *Kicking the Football Soccer Style,* ed. Ray Siegener (New York: Atheneum, 1972), 6–7.

52.   *Admissions Policy for the Undergraduate Schools of the University of Pennsylvania* (McGill Report), 1 August 1967, Dan M. McGill, chairman, 5.

53.   *Toward an Ivy Group Handbook,* 1967, 2, Personal Files of Jeremiah Ford II.

54.   Mark Lieberman, "Pride and Awareness," *Daily Pennsylvanian,* 4 March 1968, 5.

55.   Fred Shabel, Personal interview, 11 October 1985.

56.   Dan Rottenberg, "The Man Who Broke the Mold," *Daily Pennsylvanian,* 2 March 1964, 8. In his 1985 book, *Fight on Pennsylvania: A Century of Red and Blue Football* (Philadelphia: University of Pennsylvania Press), Rottenberg states that Penn lost in the first period of Ivy league competition because Ford was "simon-pure." Like Shabel and others, Rottenberg thought that Penn's eventual move away from Ford to Harry Fields was an inevitable response to a miserable 1964 football season and a reflection of a change in campus attitudes from passive to more aggressive. In fact, Ford was anything but passive in his promotion of Penn as a moral beacon. The shift, then, was one of a more subtle nature and took place within trustee circles, not necessarily as a reflection of "campus" attitudes.

57.   Mark Lieberman, "A Real Sport," *Daily Pennsylvanian,* 18 November 1968, 2.

58.   Guy M. Blynn, "The Rape of the Quaker," *Daily Pennsylvanian,* 22 October 1969, 6; Shabel, Personal Interview; Steve Bilsky, Personal Interview, 23 July 1985.

59.   *Daily Pennsylvanian,* 5 May 1971, 3.

60.   Bob Savett and Mark Pearlman, "Ivy League: Whither Thou Goest?" *Daily Pennsylvanian,* 4 March 1970, 6; Peter Eglick and John Riley, "Days of

Glory Renewed: Making, Breaking, and Remaking an Athletic Powerhouse,"
Daily Pennsylvanian, 18 January 1971, 3; 19 January 1971, 3; 20 January
1971, 3, 5; 21 January 1971, 3, 6; 22 January 1971, 3.

61. Harrison Clement Jr., Personal Interview, 11 October 1985.

62. Bruce Jacobsohn, Personal Interview, 4 February 1986.

63. James S. Riepe, Personal Interview, 22 January 1986.

64. Clement, Personal Interview.

65. John Ketwig, *"and a hard rain fell,"* cited in John F. Kelly,
"Exorcising Vietnam," *Baltimore Sun,* 23 April 1985, 2.

66. Phil Shimkin, "To Win and to Win and to Win," *Daily
Pennsylvanian,* 1 February 1973, 1; Riepe, Personal Interview.

67. Gaylord Harnwell, Annual Report of the President, University of
Pennsylvania, 1969–70, 1.

68. Bester, "University of Pennsylvania," 166; Nicholas Hendershot,
Personal Interview, 19 September 1985.

69. *Daily Pennsylvanian,* 10 December 1969, 13.

70. Tony Kovatch, "Friedl Not out to Make Friends," *Daily
Pennsylvanian,* 28 October 1970, 6.

71. Jeff Rothbard, "Heavy Lies the Head That Bears the Crown," *Daily
Pennsylvanian,* 5 May 1971, 16.

CHAPTER FOUR: WHEN FALLS THE COLISEUM

1. George Gipe, *The Great American Sports Book* (Garden City, N.Y.:
Dolphin, Doubleday and Co., 1978), 451; John F. Kennedy, "The Soft
American," *Sports Illustrated* 13 (26 December 1960): 14–17.

2. J. William Fulbright, "The Two Americas," from *The Arrogance of
Power,* cited in Lora, *America in the 60's,* 203.

3. See Gila Hayim, "The Intellectual Base of Counter-Culture" (Ph.D.
diss., University of Pennsylvania, 1972), 109, for a discussion of this idea.

4. Lyndon B. Johnson, 28 July 1965 and 3 August 1965, from
Vietnam: A Television History ("LBJ Goes to War" episode), 1983.

5. Landon Y. Jones, *Great Expectations: America and the Baby Boom
Generation* (New York: Ballantine Books, 1980), 111; Arthur Schlesinger Jr.,
Violence: America in the Sixties (New York: Signet Books, 1968), ix.

6. Lance Morrow, "A Bloody Rite of Passage," *Time* 125 (15 April
1985): 22.

7. See George Gerbner; Larry Gross; Nancy Signorielli; Michael
Morgan; and Marilyn Jackson-Beeck, *Trends in Network Television Drama and
Viewer Conceptions of Social Reality, 1967–1978,* Violence Profile No. 10,
Annenberg School of Communications, University of Pennsylvania, April

1979; and a summary of their 1967–68 work in *Daily Pennsylvanian,* 16 September 1969, 1.

8.   *Sports Illustrated* 21 (12 October 1964): 36; 21 (19 October 1964): 43.

9.   Ibid., 13 (21 October 1960); *Life* 61 (14 October 1966): front cover.

10.   *Esquire* 68 (July 1967): 58.

11.   Schlesinger, *Violence: America in the Sixties,* 30.

12.   *Sports Illustrated* 40 (21 January 1974): 11.

13.   Ivy Group Agreement, 1954, 2. The agreement did give indication that the Ivy members were nervous about the appearance of differentiated athletes. It spelled out academic control of athletics to ensure "harmony" with educational goals.

14.   Dr. James Fisher, Personal Interview, 15 July 1997; Russell B. Goodman to editor, *Daily Pennsylvanian,* 13 December 1965, 1.

15.   *People* 46 (15 July 1996): 84; *Sports Illustrated* 30 (16 June 1969): 6; Kunen, *The Strawberry Statement,* 41–42.

16.   Bruce Jacobsohn, Personal Interview, 4 February 1986; Phil Hoag, Personal Interview, 20 February 1997.

17.   Theodore Roszak, *The Making of a Counterculture: Reflections on the Technocratic Society and Its Youthful Opposition* (Garden City, N.Y.: Anchor Books, Doubleday and Co., 1968), 64.

18.   Gary C. Burns, "Utopia and Dystopia in Popular Song Lyrics: Rhetorical Visions in the United States, 1963–1972" (Ph.D. diss., Northwestern University, 1981).

19.   Harry S. Ashmore, "Where Have All the Liberals Gone," in *The Establishment and All That* (Santa Barbara, Calif.: Center for the Study of Democratic Institutions, 1970), 57.

20.   Hayim, "The Intellectual Base of Counter-Culture," 111–18.

21.   Philip Arkow, "Psychedelphia Comes to Arch Street," *Daily Pennsylvanian,* 2 March 1967, 3.

22.   See Nicholas Von Hoffman, *We Are the People Our Parents Warned Us Against* (Greenwich, Conn.: Fawcett Publications, 1968).

23.   Norman Mailer, *Armies of the Night* (New York: Signet Books, 1968), 178.

24.   Martin Ralbovsky, *The Namath Effect* (Englewood Cliffs, N.J.: Prentice-Hall, 1976), 111.

25.   Kenneth Keniston, "The Agony of the Counterculture," *Educational Record* 52 (summer 1971): 205–11.

26.   Historian William Susman found Freudian thought to be just the final blow in a centuries-long series of developments that suggested that

humans did not have full control of their destinies. He cites as specific examples the sixteenth-century Copernican removal of humans from the universe's center and Darwinian thought that undermined, in the nineteenth century, the role of reason in civilization by noting the human place in the animal kingdom. Freud introduced a new view of the importance of the unconscious. Susman, "'Personality' and the Making of Twentieth-Century Culture."

27.   Ibid., 4.

28.   Howard Senzel, *Baseball and the Cold War* (New York: Harcourt, Brace, Jovanovich, 1977), 46.

29.   Vice President Spiro T. Agnew's Address to the First Annual Vince Lombardi Award Dinner, Houston, Tex., 21 January 1971, published in Coyne Jr., *The Impudent Snobs*, 446.

30.   See Michael Oriard, *Reading Football: How the Popular Press Created an American Spectacle* (Chapel Hill: University of North Carolina Press, 1993), 18, for a discussion of why the interpretation of football as enactment of imperialism is limited and muddled.

31.   *Life* 71 (3 December 1971).

32.   Jerry Kramer, *Instant Replay: The Green Bay Diary of Jerry Kramer* (New York: Signet Books, 1968), 124.

33.   Richard Crepeau, "Punt or Bunt," *Journal of Sport History* 3 (winter 1976): 205–12.

34.   Merrell Noden, "Catching up With . . ." *Sports Illustrated* 87 (18 August 1997): 7.

35.   David Halberstam, *The Amateurs* (New York: Penguin Books, 1985), 109–10.

36.   Major league baseball star Dave Winfield was one of those on the Minnesota bench who joined the melee. In his autobiography Winfield says that Taylor claimed that Witte had first spit at him. Dave Winfield with Tom Parker, *Winfield* (New York: W. W. Norton and Co., 1988), 79–82.

37.   William F. Reed, "An Ugly Affair in Minneapolis," *Sports Illustrated* 36 (7 February 1972): 18–21.

38.   Ibid., 21.

39.   Tom Keys, "Where Were Police as Buckeyes Fell?" *Columbus Citizen-Journal*, 27 January 1972, 22; 1 February 1972, 9.

40.   Christopher Lasch, *The Culture of Narcissism: American Life in an Age of Diminishing Expectations* (New York: W. W. Norton and Co., 1978), 117.

41.   *Sports Illustrated* 23 (August 1965): 12.

42.   Harry Edwards, *The Revolt of the Black Athlete* (New York: Free Press, 1969): xiv–xvi, 142–66.

43.   *New York Times,* 18 October 1969, 40; 17 October 1969, 58, 59; *Baltimore Sun,* 17 October 1969, C1.

44.   *Baltimore Sun,* 17 October 1969, C1; Arthur Daley, "Sports of the Times," *New York Times,* 17 October 1969, 59; George Vecsey, "After the Game, Delirious Rooters Tear up Field," *New York Times,* 17 October 1969, 59; 17 October 1969, 1; Robert Lipsyte, "Sports of the Times," *New York Times,* 18 October 1969, 40.

45.   George Kiseda, "Gene Mauch (Of All People) Saves Last Day," *Philadelphia Bulletin,* 1 October 1970, 35.

46.   Bill Conlin, "Connie Mack Stadium Expires with a Smash," *Philadelphia Daily News,* 2 October 1970, 3; Frank Dolson, "Nostalgic Evening Ends in Nightmare," *Philadelphia Inquirer,* 2 October 1970, 27; Jim Barniak, "Farewell Party a Real Steal," *Philadelphia Bulletin,* 2 October 1970, 31; *Philadelphia Bulletin,* 2 October 1970, 35.

47.   *Philadelphia Daily News,* 2 October 1970, 3; Kiseda, "Gene Mauch (Of All People) Saves Last Day," 35; Conlin, "Connie Mack Stadium Expires with a Smash," 3.

48.   *Ohio State Lantern,* 23 November 1970, 1.

49.   Joseph L. Wagner, "Looting, Violence Mar Party," *Columbus Citizen-Journal,* 23 November 1970, 1; *Ohio State Lantern,* 23 November 1970, 1.

50.   Wagner, "Looting, Violence Mar Party," 1.

51.   Kunen, *The Strawberry Statement,* 116.

52.   Columbus *Citizen-Journal,* 24 November 1970, 1.

53.   Arthur Hirsch, "Smash-Mouth Sarcasm," *Baltimore Sun,* 4 September 2000, 2F.

54.   *Baltimore Sun,* 18 October 1971, 1; *New York Times,* 18 October 1971, 50.

55.   *Pittsburgh Press,* letters to editor, 20 October 1971, 26; Gilbert Love, "Let's Repair City's Image," *Pittsburgh Press,* 20 October 1971, 25; Mary O'Hara, "A World 'Serious' Bobble," *Pittsburgh Press,* 20 October 1971, 52; Margie Carlin, "Delirium Reigns as World Champs Come Home," *Pittsburgh Press,* 18 October 1971, 9.

56.   *Columbus Citizen-Journal,* 25 November 1970, 11.

57.   Orrin Klapp, *Collective Search for Identity* (New York: Holt, Rinehart, and Winston, 1969), 14–18.

CHAPTER FIVE: THE GREATEST

1.   Robert Lipsyte, *SportsWorld: An American Dreamland* (New York: Quadrangle, 1975), 81; Thomas Hauser, *Muhammad Ali: His Life and Times,*

63; David Remnick, *King of the World: Muhammad Ali and the Rise of an American Hero* (New York: Vintage Books, 1998), 158. In Remnick's version, Ali checks to make sure that Lennon is smiling. The fact that he was, given Lennon's nettlesome ways, doesn't mean he wasn't serious.

2.   *New York Journal American,* 22 February 1996, cited in Thomas Hauser, *Muhammad Ali: His Life and Times,* 145–46.

3.   *Muhammad Ali: The Greatest,* directed and produced by Martin Davidson, Arts and Entertainment, 1996.

4.   Ibid.

5.   Ibid.

6.   Thorstein Veblen, excerpt from *The Theory of the Leisure Class* (1899), in *Sport and Society: An Anthology,* ed. John T. Talamini and Charles H. Page (Boston: Little, Brown and Co., 1973), 52.

7.   Gail Bederman, *Manliness and Civilization: A Cultural History of Gender and Race in the United States, 1880–1917* (Chicago: University of Chicago Press, 1995), 15, 20, 25.

8.   Eugene D. Genovese, *Roll, Jordan, Roll: The World the Slaves Made* (New York: Vintage Books, Random House, 1976), 458.

9.   Lillian Smith, *Killers of the Dream,* rev. ed. (New York: W. W. Norton and Co., 1961). Evidence of the ongoing existence of the fear was seen in the 1992 rape trial of black heavyweight boxer Mike Tyson. His white counsel settled upon a defense strategy that portrayed Tyson as a sexual animal of such renown and obvious intent that his accuser should have known to avoid him. Tyson was convicted.

10.   See C. Vann Woodward, *The Strange Career of Jim Crow,* 3d rev. ed. (New York: Oxford University Press, 1974), 149–88.

11.   Barry Kessler and David Zang, *The Play Life of a City: Baltimore's Recreation and Parks, 1900–1955* (Baltimore: Baltimore City Life Museums, 1989), 33.

12.   "The Astonishing John Wideman," *Look* 27 (21 May 1963): 36.

13.   Jerry L. Avorn et al., *Up Against the Ivy Wall: A History of the Columbia Crisis* (New York: Atheneum, 1968), 60–61; Russell Sackett, "Plotting a War on 'Whitey,'" *Life* 60 (10 June 1966): 100; Nicholas von Hoffman, *We Are the People Our Parents Warned Us Against* (Greenwich, Conn.: Fawcett Publications, 1968), 102.

14.   Lipsyte, *SportsWorld,* 252.

15.   *Muhammad Ali: The Whole Story,* produced by Joseph Consentino, directed by Sandra and Joseph Consentino, Turner Network Television, 1997.

16.   Hauser, *Muhammad Ali: His Life and Times,* 266.

17.   *Daily Pennsylvanian,* 4 October 1965, 2.

18. *Muhammad Ali: The Greatest,* 1996.

19. Hauser, *Muhammad Ali: His Life and Times,* 145.

20. Ibid., 166; *Fields of Fire: Sports in the 60s,* produced by George Roy, directed and written by Steven Stern, Home Box Office in association with Black Canyon Productions, 1995.

21. Lionel Tiger, *Men in Groups* (New York: Random House, 1969), 115–25.

22. *Muhammad Ali: The Whole Story,* 1997.

23. Ibid.

24. *Muhammad Ali: The Greatest,* 1996.

25. Norman Mailer, "Ego," *Life* 70 (19 March 1971): 22.

26. *Muhammad Ali: The Whole Story,* 1997; *Muhammad Ali: The Greatest,* 1996; *Life* 59 (3 December 1965): 42A.

27. *Muhammad Ali: The Greatest,* 1996.

28. Ibid.

29. *New York Post,* 7 April 1973, cited in Hauser, *Muhammad Ali: His Life and Times,* 253.

30. Douglas Pike, "The Viet Cong Strategy of Terror," monograph, U.S. Mission, Saigon, February 1970, 9, cited by Frances Fitzgerald, *Fire in the Lake: The Vietnamese and the Americans in Vietnam* (New York: Vintage Books, Random House, 1972), 505. See also Fitzgerald's chapter, "Guerillas," 507–17.

31. Sam Angeloff, "Tough, Punishing Work—But Dawkins Asked for It," *Life* 60 (8 April 1966): 96.

32. Hauser, *Muhammad Ali: His Life and Times,* 267.

33. Joan Paul, Richard V. McGhee, and Helen Fant, "The Arrival and Ascendance of Black Athletes in the Southeastern Conference, 1966–1980," *Phylon* 45 (December 1984): 284–97.

34. Peter Andrews, Personal Interview, 17 December 1985.

35. Martin Kane, "An Assessment of Black Is Best," *Sports Illustrated* 34 (18 January 1971): 83.

36. See Peter Axthelm, *The City Game: Basketball in New York* (New York: Harper's Magazine Press, 1970), and David Halberstam, *The Breaks of the Game* (New York: Alfred A. Knopf, 1981), for journalistic impressions of this idea.

37. Andrews, Personal Interview.

38. Mark Lieberman, "Pride and Awareness," *Daily Pennsylvanian,* 4 March 1968, 5.

39. Tex Maule, "Make No Mistakes About It," *Sports Illustrated* 28 (29 January 1968): 25.

40.   Martin Kane, "The Art of Ali," *Sports Illustrated* 30 (5 May 1969): 48–57.

41.   Harold Schecter, "The Myth of the Eternal Child in Sixties America," in *The Popular Culture Reader,* ed. Jack Nachbar, Deborah Weiser, John L. Wright (Bowling Green, Ohio: Bowling Green University Press, 1978): 69–70.

42.   Schecter, "The Myth," 70.

43.   Hauser, *Muhammad Ali: His Life and Times,* 276.

44.   Ibid., 171.

45.   Ibid., 168.

46.   Schecter, "The Myth," 69.

47.   Hauser, *Muhammad Ali: His Life and Times,* 188–89.

48.   Mark Kram, "Lawdy, Lawdy, He's Great," *Sports Illustrated* 43 (13 October 1975): 26.

49.   Gerald Early, *The Muhammad Ali Reader,* ed. Gerald Early (New York: Rob Weisbach Books, 1998), xiii–xiv.

50.   Hauser, *Muhammad Ali: His Life and Times,* 158.

CHAPTER SIX: TERRAPIN SOUP

1.   Underwood, "The Desperate Coach" (1 September 1969): 24.

2.   Mark Carp, Personal interview, 15 August 2000.

3.   Underwood, "The Desperate Coach" (1 September 1969): 24.

4.   Dave Bourdon, "Football, '67: A Long Day's Journey," *Diamondback,* 24 May 1968, 3C.

5.   Underwood, "The Desperate Coach" (1 September 1969): 24.

6.   Jeff Greenfield, *No Peace, No Place: Excavations along the Generational Fault* (Garden City, N.Y.: Doubleday and Co., 1973), 101–34; Kunen, *The Strawberry Statement,* 30.

7.   Bourdon, "'Nobody Wants to Play for You,'" 12.

8.   Ernie Torain, Personal Interview, 29 August 2000.

9.   Peter Clecak, *America's Quest for the Ideal Self: Dissent and Fulfillment in the 60's and 70's* (New York: Oxford University Press, 1983), 280.

10.   Allen J. Matusow, *The Unraveling of America: A History of Liberalism in the 1960's* (New York: Harper and Row, 1984), 127.

11.   Leonard Shecter, "The Toughest Man in Pro Football," *Esquire* 68 (January 1968): 146.

12.   William E. Leuchtenburg, *A Troubled Feast: American Society since 1945* (Boston: Little, Brown and Co., 1983), 234–35.

13.   Philip E. Slater, *The Pursuit of Loneliness: American Culture at the Breaking Point* (Boston: Beacon Press, 1970), 61–62.

14.   Ibid., 4.

15.   Thomas J. Cottle, *Time's Children: Impressions of Youth,* with a foreword by David Riesman (Boston: Little, Brown and Co., 1971), 329–30.

16.   Marshall Berman, "Faust in the 60's," in *The Sixties,* ed. Gerald Howard (New York: Washington Square Press, 1982), 496.

17.   Harvey C. Greisman, "Requiem for the Counter-Culture" (Ph.D. diss., Syracuse University, 1973), 7.

18.   Hunter S. Thompson, "The 'Hashbury' Is the Capital of the Hippies," in *American Society since 1945,* ed. William L. O'Neill (Chicago: Quadrangle Books, 1969), 132.

19.   Dave Bourdon, "Those Dumb Animals," *Diamondback,* 1 April 1968, n.p.

20.   See David M. Potter, *People of Plenty: Economic Abundance and the American Character* (Chicago: University of Chicago Press, 1954), 189–208, for a discussion of permissive and authoritarian rearing and the changes that abundance produced in family structure, child rearing, and peer groups; see also Clecak, *America's Quest for the Ideal Self,* 109.

21.   Melvin L. Kohn and Carmi Schooler, "Class, Occupation, and Orientation," *American Sociological Review* 34 (October 1969): 659–78.

22.   "To Keep Pace with America," *Pennsylvania Gazette* 64 (April 1966): n.p.

23.   *Pennsylvania Gazette* 67 (May 1969): 3–4; 67 (June 1969): 3–4.

24.   Jerry Avorn et al., *Up Against the Ivy Wall: A History of the Columbia Crisis* (New York: Atheneum, 1968), 119.

25.   Underwood, "Desperate Coach" (25 August 1969): 40.

26.   "Ward on Rampage Against DBK," *Diamondback,* 8 October 1968, 1.

27.   Ibid.; Jeff Isner, "'Bourdon Doesn't Know Much,'" *Diamondback,* 8 October 1968, 1.

28.   Underwood, "The Desperate Coach" (1 September 1969): 24.

29.   Carp, Personal Interview.

30.   Alfred Bester, "The University of Pennsylvania," *Holiday* 32 (November 1962): 177.

31.   John W. Stewart, "Ward Seen Dismissed or Quitting," *Baltimore Sun,* 5 March 1969, C1.

32.   Dave Bourdon, "Ward—Under the Gun?" *Diamondback,* 11 September 1968, 24.

33.   Underwood, "The Desperate Coach" (1 September 1969): 25.

34.   Ibid., 24.

35.   Ibid., 25.

36. Ibid.; Bourdon, "'Nobody Wants to Play for You,'" 13.

37. Underwood, "The Desperate Coach" (1 September 1969): 25.

38. Dave Bourdon, "'Greatest Day' Ward Says of First Victory," *Diamondback,* 14 October 1968, 18A.

39. Bourdon, "Ward on Rampage," 1.

40. Bourdon, "'Nobody Wants to Play for You,'" 13.

41. Dave Bourdon, "Gridders Request Ward Firing," *Diamondback,* 28 February 1969, 1.

42. Ibid., 1.

43. Neil D. Isaacs, *Jock Culture, U.S.A.* (New York: W. W. Norton and Co., 1978), 172.

44. Bourdon, "Gridders Request Ward Firing," 1.

45. Torain, Personal Interview.

46. Bourdon, "'Nobody Wants to Play for You,'" 14.

47. *Fields of Fire: Sports in the 60s,* produced by George Roy, directed and written by Steven Stern, Home Box Office in association with Black Canyon Productions, 1995.

48. Bob Ibach, "Van Heusen Gets His Kicks," *Diamondback,* 23 May 1969, 28A; Torain, Personal Interview.

49. Bourdon, "'Nobody Wants to Play for You,'" 15.

50. Ibach, "Van Heusen Gets His Kicks," 28A.

51. Torain, Personal Interview.

52. Fred Shabel, Personal Interview, 11 October 1985.

53. Torain, Personal Interview.

54. Dave Bourdon, "Requiem for Bob Ward," *Diamondback,* 7 March 1969, 14.

55. Bourdon, "Terps, Ward Set for Showdown," 18.

56. John W. Stewart, "Maryland's Greatest Football Hero Leaves with 'Great Regret' But 'No Bitterness,'" *Baltimore Sun,* 6 March 1969, C1.

57. Isaacs, *Jock Culture, U.S.A.,* 172; Underwood, "The Desperate Coach" (1 September 1969): 25.

58. Mark Carp, "And God Created Kehoe . . . or Vice Versa," *Diamondback,* 23 May 1969, 30A.

59. Underwood, "The Desperate Coach" (1 September 1969): 22.

60. Ibid., 25.

61. AFCA Board of Trustees Minutes, Atlanta, Ga., 28 June 1969; Washington, D.C., 12 January 1970.

62. Robert Ward, Personal Interview, 2 March 2000; Bourdon, "'Nobody Wants to Play for You,'" 15.

63.   Mark Carp, "James Kehoe, A.D.," *Diamondback,* 13 February 1969, 19; Jeff Isner, "Fellows: Too Nice to Be a Winner?" *Diamondback,* 12 March 1969, 10.

64.   Cited in George Gipe, *The Great American Sports Book* (Garden City, N.Y.: Dolphin Books, Doubleday, 1978), 494.

65.   Torain, Personal Interview.

66.   William Nack and Lester Munson, "Out of Control," *Sports Illustrated* 93 (24 July 2000): 90.

67.   See Peter Burke, *Popular Culture in Early Modern Europe* (New York: Harper and Row, 1978), 185–91.

CHAPTER SEVEN: THE BAD NEWS BEARS

1.   "50 Top-Grossing Films," *Variety* 21 (April 1976): 11; (28 April 1976): 13; (5 May 1976): 9; (12 May 1976): n.p.; (19 May 1976): 15; (26 May 1976): 9.

2.   Anne LaRiviere, "A Voice for More Joy in Sports," *Los Angeles Times,* 9 April 1976, N1.

3.   Ellen W. Gerber, Jan Felshin, Pearl Berlin, Waneen Wyrick, *The American Woman in Sport* (Reading, Mass.: Addison-Wesley, 1974), 217–18.

4.   *Los Angeles Times,* 4 April 1976, H1.

5.   *Sports Illustrated* 23 (9 August 1965): 26.

6.   Landon Y. Jones, *Great Expectations: America and the Baby Boom Generation* (New York: Ballantine Books, 1980), 65.

7.   Stanley Kauffmann, "The Film Generation: Celebration and Concern," *World on Film* (New York: Harper and Row, 1966), 422.

8.   Thomas J. Cottle, *Time's Children: Impressions of Youth,* with a foreword by David Riesman (Boston: Little, Brown and Co., 1971), xxii–xxiii; Jeff Greenfield, *No Peace, No Place: Excavations along the Generational Fault* (New York: Doubleday and Co., 1973), 28. It is Greenfield's contention that this willingness to act was the crucial distinction between those on either side of the generational fault.

9.   For theories of generational discontinuity see Margaret Mead, *Culture and Commitment: A Study of the Generation Gap* (New York: Basic Books, 1970), and Vern L. Bengston, "The Generation Gap: A Review and Typology of Social-Psychological Perspectives," in *The New Pilgrims: Youth Protest in Transition,* ed. Philip G. Altbach and Robert S. Laufer (New York: David McKay Co., 1972), 195–217. Anthony Lukas, in *Don't Shoot—We Are Your Children,* 4th ed. (New York: Random House, 1972), 461, argues for a "reality gap" as a more important divider of ideas than a generation gap.

10.   *Variety's Film Reviews,* 7 April 1976.

11.   Tom Milne, "The Bad News Bears," *Monthly Film Bulletin* 43 (November 1976): 228.

12.   In a poll taken by *USA Today* it finished twenty-second; *USA Today,* 15 July 1998, 1, 2C.

13.   *Sports on the Silver Screen,* produced by Leslie Farrell, directed by Ross Greenburg and Rick Bernstein, Home Box Office, 1997.

14.   Susman, "'Personality' and the Making of Twentieth-Century Culture," 273–74, 277.

15.   Frank Deford, "All-America, All the Way," *Sports Illustrated* 36 (21 February 1972): 69–70.

Index

About the Author

David W. Zang is a sports historian and Director of Sport Studies at Towson University. He is also the author of *Fleet Walker's Divided Heart: The Life of Baseball's First Black Major Leaguer* (Nebraska, 1995).